12/20/91

Emily Elizabeth

Best wishes on
this day of your christening.
May your life be full of joy
and happiness and the love
of a good book.

All our love Vicente
Cynthia, Josephine
and Josephine Orlandella

A CHILD'S BOOK OF STORIES

A CHILD'S BOOK OF STORIES

WITH PICTURES BY
Jessie Willcox Smith

LONGMEADOW PRESS

This book is printed on acid-free paper. It surpasses the standards set for Permanence of Paper for Printed Library Materials.

Copyright © 1986 by dilithium Press, Ltd., Children's Classics Division. All rights reserved.

This 1986 edition is published exclusively by Longmeadow Press, 201 High Ridge Road, P.O. Box 10218, Stamford, CT 06904, by arrangement with Outlet Book Company, Inc., a Random House Company, 225 Park Avenue South, New York, New York 10003.

Printed and Bound in the United States of America

Cover design by Jesse Cohen

ISBN 0-681-40197-4

10 9 8 7 6 5

Contents

And Alphabetical Index

v

CONTENTS

CONTENTS

vii

Color Plates

TO

ADA, EVA, AND MERVYN

Foreword

THIS is a child's garden: the colors, the wonder, the miracle of discovery, and the comfort of the known. Though its pages may become worn with use and reuse, it will remain forever new. Here you will find eighty-six of the best-known and best-loved children's stories, not only of the English language but of the written word; many of the stories have been translated into English time and time again over the centuries. This edition has brought together the definitive versions of each story, fable, and folk tale, with an eye not only to authenticity but also to similarity of style, so that the resulting book takes on the character of a unified piece, if not written by the same author, at least with the same audience in mind. And this special edition is beautifully enriched with the magnificent illustrations of Jessie Willcox Smith in stunning jewel-tone colors.

All the familiar titles are here. And, in addition to the classics of eternal popularity and availability, we find many that may not have arrived at the level of stardom of a "Little Red Riding Hood" but which may, with new generations of readers and a different temper of the times, find a similar place in the rankings of young readers' favorites. Among today's youth, for example, "The Pancake" may perhaps prove a more popular treat than a "Gingerbread Man." The stories are very similar in content and style, but "The Pancake" may catch the fancy of the modern child in a way that "The Gingerbread Man" could not. The scientific emphasis in education today, which has taken over most aspects of the child's world, should make the explanation fables more provocative. "The Magpie's Nest" explains why bird's nests are made as they are; and "The Foolhardy Frogs and the Stork" supplements elementary science classes. "Mr. Miacca" is a quick and effective little tale reminding children not to wander from their own back (or front) yards. "Diamonds and Toads" is an equally effective deterrent to cruel behavior. "The History of the Five Little Pigs" takes the old favorite parent-and-child verse game and elaborates on it, explaining just what really happened to each little pig, and why.

It is important to the success of a children's book that each young reader experience two things: a sense of the familiar, which enables the child to feel at home with the book, and a sense of discovery, which delights and surprises while stimulating learning and understanding. This book, with its old favorites and lesser known gems, meets these qualifications perfectly.

Of equal importance in this edition are the striking illustrations of Jessie Willcox Smith. In her unique style, she has brought each story she has illustrated gloriously to life—but that life surpasses realism and unlocks the gates to a private and protected world where children's feelings are the only things that really matter. Yet the children are sweet children—not arrogant or spoiled. All of Smith's children are innocents, but believable innocents. Theirs are real faces, and her adults are real adults—not excessively beautiful or ugly, for Smith knew how to create credibility and loveliness simultaneously. The witch in "Hansel and Gretel" will not create nightmares any more than the wolf in "Red Riding Hood." Wickedness is cloaked with just enough fantasy to remove it from troublesome intrusion into the child's mind, in the same way that beauty, in these illustrations, is real enough to make it believable.

This child's garden of stories is at once an old friend and a new best friend. Just as a garden is reborn each spring, so these stories are reborn with each new encounter. But, luckily for us all, spring and summer are always just an arm's reach away.

PATRICIA BARRETT PERKINS

Baltimore, Maryland
1986

A CHILD'S BOOK OF STORIES

HANSEL AND GRETTEL

O NCE upon a time there dwelt on the outskirts of a large forest a poor woodcutter with his wife and two children; the boy was called Hansel and the girl Grettel. He had always little enough to live on, and once, when there was a great famine in the land, he could n't even provide them with daily bread. One night, as he was tossing about in bed, full of cares and worry, he sighed and said to his wife: "What's to become of us? How are we to support our poor children, now that we have nothing more for ourselves?" "I'll tell you what, husband," answered the woman; "early to-morrow morning we'll take the children out into the thickest part of the wood; there we shall light a fire for them and give them each a piece of bread; then we'll go on to our work and leave them alone. They won't be able to find their way home, and we shall thus be rid of them." "No, wife," said her husband, "that I won't do; how could I find it in my heart to leave my children alone in the wood? The wild beasts would soon come and tear them to pieces." "Oh! you fool," said she, "then we must all four die of hunger, and you may just as well go and plane the boards for our coffins;" and she left him no peace till he consented. "But I can't help feeling sorry for the poor children," added the husband.

The children, too, had not been able to sleep for hunger, and had heard what their stepmother had said to their father. Grettel wept bitterly and spoke to Hansel: "Now it's all up with us." "No, no, Grettel," said Hansel, "don't fret yourself; I'll be

1

able to find a way of escape, no fear." And when the old people had fallen asleep he got up, slipped on his little coat, opened the back door, and stole out. The moon was shining clearly, and the white pebbles which lay in front of the house glittered like bits of silver. Hansel bent down and filled his pocket with as many of them as he could cram in. Then he went back and said to Grettel, " Be comforted, my dear little sister, and go to sleep: God will not desert us," and he lay down in bed again.

At daybreak, even before the sun was up, the woman came and woke the two children: " Get up, you lie-abeds, we 're all going to the forest to fetch wood." She gave them each a bit of bread and spoke: " There 's something for your luncheon, but don't you eat it up before, for it 's all you 'll get." Grettel took the bread under her apron, as Hansel had the stones in his pocket. Then they all set out together on the way to the forest. After they had walked for a little, Hansel stood still and looked back at the house, and this manœuvre he repeated again and again. His father observed him and spoke: " Hansel, what are you gazing at there, and why do you always remain behind? Take care, and don't lose your footing." " Oh! father," said Hansel, " I am looking back at my white kitten, which is sitting on the roof, waving me a farewell." The woman exclaimed: " What a donkey you are! That is n't your kitten, that 's the morning sun shining on the chimney." But Hansel had not looked back at his kitten, but had always dropped one of the white pebbles out of his pocket on to the path.

When they had reached the middle of the forest the father said: " Now, children, go and fetch a lot of wood, and I 'll light a fire that you may n't feel cold." Hansel and Grettel heaped up brushwood till they had made a pile nearly the size of a small hill. The brushwood was set fire to, and when the flames leaped high the woman said: " Now lie down at the fire, children, and rest yourselves: we are going into the forest to cut down wood;

2

when we 've finished we 'll come back and fetch you." Hansel and Grettel sat down beside the fire, and at mid-day ate their little bits of bread. They heard the strokes of the ax, so they thought their father was quite near. But it was no ax they heard, but a bough he had tied on to a dead tree, and that was blown about by the wind. And when they had sat for a long time their eyes closed with fatigue, and they fell fast asleep. When they awoke at last it was pitch-dark. Grettel began to cry and said: " How are we ever to get out of the wood? " But Hansel comforted her. " Wait a bit," he said, " till the moon is up, and then we 'll find our way sure enough." And when the full moon had risen he took his sister by the hand and followed the pebbles, which shone like new threepenny bits and showed them the path. They walked all through the night, and at daybreak reached their father's house again. They knocked at the door, and when the woman opened it she exclaimed: " You naughty children, what a time you 've slept in the wood! We thought you were never going to come back." But the father rejoiced, for his conscience had reproached him for leaving his children behind by themselves.

Not long afterward there was again great dearth in the land, and the children heard their mother address their father thus in bed one night: " Everything is eaten up once more; we have only half a loaf in the house, and when that 's done it 's all up with us. The children must be got rid of; we 'll lead them deeper into the wood this time, so that they won't be able to find their way out again. There is no other way of saving ourselves." The man's heart smote him heavily, and he thought, " Surely it would be better to share the last bite with one's children! " But his wife would n't listen to his arguments, and did nothing but scold and reproach him. If a man yields once he 's done for, and so, because he had given in the first time, he was forced to do so the second.

3

But the children were awake and had heard the conversation. When the old people were asleep Hansel got up and wanted to go out and pick up pebbles again, as he had done the first time; but the woman had barred the door and Hansel couldn't get out. But he consoled his little sister and said: "Don't cry, Grettel, and sleep peacefully, for God is sure to help us."

At early dawn the woman came and made the children get up. They received their bit of bread, but it was even smaller than the time before. On the way to the wood Hansel crumbled it in his pocket, and every few minutes he stood still and dropped a crumb on the ground. "Hansel, what are you stopping and looking about you for?" said the father. "I'm looking back at my little pigeon, which is sitting on the roof waving me a farewell," answered Hansel. "Fool!" said the wife; "that isn't your pigeon, it's the morning sun glittering on the chimney." But Hansel gradually threw all his crumbs on to the path. The woman led the children still deeper into the forest, further than they had ever been in their lives before. Then a big fire was lit again, and the mother said: "Just sit down there, children, and if you're tired you can sleep a bit; we're going into the forest to cut down wood, and in the evening when we're finished we'll come back to fetch you." At mid-day Grettel divided her bread with Hansel, for he had strewn his all along their path. Then they fell asleep, and evening passed away, but nobody came to the poor children. They didn't awake till it was pitch-dark, and Hansel comforted his sister, saying: "Only wait, Grettel, till the moon rises, then we shall see the bread-crumbs I scattered along the path; they will show us the way back to the house." When the moon appeared they got up, but they found no crumbs, for the thousands of birds that fly about the woods and fields had picked them all up. "Never mind," said Hansel to Grettel; "you'll see we'll still find a way out"; but all the same they did not. They wandered about the whole night, and the next day, from morning till evening, but they could not find a path out of the wood. They were very hungry, too, for they had nothing to eat but a few berries they found growing on the ground. And at last they were so tired that their legs refused to carry them any longer, so they lay down under a tree and fell fast asleep.

On the third morning after they had left their father's house they set about their wandering again, but only got deeper and deeper into the wood, and now they felt that if help did not come to them soon they must perish. At mid-day they saw a beautiful little snow-white bird sitting on a branch, which sang so sweetly that they stopped still and listened to it. And when its song was finished it flapped its wings and flew on in front of them. They followed it and came to a little house, on the roof of which it perched; and when they came quite near they saw that the cottage was made of bread and roofed with cakes, while the window was made of transparent sugar. " Now we 'll set to," said Hansel, " and have a regular blow-out. I 'll eat a bit of the roof, and you, Grettel, can eat some of the window, which you 'll find a sweet morsel." Hansel stretched up his hand and broke off a little bit of the roof to see what it was like, and Grettel went to the casement and began to nibble at it. Thereupon a shrill voice called out from the room inside:

> " Nibble, nibble, little mouse,
> Who 's nibbling my house? "

The children answered,

> " 'T is Heaven's own child,
> The tempest wild,"

and went on eating, without putting themselves about. Hansel, who thoroughly appreciated the roof, tore down a big bit of it, while Grettel pushed out a whole round window-pane, and sat

5

down the better to enjoy it. Suddenly the door opened and an ancient dame leaning on a staff hobbled out. Hansel and Grettel were so terrified that they let what they had in their hands fall. But the old woman shook her head and said: "Oh, ho! you dear children, who led you here? Just come in and stay with me; no ill shall befall you." She took them both by the hand and led them into the house, and laid a most sumptuous dinner before them — milk and sugared pancakes, with apples and nuts. After they had finished, two beautiful little white beds were prepared for them, and when Hansel and Grettel lay down in them they felt as if they had got into heaven.

The old woman had appeared to be most friendly, but she was really an old witch who had waylaid the children, and had only built the little bread house in order to lure them in. When any one came into her power she killed, cooked, and ate him, and held a regular feast-day for the occasion. Now, witches have red eyes and cannot see far, but, like beasts, they have a keen sense of smell and know when human beings pass by. When Hansel and Grettel fell into her hands she laughed maliciously and said jeeringly: "I've got them now; they sha'n't escape me." Early in the morning, before the children were awake, she arose, and when she saw them both sleeping so peacefully, with their round rosy cheeks, she muttered to herself: "That'll be a dainty bite." Then she seized Hansel with her bony hand and carried him into a little stable, and barred the door on him; he might scream as much as he liked, it did him no good. Then she went to Grettel, shook her till she awoke, and cried: "Get up, you lazy-bones; fetch water and cook something for your brother. When he's fat I'll eat him up." Grettel began to cry bitterly, but it was of no use: she had to do what the wicked witch bade her.

So the best food was cooked for poor Hansel, but Grettel got nothing but crab-shells. Every morning the old woman hobbled out to the stable and cried: "Hansel, put out your finger, that I may feel if you are getting fat." But Hansel always stretched out a bone, and the old dame, whose eyes were dim, could n't see it, and thinking always it was Hansel's finger, wondered why he fattened so slowly. When four weeks passed and Hansel still remained thin, she lost patience and determined to wait no longer. "Hi! Grettel," she called to the girl, "be quick and get some water. Hansel may be fat or thin, I 'm going to kill him to-morrow and cook him." Oh! how the poor little sister sobbed as she carried the water, and how the tears rolled down her cheeks! "Kind Heaven help us now!" she cried; "if only the wild beasts in the wood had eaten us, then at least we should have died together." "Just hold your peace," said the old hag; "it won't help you."

Early in the morning Grettel had to go out and hang up the kettle full of water and light the fire. "First we 'll bake," said the old dame; "I 've heated the oven already and kneaded the dough." She pushed Grettel out to the oven, from which fiery flames were already issuing. "Creep in," said the witch, "and see if it 's properly heated, so that we can shove in the bread." For when she had got Grettel in she meant to close the oven and let the girl bake, that she might eat her up too. But Grettel perceived her intention and spoke: "I don't know how I 'm to do it; how do I get in?" "You silly goose!" said the hag, "the opening is big enough; see, I could get in myself"; and she crawled toward it and poked her head into the oven. Then Grettel gave her a shove that sent her right in, shut the iron door, and drew the bolt. Gracious! how she yelled! it was quite horrible; but Grettel fled, and the wretched old woman was left to perish miserably.

Grettel flew straight to Hansel, opened the little stable door, and cried: "Hansel, we are free; the old witch is dead." Then Hansel sprang like a bird out of a cage when the door is opened.

How they rejoiced, and fell on each other's necks, and jumped for joy, and kissed one another! And as they had no longer any cause for fear, they went into the old hag's house, and there they found, in every corner of the room, boxes with pearls and precious stones. "These are even better than pebbles," said Hansel, and crammed his pockets full of them; and Grettel said, "I too will bring something home"; and she filled her apron full. "But now," said Hansel, "let's go and get well away from the witch's wood." When they had wandered about for some hours they came to a big lake. "We can't get over," said Hansel; "I see no bridge of any sort or kind." "Yes, and there's no ferry-boat either," answered Grettel; "but look, there swims a white duck; if I ask her she'll help us over"; and she called out:

"Here are two children, mournful very,
Seeing neither bridge nor ferry;
Take us upon your white back,
And row us over quack, quack!"

The duck swam toward them, and Hansel got on her back and bade his little sister sit beside him. "No," answered Grettel, "we should be too heavy a load for the duck: she shall carry us across separately." The good bird did this, and when they were landed safely on the other side and had gone on for awhile, the wood became more and more familiar to them, and at length they saw their father's house in the distance. Then they set off to run, and bounding into the room fell on their father's neck. The man had not passed a happy hour since he left them in the wood, but the woman had died. Grettel shook out her apron so that the pearls and precious stones rolled about the room, and Hansel threw down one handful after the other out of his pocket. Thus all their troubles were ended, and they all lived happily ever afterward.

My story is done. See! there runs a little mouse; any one who catches it may make himself a large fur cap out of it.

GOLDILOCKS; OR, THE THREE BEARS

LITTLE GOLDILOCKS was a pretty girl who lived once upon a time in a far-off country.

One day she was sitting on the hearth-rug playing with her two kittens, and you would have thought she was as happy as a queen, and quite contented to stay where she was instead of wanting to run about the world meddling with other people's property. But it happened that she was a rather mischievous little maid, and could not resist teasing her pets, so one of them scratched her and then she would play with them no longer.

She went away into the wood behind her mother's house, and it was such a warm, pleasant day that she wandered on and on until she came to a part of the wood where she had never been before.

Now, in this wood there lived a family of three Bears. The first was a Great Big Bear, the second was a Middling-sized Bear, and the third was a Little Teeny Tiny Bear, and they all lived together in a funny little house, and were very happy.

Goldilocks stopped when she came to the Bears' house, and began to wonder who lived there.

" I 'll just look in and see," she said, and so she did; but there was no one there, for the Bears had all gone out for a morning walk, whilst the soup they were going to have for dinner cooled upon the table.

Goldilocks was rather hungry after her walk, and the soup smelled so good that she began to wish the people of the house would come home and invite her to have some. But although she looked everywhere, under the table and into the cupboards, she could find no one, and at last she could resist no longer, but made up her mind to take just a little sip to see how the soup tasted. The soup had been put into three bowls — a Great Big Bowl for the Great Big Bear, a Middling-sized Bowl for the Middling-sized Bear, and a Teeny Tiny Bowl for the Teeny Tiny Bear. Beside each bowl lay a spoon, and Goldilocks took one and helped herself to a spoonful of soup from the Great Big Bowl.

Ugh! how it burned her mouth; it was so hot with pepper that she did not like it at all; still, she was very hungry, so she thought she would try again.

This time she took a sip of the Middling-sized Bear's soup, but she liked it no better, for it was too salt. But when she tasted the Teeny Tiny Bear's soup it was just as she liked it; so she ate it up every drop, without thinking twice about it.

When she had finished her dinner she noticed three chairs standing by the wall. One was a Great Big Chair, and she climbed upon that and sat down. Oh! how hard it was! She was sure she could not sit there for long, so she climbed up on the next, which was only a Middling-sized Chair, but that was too soft for her taste; so she went on to the last, which was a Teeny Tiny Chair and just suited her.

It was so comfortable that she sat on and on until, if you 'll believe it, she actually sat the bottom out. Then, of course, she was comfortable no longer, so she got up and wondered what she should do next.

There was a staircase in the Bears' house, and Goldilocks thought she would see where it led to. So up she went, and when she reached the top she laughed outright, for she came to the Bears' bedroom, and it was the funniest room she had ever seen. In the middle of the room stood a Great Big Bed, on one side of it there was a Middling-sized Bed, and on the other side there was a Teeny Tiny Bed.

Goldilocks was sleepy, so she thought she would lie down on one of the beds and have a little nap. First she got upon the Great Big Bed, but it was just as hard as the Great Big Chair had been; so she jumped off and tried the Middling-sized Bed, but it was so soft that she sank right down into the feather cushions and was nearly smothered.

"I will try the Teeny Tiny Bed," she said, and so she did, and she found it so very comfortable that she soon fell fast asleep.

Whilst she lay there, dreaming of all sorts of pleasant things, the three Bears who lived in the little house came home from their walk, very hungry and quite ready for their dinners.

But, oh! dear me! how cross the Great Big Bear looked when he saw his spoon had been used and thrown under the table.

"WHO HAS BEEN TASTING MY SOUP?" he cried angrily, in a Great Big Voice.

"AND WHO HAS BEEN TASTING MINE?" cried the Middling-sized Bear, in a Middling-sized Voice.

"*But who has been tasting mine, and tasted it all up?*" cried the poor little Teeny Tiny Bear, in a Teeny Tiny Voice, with tears running down his Teeny Tiny Face.

When the Great Big Bear went to sit down in his Great Big Chair, he cried out in his Great Big Voice:

"WHO HAS BEEN SITTING ON MY CHAIR?"

And the Middling-sized Bear cried, in a Middling-sized Voice:

"WHO HAS BEEN SITTING ON MY CHAIR?"

But the Teeny Tiny Bear cried out in a Teeny Tiny Voice of anger:

"*Who has been sitting on my chair, and sat the bottom out?*"

By this time the Bears were sure that some one had been in

their house quite lately; so they looked about to see if some one were not there still.

There was certainly no one downstairs, so they went up the staircase to their bedroom.

As soon as the Great Big Bear looked at his bed, he cried out in his Great Big Voice:

"WHO HAS BEEN LYING ON MY BED?"

And the Middling-sized Bear, seeing that the coverlet was all rumpled, cried out, in a Middling-sized Voice:

"WHO HAS BEEN LYING ON MY BED?"

But the Teeny Tiny Bear cried out, in a Teeny Tiny Voice of astonishment:

"*Who has been lying on my bed, and lies there still?*"

Now, when the Great Big Bear began to speak, Goldilocks dreamed that there was a bee buzzing in the room, and when the Middling-sized Bear began to speak, she dreamed that it was flying out of the window; but when the Teeny Tiny Bear began to speak, she dreamed that the bee had come back and stung her on the ear, and up she jumped. Oh! how frightened she was when she saw the three Bears standing beside her.

She hopped out of bed and in a second was out through the open window. Never stopping to wonder if the fall had hurt her, she got up and ran and ran and ran until she could go no farther, always thinking that the Bears were close behind her. And when at length she fell down in a heap on the ground, because she was too tired to run any more, it was her own mother who picked her up, because in her fright she had run straight home without knowing it.

SNOW-WHITE AND ROSE-RED

A POOR widow once lived in a little cottage with a garden in front of it, in which grew two rose-trees, one bearing white roses and the other red. She had two children, who were just like the two rose-trees; one was called Snow-white and the other Rose-red, and they were the sweetest and best children in the world, always diligent and always cheerful; but Snow-white was quieter and more gentle than Rose-red. Rose-red loved to run about the fields and meadows and to pick flowers and catch butterflies; but Snow-white sat at home with her mother and helped her in the household, or read aloud to her when there was no work to do. The two children loved each other so dearly that they always walked about hand in hand whenever they went out together, and when Snow-white said, "We will never desert each other," Rose-red answered, "No, not as long as we live;" and the mother added: "Whatever one gets she shall share with the other." They often roamed about in the woods gathering berries and no beast offered to hurt them; on the contrary, they came up to them in the most confiding manner; the little hare would eat a cabbage leaf from their hands, the deer grazed beside them, the stag would bound past them merrily, and the birds remained on the branches and sang to them with all their might. No evil ever befell them; if they tarried late in the wood and night overtook them, they lay down together on the moss and slept till morning, and their mother knew they were quite safe and never felt anxious about them. Once, when they had slept the night in the wood and had been wakened by the morning sun, they perceived a beautiful child in a shining white robe sitting close to their resting-place. The figure got up, looked at them kindly, but said nothing, and vanished into the wood. And when they looked round about them they became aware that they had slept quite close to a precipice, over which they would certainly have fallen had they gone on a few steps further in the darkness. And when they told their mother of their adventure, she said what they had seen must have been the angel that guards good children.

Snow-white and Rose-red kept their mother's cottage so beautifully clean and neat that it was a pleasure to go into it. In summer Rose-red looked after the house, and every morning before her mother awoke she placed a bunch of flowers before the bed, from each tree a rose. In winter Snow-white lit the fire and put on the kettle, which was made of brass, but so beautifully polished that it shone like gold. In the evening when the snowflakes fell their mother said, "Snow-white, go and close the shutters;" and they drew round the fire, while the mother put on her spectacles and read aloud from a big book, and the two girls listened and sat and spun. Beside them on the ground lay a little lamb, and behind them perched a little white dove with its head tucked under its wings.

One evening as they sat thus cozily together some one knocked at the door as though he desired admittance. The mother said: "Rose-red, open the door quickly; it must be some traveler seeking shelter." Rose-red hastened to unbar the door, and thought she saw a poor man standing in the darkness outside; but it was no such thing, only a bear, who poked his thick black head through the door. Rose-red screamed aloud and sprang back in terror, the lamb began to bleat, the dove flapped its wings, and Snow-white ran and hid behind her mother's bed. But the bear began to speak, and said: "Don't be afraid: I won't hurt you,

I am half-frozen, and only wish to warm myself a little." "My poor bear," said the mother, "lie down by the fire, only take care you don't burn your fur." Then she called out: "Snow-white and Rose-red, come out; the bear will do you no harm; he is a good, honest creature." So they both came out from their hiding-places, and gradually the lamb and dove drew near too, and they all forgot their fear. The bear asked the children to beat the snow a little out of his fur, and they fetched a brush and scrubbed him till he was dry. Then the beast stretched himself in front of the fire and growled quite happily and comfortably. The children soon grew quite at their ease with him and led their helpless guest a fearful life. They tugged his fur with their hands, put their small feet on his back, and rolled him about here and there, or took a hazel wand and beat him with it; and if he growled they only laughed. The bear submitted to everything with the best possible good-nature, only when they went too far he cried: " Oh! children, spare my life!

> " ' Snow-white and Rose-red,
> Don't beat your lover dead.' "

When it was time to retire for the night and the others went to bed, the mother said to the bear: " You can lie there on the hearth, in Heaven's name; it will be shelter for you from the cold and wet." As soon as day dawned the children let him out, and he trotted over the snow into the wood. From this time on the bear came every evening at the same hour, and lay down by the hearth and let the children play what pranks they liked with him; and they got so accustomed to him that the door was never shut till their black friend had made his appearance.

When spring came and all outside was green, the bear said one morning to Snow-white: " Now I must go away and not return again the whole summer." " Where are you going to, dear bear?" asked Snow-white. "I must go to the wood and protect my treasure from the wicked dwarfs. In winter, when the earth is frozen hard, they are obliged to remain underground, for they can't work their way through; but now, when the sun has thawed and warmed the ground, they break through and come up above to spy the land and steal what they can: what once falls into their hands and into their caves is not easily brought back to light." Snow-white was quite sad over their friend's departure, and when she unbarred the door for him the bear, stepping out, caught a piece of his fur in the door-knocker, and Snow-white thought she caught sight of glittering gold beneath it, but she couldn't be certain of it; and the bear ran hastily away and soon disappeared behind the trees.

A short time after this the mother sent the children into the wood to collect fagots. They came in their wanderings upon a big tree which lay felled on the ground, and on the trunk among the long grass they noticed something jumping up and down, but what it was they couldn't distinguish. When they approached nearer they perceived a dwarf with a wizened face and a beard a yard long. The end of the beard was jammed into a cleft of the tree, and the little man sprang about like a dog on a chain, and didn't seem to know what he was to do. He glared at the girls with his fiery red eyes and screamed out: "What are you standing there for? Can't you come and help me?" "What were you doing, little man?" asked Rose-red. "You stupid, inquisitive goose!" replied the dwarf; "I wanted to split the tree, in order to get little chips of wood for our kitchen fire; those thick logs that serve to make fires for coarse, greedy people like yourselves quite burn up all the little food we need. I had successfully driven in the wedge and all was going well, but the wood was so slippery that it suddenly sprang out, and the tree closed up so rapidly that I had no time to take my beautiful white beard out, so here I am stuck fast and I can't get

16

away; and you silly, smooth-faced, milk-and-water girls just stand and laugh! Ugh! what wretches you are!"

The children did all in their power, but they could n't get the beard out; it was wedged in far too firmly. " I will run and fetch somebody," said Rose-red. " Crazy blockheads!" snapped the dwarf; "what's the good of calling any one else? You're already too many for me. Does nothing better occur to you than that?" " Don't be so impatient," said Snow-white. " I 'll see you get help." And taking her scissors out of her pocket she cut the end off his beard. As soon as the dwarf felt himself free he seized a bag full of gold which was hidden among the roots of the tree, lifted it up, and muttered aloud: " Drat these rude wretches, cutting off a piece of my splendid beard! " With these words he swung the bag over his back and disappeared without as much as looking at the children again.

Shortly after this Snow-white and Rose-red went out to get a dish of fish. As they approached the stream they saw something which looked like an enormous grasshopper springing toward the water as if it were going to jump in. They ran forward and recognized their old friend the dwarf. " Where are you going to?" asked Rose-red. " You're surely not going to jump into the water?" " I 'm not such a fool," screamed the dwarf. " Don't you see that fish is trying to drag me in?" The little man had been sitting on the bank fishing, when unfortunately the wind had entangled his beard in the line; and when immediately afterward a big fish bit, the feeble little creature had no strength to pull it out. The fish had the upper fin and dragged the dwarf toward him. He clung on with all his might to every rush and blade of grass, but it did n't help him much. He had to follow every movement of the fish and was in great danger of being drawn into the water. The girls came up just at the right moment, held him firm, and did all they could to disentangle his beard from the line; but in vain — beard and line were in a hopeless muddle. Nothing remained but to produce the scissors and cut the beard, by which a small part of it was sacrificed.

When the dwarf perceived what they were about he yelled to them: " Do you call that manners, you toadstools! to disfigure a fellow's face? It was n't enough that you shortened my beard before, but you must now needs cut off the best of it. I can't appear like this before my own people. I wish you 'd been at Jericho first." Then he fetched a sack of pearls that lay among the rushes, and without saying another word he dragged it away and disappeared behind a stone.

It happened that soon after this the mother sent the two girls to the town to buy needles, thread, laces, and ribbons. Their road led over a heath where huge bowlders of rock lay scattered here and there. While trudging along they saw a big bird hovering in the air, circling slowly above them, but always descending lower, till at last it settled on a rock not far from them. Immediately afterward they heard a sharp, piercing cry. They ran forward and saw with horror that the eagle had pounced on their old friend the dwarf and was about to carry him off. The tender-hearted children seized a hold of the little man, and struggled so long with the bird that at last he let go his prey. When the dwarf had recovered from the first shock he screamed in his screeching voice: " Could n't you have treated me more carefully? You have torn my thin little coat all to shreds, useless, awkward hussies that you are!" Then he took a bag of precious stones and vanished under the rocks into his cave. The girls were accustomed to his ingratitude, and went on their way and did their business in town. On their way home, as they were again passing the heath, they surprised the dwarf pouring out his precious stones on an open space, for he had thought no one would pass by at so late an hour. The evening sun shone on the glittering stones, and they glanced and gleamed so beautifully

HANSEL AND GRETTEL

Page 6

GOLDILOCKS, OR THE THREE BEARS

Page 10

that the children stood still and gazed on them. "What are you standing there gaping for?" screamed the dwarf, and his ashen-gray face became scarlet with rage. He was about to go off with these angry words, when a sudden growl was heard and a black bear trotted out of the wood. The dwarf jumped up in a great fright, but he had n't time to reach his place of retreat, for the bear was already close to him. Then he cried in terror: "Dear Mr. Bear, spare me! I 'll give you all my treasure. Look at these beautiful precious stones lying there. Spare my life! What pleasure would you get from a poor feeble little fellow like me? You won't feel me between your teeth. There, lay hold of these two wicked girls — they will be a tender morsel for you, as fat as young quails; eat them up, for Heaven's sake." But the bear, paying no attention to his words, gave the evil little creature one blow with his paw and he never moved again.

The girls had run away, but the bear called after them: "Snow-white and Rose-red, don't be afraid. Wait, and I 'll come with you." Then they recognized his voice and stood still, and when the bear was quite close to them his skin suddenly fell off, and a beautiful man stood beside them, all dressed in gold. "I am a king's son," he said, "and have been doomed by that unholy little dwarf, who had stolen my treasure, to roam about the woods as a wild bear till his death should set me free. Now he has got his well-merited punishment."

Snow-white married him and Rose-red his brother, and they divided the great treasure the dwarf had collected in his cave between them. The old mother lived for many years peacefully with her children; and she carried the two rose-trees with her, and they stood in front of her window, and every year they bore the finest red and white roses.

BEAUTY AND THE BEAST

ONCE upon a time, in a very far-off country, there lived a merchant who had been so fortunate in all his undertakings that he was enormously rich. As he had, however, six sons and six daughters, he found that his money was not too much to let them all have everything they fancied, as they were accustomed to do.

But one day a most unexpected misfortune befell them. Their house caught fire and was speedily burned to the ground, with all the splendid furniture, the books, pictures, gold, silver, and precious goods it contained; and this was only the beginning of their troubles. Their father, who had until this moment prospered in all ways, suddenly lost every ship he had upon the sea, either through pirates, shipwreck, or fire. Then he heard that his clerks in distant countries, whom he trusted entirely, had proved unfaithful, and at last from great wealth he fell into the direst poverty.

All that he had left was a little house in a desolate place at least a hundred leagues from the town in which he had lived, and to this he was forced to retreat with his children, who were in despair at the idea of leading such a different life. Indeed, the daughters at first hoped that their friends, who had been so numerous while they were rich, would insist on their staying in their houses now they no longer possessed one. But they soon found that they were left alone, and that their former friends even attributed their misfortunes to their own extravagance, and showed no intention of offering them any help. So nothing was left for them but to take their departure to the cottage, which stood in the midst of a dark forest, and seemed to be the most dismal place upon the face of the earth.

As they were too poor to have any servants, the girls had to work hard, like peasants, and the sons, for their part, cultivated the fields to earn their living. Roughly clothed, and living in the simplest way, the girls regretted unceasingly the luxuries and amusements of their former life; only the youngest tried to be brave and cheerful. She had been as sad as any one when misfortune first overtook her father, but, soon recovering her natural gayety, she set to work to make the best of things, to amuse her father and brothers as well as she could, and to try to persuade her sisters to join her in dancing and singing. But they would do nothing of the sort, and because she was not as doleful as themselves they declared that this miserable life was all she was fit for. But she was really far prettier and cleverer than they were; indeed, she was so lovely that she was always called Beauty. After two years, when they were all beginning to get used to their new life, something happened to disturb their tranquillity. Their father received the news that one of his ships, which he had believed to be lost, had come safely into port with a rich cargo.

All the sons and daughters at once thought that their poverty was at an end and wanted to set out directly for the town, but their father, who was more prudent, begged them to wait a little, and though it was harvest-time and he could ill be spared, determined to go himself first to make inquiries. Only the youngest daughter had any doubt but that they would soon again be as rich as they were before, or at least rich enough to live comfortably in some town where they would find amusement and gay companions once more. So they all loaded their father with commissions for jewels and dresses which it would have taken a fortune to buy; only Beauty, feeling sure that it was of no use, did not ask for anything. Her father, noticing her silence, said: "And what shall I bring for you, Beauty?"

"The only thing I wish for is to see you come home safely," she answered.

But this reply vexed her sisters, who fancied she was blaming them for having asked for such costly things. Her father was pleased, but as he thought that at her age she certainly ought to like pretty presents, he told her to choose something.

"Well, dear father," she said, "as you insist upon it, I beg that you will bring me a rose. I have not seen one since we came here, and I love them so much."

So the merchant set out and reached the town as quickly as possible, but only to find that his former companions, believing him to be dead, had divided between them the goods which the ship had brought; and after six months of trouble and expense he found himself as poor as when he started, having been able to recover only just enough to pay the cost of his journey. To make matters worse, he was obliged to leave the town in the most terrible weather, so that by the time he was within a few leagues of his home he was almost exhausted with cold and fatigue. Though he knew it would take some hours to get through the forest, he was so anxious to be at his journey's end that he resolved to go on; but night overtook him, and the deep snow and bitter frost made it impossible for his horse to carry him any further. Not a house was to be seen. The only shelter he could get was the hollow trunk of a great tree, and there he crouched all the night, which seemed to him the longest he had ever known. In spite of his weariness the howling of the wolves kept him awake, and even when at last the day broke he was not much better off, for the falling snow had covered up every path and he did not know which way to turn.

At length he made out some sort of track, and though at the beginning it was so rough and slippery that he fell down more than once, it presently became easier and led him into an avenue of trees which ended in a splendid castle. It seemed to the merchant very strange that no snow had fallen in the avenue, which was entirely composed of orange-trees, covered with flowers and fruit. When he reached the first court of the castle he saw before him a flight of agate steps, and went up them and passed through several splendidly furnished rooms. The pleasant warmth of the air revived him and he felt very hungry; but there seemed to be nobody in all this vast and splendid palace whom he could ask to give him something to eat. Deep silence reigned everywhere, and at last, tired of roaming through empty rooms and galleries, he stopped in a room smaller than the rest, where a clear fire was burning and a couch was drawn up cozily close to it. Thinking that this must be prepared for some one who was expected, he sat down to wait till he should come, and very soon fell into a sweet sleep.

When his extreme hunger wakened him after several hours he was still alone, but a little table, upon which was a good dinner, had been drawn up close to him, and as he had eaten nothing for twenty-four hours he lost no time in beginning his meal, hoping that he might soon have an opportunity of thanking his considerate entertainer, whoever it might be. But no one appeared, and even after another long sleep, from which he awoke completely refreshed, there was no sign of anybody, though a fresh meal of dainty cakes and fruit was prepared upon a little table at his elbow. Being naturally timid, the silence began to terrify him, and he resolved to search once more through all the rooms; but it was of no use. Not even a servant was to be seen; there was no sign of life in the palace! He began to wonder what he should do, and to amuse himself by pretending that all the treasures he saw were his own, and considering how he would divide them among his children. Then he went down into the garden, and though it was winter everywhere else, here the sun shone, and the birds sang, and the flowers bloomed, and the air was soft and sweet. The merchant, in ecstasies with all he saw and heard, said to himself:

"All this must be meant for me. I will go this minute and bring my children to share all these delights."

In spite of being so cold and weary when he reached the castle, he had taken his horse to the stable and fed it. Now he thought he would saddle it for his homeward journey, and he turned down the path which led to the stable. This path had a hedge of roses on each side of it, and the merchant thought he had never seen or smelled such exquisite flowers. They reminded him of his promise to Beauty, and he stopped and had just gathered one to take to her when he was startled by a strange noise behind him. Turning round he saw a frightful beast, which seemed to be very angry and said in a terrible voice:

"Who told you that you might gather my roses? Was it not enough that I allowed you to be in my palace and was kind to you? This is the way you show your gratitude, by stealing my flowers! But your insolence shall not go unpunished." The merchant, terrified by these furious words, dropped the fatal rose, and throwing himself on his knees cried: "Pardon me, noble sir. I am truly grateful to you for your hospitality, which was so magnificent that I could not imagine that you would be offended by my taking such a little thing as a rose." But the beast's anger was not lessened by this speech.

"You are very ready with excuses and flattery," he cried; "but that will not save you from the death you deserve."

"Alas!" thought the merchant, "if my daughter Beauty could only know what danger her rose has brought me into!"

And in despair he began to tell the beast all his misfortunes and the reason of his journey, not forgetting to mention Beauty's request.

24

"A king's ransom would hardly have procured all that my other daughters asked," he said, "but I thought that I might at least take Beauty her rose. I beg you to forgive me, for you see I meant no harm."

The beast considered for a moment, and then he said in a less furious tone:

"I will forgive you on one condition — that is, that you will give me one of your daughters."

"Ah!" cried the merchant, "if I were cruel enough to buy my own life at the expense of one of my children's, what excuse could I invent to bring her here?"

"No excuse would be necessary," answered the beast. "If she comes at all she must come willingly. On no other condition will I have her. See if any one of them is courageous enough and loves you well enough to come and save your life. You seem to be an honest man, so I will trust you to go home. I give you a month to see if either of your daughters will come back with you and stay here, to let you go free. If neither of them is willing you must come alone, after bidding them good-by forever, for then you will belong to me. And do not imagine that you can hide from me, for if you fail to keep your word I will come and fetch you!" added the beast grimly.

The merchant accepted this proposal, though he did not really think any of his daughters would be persuaded to come. He promised to return at the time appointed, and then, anxious to escape from the presence of the beast, he asked permission to set off at once. But the beast answered that he could not go until the next day.

"Then you will find a horse ready for you," he said. "Now go and eat your supper and await my orders."

The poor merchant, more dead than alive, went back to his room, where the most delicious supper was already served on the little table which was drawn up before a blazing fire. But he was too terrified to eat, and only tasted a few of the dishes, for fear the beast should be angry if he did not obey his orders. When he had finished he heard a great noise in the next room, which he knew meant that the beast was coming. As he could do nothing to escape his visit, the only thing that remained was to seem as little afraid as possible; so when the beast appeared and asked roughly if he had supped well, the merchant answered humbly that he had, thanks to his host's kindness. Then the beast warned him to remember their agreement and to prepare his daughter exactly for what she had to expect.

"Do not get up to-morrow," he added, "until you see the sun and hear a golden bell ring. Then you will find your breakfast waiting for you here, and the horse you are to ride will be ready in the court-yard. He will also bring you back again when you come with your daughter a month hence. Farewell. Take a rose to Beauty, and remember your promise."

The merchant was only too glad when the beast went away, and though he could not sleep for sadness, he lay down until the sun rose. Then, after a hasty breakfast, he went to gather Beauty's rose and mounted his horse, which carried him off so swiftly that in an instant he had lost sight of the palace, and he was still wrapped in gloomy thoughts when it stopped before the door of the cottage.

His sons and daughters, who had been very uneasy at his long absence, rushed to meet him, eager to know the result of his journey, which, seeing him mounted upon a splendid horse and wrapped in a rich mantle, they supposed to be favorable. But he hid the truth from them at first, only saying sadly to Beauty as he gave her the rose:

"Here is what you asked me to bring you. You little know what it has cost."

But this excited their curiosity so greatly that presently he told them his adventures from beginning to end, and then they

were all very unhappy. The girls lamented loudly over their
lost hopes, and the sons declared that their father should not
return to this terrible castle, and began to make plans for killing the beast if it should come to fetch him. But he reminded
them that he had promised to go back. Then the girls were
very angry with Beauty and said it was all her fault, and that
if she had asked for something sensible this would never have
happened, and complained bitterly that they should have to suffer
for her folly.

Poor Beauty, much distressed, said to them:

" I have indeed caused this misfortune, but I assure you I
did it innocently. Who could have guessed that to ask for a
rose in the middle of summer would cause so much misery? But
as I did the mischief it is only just that I should suffer for it.
I will therefore go back with my father to keep his promise."

At first nobody would hear of this arrangement, and her
father and brothers, who loved her dearly, declared that nothing
should make them let her go; but Beauty was firm. As the
time drew near she divided all her little possessions between her
sisters and said good-by to every thing she loved, and when the
fatal day came she encouraged and cheered her father as they
mounted together the horse which had brought him back. It
seemed to fly rather than gallop, but so smoothly that Beauty
was not frightened; indeed, she would have enjoyed the journey
if she had not feared what might happen to her at the end of
it. Her father still tried to persuade her to go back, but in vain.
While they were talking the night fell, and then, to their great
surprise, wonderful colored lights began to shine in all directions,
and splendid fireworks blazed out before them. All the forest
was illuminated by them, and even felt pleasantly warm, though
it had been bitterly cold before. This lasted until they reached
the avenue of orange-trees, where were statues holding flaming
torches, and when they got nearer to the palace they saw that

it was illuminated from the roof to the ground, and music sounded softly from the court-yard. "The beast must be very hungry," said Beauty, trying to laugh, "if he makes all this rejoicing over the arrival of his prey."

But in spite of her anxiety she could not help admiring all the wonderful things she saw.

The horse stopped at the foot of the flight of steps leading to the terrace, and when they had dismounted her father led her to the little room he had been in before, where they found a splendid fire burning and the table daintily spread with a delicious supper.

The merchant knew that this was meant for them, and Beauty, who was rather less frightened now that she had passed through so many rooms and seen nothing of the beast, was quite willing to begin, for her long ride had made her very hungry. But they had hardly finished their meal when the noise of the beast's footsteps was heard approaching, and Beauty clung to her father in terror, which became all the greater when she saw how frightened he was. But when the beast really appeared, though she trembled at the sight of him, she made a great effort to hide her horror and saluted him respectfully.

This evidently pleased the beast. After looking at her he said, in a tone that might have struck terror into the boldest heart, though he did not seem to be angry:

"Good-evening, old man. Good-evening, Beauty."

The merchant was too terrified to reply, but Beauty answered sweetly:

"Good-evening, Beast."

"Have you come willingly?" asked the beast. "Will you be content to stay here when your father goes away?"

Beauty answered bravely that she was quite prepared to stay.

"I am pleased with you," said the beast. "As you have come

of your own accord, you may stay. As for you, old man," he added, turning to the merchant, " at sunrise to-morrow you will take your departure. When the bell rings get up quickly and eat your breakfast, and you will find the same horse waiting to take you home; but remember that you must never expect to see my palace again."

Then turning to Beauty he said:

" Take your father into the next room and help him to choose everything you think your brothers and sisters would like to have. You will find two traveling-trunks there; fill them as full as you can. It is only just that you should send them something very precious as a remembrance of yourself."

Then he went away after saying " Good-bye, Beauty; good-bye, old man "; and though Beauty was beginning to think with great dismay of her father's departure, she was afraid to disobey the beast's orders, and they went into the next room, which had shelves and cupboards all round it. They were greatly surprised at the riches it contained. There were splendid dresses fit for a queen, with all the ornaments that were to be worn with them; and when Beauty opened the cupboards she was quite dazzled by the gorgeous jewels that lay in heaps upon every shelf. After choosing a vast quantity, which she divided between her sisters — for she had made a heap of the wonderful dresses for each of them — she opened the last chest, which was full of gold.

" I think, father," she said, " that as the gold will be more useful to you we had better take out the other things again and fill the trunks with it." So they did this; but the more they put in the more room there seemed to be, and at last they put back all the jewels and dresses they had taken out, and Beauty even added as many more of the jewels as she could carry at once; and then the trunks were not too full, but they were so heavy that an elephant could not have carried them!

" The beast was mocking us," cried the merchant. " He must

have pretended to give us all these things, knowing that I could not carry them away."

"Let us wait and see," answered Beauty. "I cannot believe that he meant to deceive us. All we can do is to fasten them up and leave them ready."

So they did this and returned to the little room, where, to their astonishment, they found breakfast ready. The merchant ate his with a good appetite, as the beast's generosity made him believe that he might perhaps venture to come back soon and see Beauty. But she felt sure that her father was leaving her forever, so she was very sad when the bell rang sharply for the second time and warned them that the time was come for them to part. They went down into the court-yard, where two horses were waiting, one loaded with the two trunks, the other for him to ride. They were pawing the ground in their impatience to start, and the merchant was forced to bid Beauty a hasty farewell; and as soon as he was mounted he went off at such a pace that she lost sight of him in an instant.

Then Beauty began to cry and wandered sadly back to her own room. But she soon found that she was very sleepy, and as she had nothing better to do she lay down and instantly fell asleep. And then she dreamed that she was walking by a brook bordered with trees and lamenting her sad fate, when a young prince, handsomer than any one she had ever seen, and with a voice that went straight to her heart, came and said to her: " Ah, Beauty! you are not so unfortunate as you suppose. Here you will be rewarded for all you have suffered elsewhere. Your every wish shall be gratified. Only try to find me out, no matter how I may be disguised, as I love you dearly, and in making me happy you will find your own happiness. Be as true-hearted as you are beautiful, and we shall have nothing left to wish for."

"What can I do, prince, to make you happy?" said Beauty.

" Only be grateful," he answered, " and do not trust too much to your eyes.   And above all, do not desert me until you have saved me from my cruel misery."

After this she thought she found herself in a room with a stately and beautiful lady, who said to her:

" Dear Beauty, try not to regret all you have left behind you, for you are destined to a better fate.   Only do not let yourself be deceived by appearances.

Beauty found her dream so interesting that she was in no hurry to awake, but presently the clock roused her by calling her name softly twelve times, and then she got up and found her dressing-table set out with everything she could possibly want; and when her toilet was finished she found dinner was waiting in the room next to hers.   But dinner does not take very long when you are all by yourself, and very soon she sat down cozily in the corner of a sofa and began to think about the charming prince she had seen in her dream.

" He said I could make him happy," said Beauty to herself. " It seems, then, that this horrible beast keeps him a prisoner. How can I set him free?   I wonder why they both told me not to trust to appearances? I don't understand it.   But after all, it was only a dream, so why should I trouble myself about it?   I had better go and find something to do to amuse myself."

So she got up and began to explore some of the many rooms of the palace.

The first she entered was lined with mirrors, and Beauty saw herself reflected on every side, and thought she had never seen such a charming room.   Then a bracelet which was hanging from a chandelier caught her eye, and on taking it down she was greatly surprised to find that it held a portrait of her unknown admirer, just as she had seen him in her dream.   With great delight she slipped the bracelet on her arm and went on into a gallery of pictures, where she soon found a portrait of the same handsome prince, as large as life and so well painted that as she studied it he seemed to smile kindly at her.

Tearing herself away from the portrait at last, she passed through into a room which contained every musical instrument under the sun, and here she amused herself for a long while in trying some of them and singing until she was tired. The next room was a library, and she saw everything she had ever wanted to read, as well as everything she had read, and it seemed to her that a whole lifetime would not be enough even to read the names of the books, there were so many. By this time it was growing dusk, and wax candles in diamond and ruby candlesticks were beginning to light themselves in every room.

Beauty found her supper served just at the time she preferred to have it, but she did not see any one or hear a sound, and though her father had warned her that she would be alone, she began to find it rather dull.

But presently she heard the beast coming, and wondered tremblingly if he meant to eat her up now.

However, as he did not seem at all ferocious, and only said gruffly, "Good-evening, Beauty," she answered cheerfully and managed to conceal her terror. Then the beast asked her how she had been amusing herself, and she told him all the rooms she had seen.

Then he asked if she thought she could be happy in his palace, and Beauty answered that everything was so beautiful that she would be very hard to please if she could not be happy. And after about an hour's talk Beauty began to think that the beast was not nearly so terrible as she had supposed at first. Then he got up to leave her and said in his gruff voice:

"Do you love me, Beauty? Will you marry me?"

"Oh! what shall I say?" cried Beauty, for she was afraid to make the beast angry by refusing.

"Say 'yes' or 'no' without fear," he replied.

"Oh! no, Beast," said Beauty hastily.

"Since you will not, good-night, Beauty," he said. And she answered, "Good-night, Beast," very glad to find that her refusal had not provoked him. And after he was gone she was very soon in bed and asleep and dreaming of her unknown prince. She thought he came and said to her:

"Ah, Beauty! why are you so unkind to me? I fear I am fated to be unhappy for many a long day still."

And then her dreams changed, but the charming prince figured in them all; and when morning came her first thought was to look at the portrait and see if it was really like him, and she found that it certainly was.

This morning she decided to amuse herself in the garden, for the sun shone and all the fountains were playing; but she was astonished to find that every place was familiar to her, and presently she came to the brook where the myrtle trees were growing where she had first met the prince in her dream, and that made her think more than ever that he must be kept a prisoner by the beast. When she was tired she went back to the palace, and found a new room full of materials for every kind of work — ribbons to make into bows and silks to work into flowers. Then there was an aviary full of rare birds, which were so tame that they flew to Beauty as soon as they saw her and perched upon her shoulders and her head.

"Pretty little creatures," she said, "how I wish that your cage was nearer to my room, that I might often hear you sing!"

So saying she opened a door and found to her delight that it led into her own room, though she had thought it was quite the other side of the palace.

There were more birds in a room further on, parrots and cockatoos that could talk, and they greeted Beauty by name. Indeed, she found them so entertaining that she took one or two back to her room, and they talked to her while she was at supper;

after which the beast paid her his usual visit and asked the same questions as before, and then with a gruff " good-night " he took his departure, and Beauty went to bed to dream of her mysterious prince. The days passed swiftly in different amusements, and after a while Beauty found out another strange thing in the palace, which often pleased her when she was tired of being alone. There was one room which she had not noticed particularly. It was empty, except that under each of the windows stood a very comfortable chair, and the first time she had looked out of the window it had seemed to her that a black curtain prevented her from seeing anything outside. But the second time she went into the room, happening to be tired, she sat down in one of the chairs, when instantly the curtain was rolled aside and a most amusing pantomime was acted before her. There were dances, and colored lights, and music, and pretty dresses, and it was all so gay that Beauty was in ecstasies. After that she tried the other seven windows in turn, and there was some new and surprising entertainment to be seen from each of them, so that Beauty never could feel lonely any more. Every evening after supper the beast came to see her, and always before saying goodnight asked her in his terrible voice:

" Beauty, will you marry me? "

And it seemed to Beauty, now she understood him better, that when she said, " No, Beast," he went away quite sad. But her happy dreams of the handsome young prince soon made her forget the poor beast, and the only thing that at all disturbed her was to be constantly told to distrust appearances, to let her heart guide her, and not her eyes, and many other equally perplexing things, which, consider as she would, she could not understand.

So everything went on for a long time, until at last, happy as she was, Beauty began to long for the sight of her father and her brothers and sisters; and one night, seeing her look very sad, the beast asked her what was the matter. Beauty had quite ceased to be afraid of him now she knew that he was really gentle in spite of his ferocious looks and his dreadful voice. So she answered that she was longing to see her home once more. Upon hearing this the beast seemed sadly distressed and cried miserably:

"Ah! Beauty, have you the heart to desert an unhappy beast like this? What more do you want to make you happy? Is it because you hate me that you want to escape?"

"No, dear Beast," answered Beauty softly, "I do not hate you, and I should be very sorry never to see you any more, but I long to see my father again. Only let me go for two months, and I promise to come back to you and stay for the rest of my life."

The beast, who had been sighing dolefully while she spoke, now replied:

"I cannot refuse you anything you ask, even though it should cost me my life. Take the four boxes you will find in the room next to your own and fill them with every thing you wish to take with you. But remember your promise and come back when the two months are over, or you may have cause to repent it, for if you do not come in good time you will find your faithful beast dead. You will not need any chariot to bring you back. Only say good-bye to all your brothers and sisters the night before you come away, and when you have gone to bed turn this ring round upon your finger and say firmly: 'I wish to go back to my palace and see my beast again.' Good-night, Beauty. Fear nothing, sleep peacefully, and before long you shall see your father once more."

As soon as Beauty was alone she hastened to fill the boxes with all the rare and precious things she saw about her, and only when she was tired of heaping things into them did they seem to be full.

Then she went to bed, but could hardly sleep for joy. And when at last she did begin to dream of her beloved prince she was grieved to see him stretched upon a grassy bank, sad and weary and hardly like himself.

"What is the matter?" she cried.

But he looked at her reproachfully and said:

"How can you ask me, cruel one? Are you not leaving me to my death perhaps?"

"Ah! don't be so sorrowful," cried Beauty. "I am only going to assure my father that I am safe and happy. I have promised the beast faithfully that I will come back, and he would die of grief if I did not keep my word!"

"What would that matter to you?" said the prince. "Surely you would not care?"

"Indeed I should be ungrateful if I did not care for such a kind beast," cried Beauty indignantly. "I would die to save him from pain. I assure you it is not his fault that he is so ugly."

Just then a strange sound woke her — some one was speaking not very far away; and opening her eyes she found herself in a room she had never seen before, which was certainly not nearly so splendid as those she was used to in the beast's palace. Where could she be? She got up and dressed hastily, and then saw that the boxes she had packed the night before were all in the room. While she was wondering by what magic the beast had transported them and herself to this strange place she suddenly heard her father's voice, and rushed out and greeted him joyfully. Her brothers and sisters were all astonished at her appearance, as they had never expected to see her again, and there was no end to the questions they asked her. She had also much to hear about what had happened to them while she was away and of her father's journey home. But when they heard that she had only come to be with them for a short time, and

then must go back to the beast's palace forever, they lamented
loudly.   Then Beauty asked her father what he thought could
be the meaning of her strange dreams, and why the prince
constantly begged her not to trust to appearances.   After much
consideration he answered:

"You tell me yourself that the beast, frightful as he is,
loves you dearly and deserves your love and gratitude for his
gentleness and kindness.   I think the prince must mean you to
understand that you ought to reward him by doing as he wishes
you to, in spite of his ugliness."

Beauty could not help seeing that this seemed very probable.
Still, when she thought of her dear prince who was so handsome, she did not feel at all inclined to marry the beast.   At
any rate, for two months she need not decide, but could enjoy
herself with her sisters.   But though they were rich now and
lived in a town again and had plenty of acquaintances, Beauty
found that nothing amused her very much; and she often
thought of the palace where she was so happy, especially as at
home she never once dreamed of her dear prince, and she felt
quite sad without him.

Then her sisters seemed to have got quite used to being
without her, and even found her rather in the way, so she would
not have been sorry when the two months were over but for her
father and brothers, who begged her to stay and seemed so
grieved at the thought of her departure that she had not the
courage to say good-bye to them.   Every day when she got up
she meant to say it at night, and when night came she put it
off again, until at last she had a dismal dream which helped her
to make up her mind.   She thought she was wandering in a
lonely path in the palace gardens, when she heard groans which
seemed to come from some bushes hiding the entrance of a
cave, and running quickly to see what could be the matter, she
found the beast stretched out upon his side, apparently dying.

He reproached her faintly with being the cause of his distress, and at the same moment a stately lady appeared and said very gravely:

"Ah! Beauty, you are only just in time to save his life. See what happens when people do not keep their promises! If you had delayed one day more you would have found him dead."

Beauty was so terrified by this dream that the next morning she announced her intention of going back at once, and that very night she said good-bye to her father and all her brothers and sisters, and as soon as she was in bed she turned her ring round upon her finger and said firmly, "I wish to go back to my palace and see my beast again," as she had been told to do.

Then she fell asleep instantly, and only woke up to hear the clock saying "Beauty, Beauty," twelve times in its musical voice, which told her at once that she was really in the palace once more. Everything was just as before, and her birds were so glad to see her; but Beauty thought she had never known such a long day, for she was so anxious to see the beast again that she felt as if supper-time would never come.

But when it did come and no beast appeared she was really frightened; so after listening and waiting for a long time she ran down into the garden to search for him. Up and down the paths and avenues ran poor Beauty, calling him in vain, for no one answered and not a trace of him could she find, until at last, quite tired, she stopped for a minute's rest and saw that she was standing opposite the shady path she had seen in her dream. She rushed down it, and, sure enough, there was the cave, and in it lay the beast — asleep, as Beauty thought. Quite glad to have found him, she ran up and stroked his head, but to her horror he did not move or open his eyes.

"Oh! he is dead, and it is all my fault," said Beauty, crying bitterly.

But then, looking at him again, she fancied he still breathed, and hastily fetching some water from the nearest fountain, she sprinkled it over his face, and to her great delight he began to revive.

" Oh, Beast, how you frightened me!" she cried, "I never knew how much I loved you until just now, when I feared I was too late to save your life."

" Can you really love such an ugly creature as I am?" said the beast faintly. "Ah! Beauty, you only came just in time. I was dying because I thought you had forgotten your promise. But go back now and rest. I shall see you again by and by."

Beauty, who had half-expected that he would be angry with her, was reassured by his gentle voice and went back to the palace, where supper was awaiting her; and afterward the beast came in as usual and talked about the time she had spent with her father, asking if she had enjoyed herself and if they had all been very glad to see her.

Beauty answered politely, and quite enjoyed telling him all that had happened to her. And when at last the time came for him to go, and he asked, as he had so often asked before, " Beauty, will you marry me?" she answered softly: "Yes, dear beast."

As she spoke a blaze of light sprang up before the windows of the palace; fireworks crackled and guns banged, and across the avenue of orange-trees, in letters all made of fireflies, was written: " Long live the prince and his bride."

Turning to ask the beast what it could all mean, Beauty found that he had disappeared, and in his place stood her long-loved prince! At the same moment the wheels of a chariot were heard upon the terrace and two ladies entered the room. One of them Beauty recognized as the stately lady she had seen in her dreams; the other was also so grand and queenly that Beauty hardly knew which to greet first.

But the one she already knew said to her companion:

"Well, queen, this is Beauty, who has had the courage to rescue your son from the terrible enchantment. They love one another, and only your consent to their marriage is wanting to make them perfectly happy."

"I consent with all my heart," cried the queen. "How can I ever thank you enough, charming girl, for having restored my dear son to his natural form?"

And then she tenderly embraced Beauty and the prince, who had meanwhile been greeting the fairy and receiving her congratulations.

"Now," said the fairy to Beauty, "I suppose you would like me to send for all your brothers and sisters to dance at your wedding?"

And so she did, and the marriage was celebrated the very next day with the utmost splendor, and Beauty and the prince lived happily ever after.

THE GOOSE-GIRL

ONCE upon a time an old queen, whose husband had been dead for many years, had a beautiful daughter. When she grew up she was betrothed to a prince who lived a great way off. Now, when the time drew near for her to be married and to depart into a foreign kingdom, her old mother gave her much costly baggage and many ornaments, gold and silver, trinkets and knick-knacks, and in fact everything that belonged to a royal trousseau, for she loved her daughter very dearly. She gave her a waiting-maid also, who was to ride with her and hand her over to the bridegroom, and she provided each of them with a horse for the journey. The princess' horse was called Falada and could speak.

When the hour for departure drew near the old mother went to her bedroom, and taking a small knife she cut her fingers till they bled; then she held a white rag under them, and letting three drops of blood fall into it, she gave it to her daughter and said: "Dear child, take great care of this rag. It may be of use to you on the journey."

So they took a sad farewell of each other, and the princess stuck the rag in front of her dress, mounted her horse, and set forth on the journey to her bridegroom's kingdom. After they had ridden for about an hour the princess began to feel very thirsty and said to her waiting-maid: "Pray get down and fetch me some water in my golden cup out of yonder stream. I would like a drink." "If you 're thirsty," said the maid, "dismount yourself and lie down by the water and drink. I don't mean to be your servant any longer." The princess was so thirsty that she got down, bent over the stream, and drank, for she was n't allowed to drink out of the golden goblet. As she drank she murmured, "Oh! Heaven, what am I to do?" and the three drops of blood replied:

> "If your mother only knew,
> Her heart would surely break in two."

But the princess was meek and said nothing about her maid's rude behavior, and quietly mounted her horse again. They rode on their way for several miles, but the day was hot and the sun's rays smote fiercely on them, so that the princess was soon overcome by thirst again. And as they passed a brook she called once more to her waiting-maid, "Pray get down and give me a drink from my golden cup," for she had long ago forgotten her maid's rude words. But the waiting-maid replied, more haughtily even than before: "If you want a drink you can dismount and get it. I don't mean to be your servant." Then the princess was compelled by her thirst to get down, and bending over the flowing water she cried and said, "Oh! Heaven, what am I to do?" and the three drops of blood replied:

> "If your mother only knew,
> Her heart would surely break in two."

And as she drank thus and leaned right over the water, the rag containing the three drops of blood fell from her bosom and floated down the stream, and she in her anxiety never even noticed her loss. But the waiting-maid had observed it with delight, as she knew it gave her power over the bride, for in losing the drops of blood the princess had become weak and powerless. When she wished to get on her horse Falada again the waiting-maid called out, "I mean to ride Falada; you must mount my beast," and this too she had to submit to. Then the waiting-maid commanded her harshly to take off her royal robes and to put on her common ones, and finally she made her swear by Heaven not to say a word about the matter when they reached the palace; and if she had n't taken this oath she would have been killed on the spot. But Falada observed everything and laid it all to heart.

The waiting-maid now mounted Falada and the real bride the worse horse, and so they continued their journey till at length they arrived at the palace yard. There was great rejoicing over the arrival, and the prince sprang forward to meet them, and taking the waiting-maid for his bride, he lifted her down from her horse and led her upstairs to the royal chamber. In the mean time the real princess was left standing below in the court-yard. The old king, who was looking out of his window, beheld her in this plight, and it struck him how sweet and gentle, even beautiful she looked. He went at once to the royal chamber and asked the bride who it was she had brought with her and had left thus standing in the court below. "Oh!" replied the bride, "I brought her with me to keep me company on the journey. Give the girl something to do, that she may n't be idle." But the old king had no work for her and could n't think of anything; so he said: "I 've a small boy who looks after the geese — she 'd better help him." The youth's name was Curdken, and the real bride was made to assist him in herding geese.

Soon after this the false bride said to the prince: "Dearest husband, I pray you grant me a favor." He answered: "That I will." "Then let the slaughterer cut off the head of the horse I rode here upon, because it behaved very badly on the journey." But the truth was she was afraid lest the horse should speak and tell how she had treated the princess. She carried her point and the faithful Falada was doomed to die. When the news came to the ears of the real princess she went to the slaughterer and secretly promised him a piece of gold if he would do something for her. There was in the town a large dark gate, through which she had to pass night and morning with the geese; would he "kindly hang up Falada's head there, that she might see it once again?" The slaughterer said he would do as she desired, chopped off the head, and nailed it firmly over the gateway.

Early next morning, as she and Curdken were driving their flock through the gate, she said as she passed under,

"Oh! Falada, 't is you hang there,"

and the head replied:

"'T is you; pass under, princess fair.
If your mother only knew,
Her heart would surely break in two."

Then she left the tower and drove the geese into a field. And when they had reached the common where the geese fed she sat down and unloosed her hair, which was of pure gold. Curdken loved to see it glitter in the sun and wanted much to pull some hair out. Then she spoke:

"Wind, wind, gently sway,
Blow Curdken's hat away;
Let him chase o'er field and wold
Till my locks of ruddy gold,
Now astray and hanging down,
Be combed and plaited in a crown."

Then a gust of wind blew Curdken's hat away, and he had to chase it over hill and dale. When he returned from the pursuit she had finished her combing and curling, and his chance of getting any hair was gone. Curdken was very angry and would n't speak to her. So they herded the geese till evening and then went home.

The next morning, as they passed under the gate, the girl said,

" Oh! Falada, 't is you hang there,"

and the head replied:

" 'T is you; pass under, princess fair.
If your mother only knew,
Her heart would surely break in two."

Then she went on her way till she came to the common, where she sat down and began to comb out her hair; then Curdken ran up to her and wanted to grasp some of the hair from her head, but she called out hastily:

" Wind, wind, gently sway,
Blow Curdken's hat away;
Let him chase o'er field and wold
Till my locks of ruddy gold,
Now astray and hanging down,
Be combed and plaited in a crown."

Then a puff of wind came and blew Curdken's hat far away, so that he had to run after it; and when he returned she had long finished putting up her golden locks, and he could n't get any hair; so they watched the geese till it was dark.

But that evening when they got home Curdken went to the old king and said: " I refuse to herd geese any longer with that girl." " For what reason?" asked the old king. " Because she does nothing but annoy me all day long," replied Curdken; and he proceeded to relate all her iniquities and said: " Every morning as we drive the flock through the dark gate she says to a horse's head that hangs on the wall,

> " ' Oh! Falada, 't is you hang there,'

and the head replies:

> " ' 'T is you; pass under, princess fair.
>   If your mother only knew,
>   Her heart would surely break in two.' "

And Curdken went on to tell what passed on the common where the geese fed and how he had always to chase his hat.

The old king bade him go and drive forth his flock as usual next day, and when morning came he himself took up his position behind the dark gate and heard how the goose-girl greeted Falada. Then he followed her through the field and hid himself behind a bush on the common. He soon saw with his own eyes how the goose-boy and the goose-girl looked after the geese, and how after a time the maiden sat down and loosed her hair, that glittered like gold, and repeated:

> " Wind, wind, gently sway,
>   Blow Curdken's hat away;
>   Let him chase o'er field and wold
>   Till my locks of ruddy gold,
>   Now astray and hanging down,
>   Be combed and plaited in a crown."

Then a gust of wind came and blew Curdken's hat away, so that he had to fly over hill and dale after it, and the girl in the mean time quietly combed and plaited her hair: all this the old king observed and returned to the palace without any one having noticed him. In the evening when the goose-girl came home he called her aside and asked her why she behaved as she did. " I may n't tell you why. How dare I confide my woes to any one? for I swore not to by Heaven, otherwise I should have lost my life." The old king begged her to tell him all, and left her no peace, but he could get nothing out of her. At last he said, " Well, if you won't tell me, confide your trouble to the iron stove there," and he went away. Then she crept to the stove and began to sob and cry and to pour out her poor little heart, and said: " Here I sit, deserted by all the world, I who am a king's daughter, and a false waiting-maid has forced me to take off my own clothes and has taken my place with my bridegroom, while I have to fulfill the lowly office of a goose-girl.

> " ' If your mother only knew,
> Her heart would surely break in two.' "

But the old king stood outside at the stove chimney and listened to her words. Then he entered the room again, and bidding her leave the stove, he ordered royal apparel to be put on her, in which she looked amazingly lovely. Then he summoned his son and revealed to him that he had got the false bride, who was nothing but a waiting-maid, while the real one, in the guise of the ex-goose-girl, was standing at his side. The young king rejoiced from his heart when he saw her beauty and learned how good she was, and a great banquet was prepared, to which every one was bidden. The bridegroom sat at the head of the table, the princess on one side of him and the waiting-maid on the other; but she was so dazzled that she did not recognize the princess in her glittering garments. Now, when they had eaten and drunk and were merry, the old king asked the waiting-maid to solve a knotty point for him. " What," said he, " should be done to a certain person who has deceived every one?" and he proceeded to relate the whole story, ending up with, " Now, what sentence should be passed?" Then the false bride answered: " She deserves to be put stark naked into a barrel lined with sharp nails, which should be dragged by two white horses up and down the street till she is dead."

" You are the person," said the king, " and you have passed sentence on yourself; and even so it shall be done to you." And when the sentence had been carried out the young king was married to his real bride, and both reigned over the kingdom in peace and happiness.

CINDERELLA; OR, THE LITTLE GLASS SLIPPER

ONCE there was a gentleman who married for his second wife the proudest and most haughty woman that was ever seen. She had by a former husband two daughters of her own humor, who were, indeed, exactly like her in all things. He had likewise, by another wife, a young daughter, but of unparalleled goodness and sweetness of temper, which she took from her mother, who was the best creature in the world.

No sooner were the ceremonies of the wedding over but the mother-in-law began to show herself in her true colors. She could not bear the good qualities of this pretty girl, and the less because they made her own daughters appear the more odious. She employed her in the meanest work of the house: she scoured the dishes, tables, etc., and scrubbed madam's chamber and those of misses, her daughters; she lay up in a sorry garret, upon a wretched straw bed, while her sisters lay in fine rooms, with floors all inlaid, upon beds of the very newest fashion, and where they had looking-glasses so large that they might see themselves at their full length from head to foot.

The poor girl bore all patiently and dared not tell her father, who would have rattled her off; for his wife governed him entirely. When she had done her work she used to go into the chimney-corner and sit down among cinders and ashes, which made her commonly be called a cinder wench; but the youngest, who was not so rude and uncivil as the eldest, called her Cinderella. However, Cinderella, notwithstanding her mean apparel, was a hundred times handsomer than her sisters, though they were always dressed very richly.

It happened that the king's son gave a ball and invited all persons of fashion to it. Our young misses were also invited, for they cut a very grand figure among the quality. They were mightily delighted at this invitation, and wonderfully busy in choosing out such gowns, petticoats, and head-clothes as might become them. This was a new trouble to Cinderella, for it was she who ironed her sisters' linen and plaited their ruffles. They talked all day long of nothing but how they should be dressed.

"For my part," said the eldest, "I will wear my red velvet suit with French trimming."

"And I," said the youngest, "shall have my usual petticoat; but then, to make amends for that, I will put on my gold-flowered manteau and my diamond stomacher, which is far from being the most ordinary one in the world."

They sent for the best tire-woman they could get to make up their head-dresses and adjust their double pinners, and they had their red brushes and patches from Mademoiselle de la Poche.

Cinderella was likewise called up to them to be consulted in all these matters, for she had excellent notions and advised them always for the best, and offered her services to dress their heads, which they were very willing she should do. As she was doing this they said to her:

"Cinderella, would you not be glad to go to the ball?"

"Alas!" said she, "you only jeer me. It is not for such as I am to go thither."

"Thou art in the right of it," replied they. "It would make the people laugh to see a cinder wench at a ball."

SNOW-WHITE AND ROSE-RED

Page 14

THE GOOSE GIRL

Page 46

CINDERELLA; OR, LITTLE GLASS SLIPPER

Any one but Cinderella would have dressed their heads awry, but she was very good and dressed them perfectly well. They were almost two days without eating, so much they were transported with joy. They broke above a dozen of laces in trying to be laced up close, that they might have a fine slender shape, and they were continually at their looking-glass. At last the happy day came. They went to court, and Cinderella followed them with her eyes as long as she could, and when she had lost sight of them she fell a-crying.

Her godmother, who saw her all in tears, asked her what was the matter.

"I wish I could — I wish I could — "

She was not able to speak the rest, being interrupted by her tears and sobbing.

This godmother of hers, who was a fairy, said to her: "Thou wishest thou couldst go to the ball. Is it not so?"

"Y-es," cried Cinderella, with a great sigh.

"Well," said her godmother, "be but a good girl, and I will contrive that thou shalt go." Then she took her into her chamber and said to her: "Run into the garden and bring me a pumpkin."

Cinderella went immediately to gather the finest she could get, and brought it to her godmother, not being able to imagine how this pumpkin could make her go to the ball. Her godmother scooped out all the inside of it, having left nothing but the rind; which done, she struck it with her wand, and the pumpkin was instantly turned into a fine coach, gilded all over with gold.

She then went to look into her mouse-trap, where she found six mice, all alive, and ordered Cinderella to lift up a little the trap-door, when, giving each mouse as it went out a little tap with her wand, the mouse was that moment turned into a fine horse, which altogether made a very fine set of six horses of a beautiful mouse-colored dapple-gray. Being at a loss for a coachman, Cinderella said:

" I will go and see if there is never a rat in the rat-trap — we may make a coachman of him."

" Thou art in the right," replied her godmother. " Go and look."

Cinderella brought the trap to her, and in it there were three huge rats. The fairy made choice of one of the three which had the largest beard, and having touched him with her wand he was turned into a fat, jolly coachman, who had the smartest whiskers eyes ever beheld. After that she said to her:

" Go again into the garden, and you will find six lizards behind the watering-pot. Bring them to me."

She had no sooner done so but her godmother turned them into six footmen, who skipped up immediately behind the coach, with their liveries all bedaubed with gold and silver, and clung as close behind each other as if they had done nothing else their whole lives. The fairy then said to Cinderella:

" Well, you see here an equipage fit to go to the ball with. Are you not pleased with it? "

" Oh! yes," cried she; " but must I go thither as I am, in these nasty rags? "

Her godmother only just touched her with her wand, and at the same instant her clothes were turned into cloth-of-gold and silver, all beset with jewels. This done, she gave her a pair of glass slippers, the prettiest in the whole world. Being thus decked out, she got up into her coach; but her godmother, above all things, commanded her not to stay till after midnight, telling her at the same time that if she stayed one moment longer the coach would be a pumpkin again, her horses mice, her coachman a rat, her footmen lizards, and her clothes become just as they were before.

She promised her godmother she would not fail of leaving

the ball before midnight, and then away she drives, scarce able to contain herself for joy. The king's son, who was told that a great princess, whom nobody knew, was come, ran out to receive her. He gave her his hand as she alighted out of the coach, and led her into the hall among all the company. There was immediately a profound silence, they left off dancing, and the violins ceased to play, so attentive was every one to contemplate the singular beauties of the unknown new-comer. Nothing was then heard but a confused noise of "Ha! how handsome she is! Ha! how handsome she is!"

The king himself, old as he was, could not help watching her and telling the queen softly that it was a long time since he had seen so beautiful and lovely a creature.

All the ladies were busied in considering her clothes and head-dress, that they might have some made next day after the same pattern, provided they could meet with such fine materials and as able hands to make them.

The king's son conducted her to the most honorable seat and afterward took her out to dance with him. She danced so very gracefully that they all more and more admired her. A fine collation was served up, whereof the young prince ate not a morsel, so intently was he busied in gazing on her.

She went and sat down by her sisters, showing them a thousand civilities, giving them part of the oranges and citrons which the prince had presented her with, which very much surprised them, for they did not know her. While Cinderella was thus amusing her sisters, she heard the clock strike eleven and three-quarters, whereupon she immediately made a courtesy to the company and hastened away as fast as she could.

On arriving home, she ran to seek out her godmother, and after having thanked her she said she could not but heartily wish she might go next day to the ball, because the king's son had desired her to.

As she was eagerly telling her godmother what had passed at the ball her two sisters knocked at the door, which Cinderella ran and opened.

"How long you have stayed!" cried she, gaping, rubbing her eyes, and stretching herself as if she had been just waked out of her sleep. She had not, however, had any manner of inclination to sleep since they went from home.

"If thou hadst been at the ball," said one of her sisters, "thou wouldst not have been tired with it. There came thither the finest princess, the most beautiful ever was seen with mortal eyes. She showed us a thousand civilities and gave us oranges and citrons."

Cinderella seemed very indifferent in the matter. Indeed, she asked them the name of that princess, but they told her they did not know it, and that the king's son was very uneasy on her account and would give all the world to know who she was. At this Cinderella, smiling, replied:

"She must, then, be very beautiful indeed. How happy you have been! Could not I see her? Ah! dear Miss Charlotte, do lend me your yellow suit of clothes which you wear every day."

"Ay, to be sure!" cried Miss Charlotte; "lend my clothes to such a dirty cinder wench as thou art! I should be a fool."

Cinderella expected well such answer and was very glad of the refusal, for she would have been sadly put to it if her sister had lent her what she asked for jestingly.

The next day the two sisters were at the ball, and so was Cinderella, but dressed more magnificently than before. The king's son was always by her and never ceased his compliments and kind speeches to her, to whom all this was so far from being tiresome that she quite forgot what her godmother had recommended to her, so that she at last counted the clock striking twelve when she took it to be no more than eleven. She then rose up and fled as nimble as a deer. The prince followed, but could not overtake her. She left behind one of her glass slippers, which the prince took up most carefully. She got home, but quite out of breath, and in her old clothes, having nothing left her of all her finery but one of the little slippers, fellow to that she dropped. The guards at the palace gate were asked if they had not seen a princess go out.

They said they had seen nobody go out but a young girl, very meanly dressed, and who had more of the air of a poor country wench than a gentlewoman.

When the two sisters returned from the ball Cinderella asked them if they had been well diverted and if the fine lady had been there.

They told her yes, but that she hurried away immediately when it struck twelve, and with so much haste that she dropped one of her little glass slippers, the prettiest in the world, which the king's son had taken up; that he had done nothing but look at her all the time at the ball, and that most certainly he was very much in love with the beautiful person who owned the glass slipper.

What they said was very true, for a few days after the king's son caused it to be proclaimed, by sound of trumpet, that he would marry her whose foot this slipper would just fit. They whom he employed began to try it upon the princesses, then the duchesses and all the court, but in vain. It was brought to the two sisters, who did all they possibly could to thrust their foot into the slipper, but they could not effect it. Cinderella, who saw all this and knew her slipper, said to them, laughing:

" Let me see if it will not fit me."

Her sisters burst out a-laughing and began to banter her. The gentleman who was sent to try the slipper looked earnestly at Cinderella, and finding her very handsome said it was but just that she should try, and that he had orders to let every one make trial.

He obliged Cinderella to sit down, and putting the slipper to her foot he found it went on very easily and fitted her as if it had been made of wax. The astonishment her two sisters were in was excessively great, but still abundantly greater when Cinderella pulled out of her pocket the other slipper and put it on her foot. Thereupon in came her godmother, who, having touched with her wand Cinderella's clothes, made them richer and more magnificent than any of those she had before.

And now her two sisters found her to be that fine, beautiful lady whom they had seen at the ball. They threw themselves at her feet to beg pardon for all the ill-treatment they had made her undergo. Cinderella took them up, and as she embraced them cried that she forgave them with all her heart and desired them always to love her.

She was conducted to the young prince, dressed as she was. He thought her more charming than ever and a few days after married her. Cinderella, who was no less good than beautiful, gave her two sisters lodgings in the palace, and that very same day matched them with two great lords of the court.

RED RIDING HOOD

THERE was once a sweet little maiden, who was loved by all who knew her; but she was especially dear to her Grandmother, who did not know how to make enough of the child. Once she gave her a little red velvet cloak. It was so becoming, and she liked it so much, that she would never wear anything else; and so she got the name of Red Riding Hood.

One day her Mother said to her: "Come here, Red Riding Hood, take this cake and bottle of wine to Grandmother; she is weak and ill, and it will do her good. Go quickly, before it gets hot, and don't loiter by the way, or run, or you will fall down and break the bottle, and there will be no wine for Grandmother. When you get there, don't forget to say 'Good-morning' prettily, without staring about you."

"I will do just as you tell me," Red Riding Hood promised her Mother.

Her Grandmother lived away in the woods a good half-hour from the village. When she got to the wood, she met a Wolf; but Red Riding Hood did not know what a wicked animal he was, so she was not a bit afraid of him.

"Good-morning, Red Riding Hood," he said.

"Good-morning, Wolf," she answered.

"Whither away so early, Red Riding Hood?"

"To Grandmother's."

"What have you got in your basket?"

"Cake and wine; we baked yesterday, so I'm taking a cake to Grannie; she wants something to make her well."

"Where does your Grandmother live, Red Riding Hood?"

"A good quarter of an hour further into the wood. Her house stands under three big oak trees, near a hedge of nut trees which you must know," said Red Riding Hood.

The Wolf thought: "This tender little creature will be a plump morsel; she will be nicer than the old woman. I must be cunning, and snap them both up."

He walked along with Red Riding Hood for a while, then he said: "Look at the pretty flowers, Red Riding Hood. Why don't you look about you? I don't believe you even hear the birds sing. You are just as solemn as if you were going to school: everything else is so gay out here in the woods."

Red Riding Hood raised her eyes, and when she saw the sunlight dancing through the trees, and all the bright flowers, she thought: "I'm sure Grannie would be pleased if I took her a bunch of fresh flowers. It is still quite early. I shall have plenty of time to pick them."

So she left the path, and wandered off among the trees to pick the flowers. Each time she picked one, she always saw another prettier one further on. So she went deeper and deeper into the forest.

In the meantime the Wolf went straight off to the Grandmother's cottage, and knocked at the door.

"Who is there?"

"Red Riding Hood, bringing you a cake and some wine. Open the door!"

"Press the latch!" cried the old woman. "I am too weak to get up."

The Wolf pressed the latch, and the door sprang open. He went straight in and up to the bed without saying a word, and ate up the poor old woman. Then he put on her nightdress and nightcap, got into bed and drew the curtains.

Red Riding Hood ran about picking flowers till she could carry no more, and then she remembered her Grandmother again. She was astonished when she got to the house to find the door open, and when she entered the room everything seemed so strange.

She felt quite frightened, but she did not know why. "Generally I like coming to see Grandmother so much," she thought. She cried: "Good-morning, Grandmother," but she received no answer.

Then she went up to the bed and drew the curtain back. There lay her Grandmother but she had drawn her cap down over her face, and she looked very odd.

"Oh, Grandmother, what big ears you have got," she said.

"The better to hear with, my dear."

"Grandmother, what big eyes you have got."

"The better to see with, my dear."

"What big hands you have got, Grandmother."

"The better to catch hold of you with, my dear."

"But Grandmother, what big teeth you have got."

"The better to eat you with, my dear."

Hardly had the Wolf said this, than he made a spring out of bed, and devoured poor little Red Riding Hood. When the Wolf had satisfied himself, he went back to bed and he was soon snoring loudly.

A Huntsman went past the house, and thought, "How loudly the old lady is snoring; I must see if there is anything the matter with her."

So he went into the house, and up to the bed, where he found the Wolf fast asleep. "Do I find you here, you old sinner?" he said. "Long enough have I sought you."

He raised his gun to shoot, when it just occurred to him

that perhaps the Wolf had eaten up the old lady, and that she might still be saved. So he took a knife and began cutting open the sleeping Wolf. At the first cut he saw the little red cloak, and after a few more slashes, the little girl sprang out, and cried: "Oh, how frightened I was, it was so dark inside the Wolf!" Next the old Grandmother came out, alive, but hardly able to breathe.

Red Riding Hood brought some big stones with which they filled the Wolf, so that when he woke and tried to spring away, they dragged him back, and he fell down dead.

They were all quite happy now. The Huntsman skinned the Wolf, and took the skin home. The Grandmother ate the cake and drank the wine which Red Riding Hood had brought, and she soon felt quite strong. Red Riding Hood thought: "I will never again wander off into the forest as long as I live, if my Mother forbids it.

THE BABES IN THE WOOD[1]

MANY years ago there lived a gentleman and his lady. The gentleman was brave and good, and the lady was gentle, beautiful, and virtuous. They were much beloved by all who knew them, for they were always trying to do good to others.

This lady and gentleman lived together very happily for many years, for they loved each other most tenderly. They had two children, who were both very young, the boy, who was the eldest, was about three years old, and the youngest, who was a girl, not quite two years old. The boy was very much like his father, and the girl was like her mother. By the end of this time the gentleman fell sick, and day after day he grew worse. His lady was so much grieved by his illness that she fell sick too. No physic, nor anything else, was of the least use to them, for they grew worse and worse; and they saw that they would soon be taken away from their little ones, and be forced to leave them in the world without father or mother.

They bore this cruel thought as well as they could, and trusted that after they were dead, their children would find some kind friend to look after them. They talked to one another tenderly about them, and at last agreed to send for the gentleman's brother, and give their darlings into his care.

As soon as the gentleman's brother heard this news he

---

[1] The best known of English ballads "The Children in the Wood" (the source of this story) was written in the latter part of the sixteenth century.

61

made all the haste he could to the bedside of the father and mother. " Ah! brother," said the dying man, " you see how short a time I have to live, yet neither death nor pain can give me half so much grief as the thought of what these dear babes will do without a parent's care. Brother, brother," continued the gentleman, putting out his hand as well as he could, and pointing to the children, " they will have none but you to be kind to them, to see them clothed and fed, and teach them to be good and happy."

" Dear, dear brother," said the dying lady, " you must be father, mother, and uncle too, to these little lambs. First let William be taught to read; and then he should be told how good his father was. And little Jane, — oh! brother, it wrings my heart to talk of her: think of the gentle usage she will stand in need of, and take her fondly on your knee, brother, and she and William, too, will repay your care with love."

The uncle then answered: " Oh! how it grieves my heart to see you, my dearest brother and sister, in this sad state! but take comfort, there may still be hope of your getting well: yet if we should happen to lose you, I will do all you can desire for your darling children. In me they shall find a father, mother, and uncle. William shall learn to read, and shall be told how good his father was, that he may turn out as good himself when he grows up to be a man. Jane shall be used with the most tender care, and shall be fondled on my knee. But, dear brother, you have said nothing of the wealth you must leave behind. I am sure you know my heart too well to think that I speak of this for any other reason than your dear children's good, and that I may be able to make use of your money only for their sake."

" Pray, brother," said the dying man, " do not grieve me with talking of any such thing; for how could you, who will be their father, mother, and uncle, once think of wronging them? Here, here, brother, is my will. You will see how I have done the best I could for my babes."

A few moments after the gentleman had said these words he pressed his cold lips to his children; the lady did the same, and in a short time they both died. The uncle shed a few tears at this sad sight, and then broke open the will, in which he found that his brother had left the little boy, William, the sum of three hundred pounds a year, when he should be twenty-one years old, and to Jane, the girl, the sum of five hundred pounds in gold, to be paid to her on the day of her marriage. But if the children should happen to die before coming of age, then all the money was to belong to their uncle. The will of the gentleman next ordered that he and his dear wife should be buried side by side in the same grave.

The two little children were now taken home to the house of their uncle, who, for some time, did just as their parents had told him upon their death-bed, and used them with great kindness. But when he had kept them about a year he forgot by degrees to think how their father and mother looked when they gave their children to his care, and how he himself had made a promise to be their father, mother, and uncle all in one. After a little more time had passed, the uncle could not help thinking that he wished he could get rid of the children, for then he should have all the money for himself; and when he had once begun to think this, he went on till he could hardly think of anything else.

At last he said to himself: "It would not be very hard for me to get rid of them so that nobody should know anything about the matter, and then the money will be mine at once."

When the cruel uncle had once made up his mind to get rid of the helpless little creatures, he was not long in finding a way to bring it about. He hired two sturdy ruffians, who had already held up many travelers in a dark, thick wood, some way off, for the sake of robbing them of their money. These two wicked men agreed with the uncle for a large sum of money to do the most cruel thing that was ever heard of; and so the uncle began to get everything ready for them.

He had told an artful story to his wife of what good it would do the children to put them forward in their learning; and how he had a friend in London who would take care of them. He then said to the poor little things: "Should you not like to see the famous town of London, where you, William, can buy a fine wooden horse to ride upon all day long, and a whip to make him gallop, and a fine sword to wear by your side? And you, Jane, shall have pretty playthings, and a nice gilded coach shall take you there."

"Oh, yes, we will go, uncle," said the children, and, with a heart as hard as stones, the uncle soon got them ready for the journey. The harmless little creatures were put into a fine coach a few days after, and along with them the two cruel wretches, who were soon to put an end to their merry prattle, and turn their smiles into tears. One of them drove the coach, and the other sat inside between little William and little Jane.

When they had reached the entrance to the dark thick wood, the two ruffians took them out of the coach, telling them they might now walk a little way and gather some flowers; and while the children were skipping about like lambs, the ruffians turned their backs to them, and began to talk about what they had to do.

"In good truth," said the one who had been sitting between the children all the way, "now I have seen their sweet faces and heard their pretty talk I have no heart to do the cruel deed: let us send the children back to their uncle."

"But, indeed, I will not," said the other; "what is their pretty talk to us?"

"Think of your own children at home," answered the first.

"Yes, but I shall get nothing to take back to them if I turn coward as you would have me do," replied the other. At last the two ruffians fell into such a passion about getting rid of the poor babes, that the one who wished to spare their lives took out the great knife he had brought to murder them with and stabbed the other to the heart, so that he fell down dead at his feet. The one who had killed him was quite at a loss what to do with the children; for he wanted to get away as fast as he could, for fear of being found in the wood.

At last he thought the only thing he could do was to leave them in the wood by themselves, and trust them to the kindness of anybody that might happen to pass by and find them there.

"Come here, my pretty ones," said he; "you must take hold of my hands and go with me." The poor children took each a hand and went on; but the tears burst from their eyes, and their little limbs shook with fear all the while.

In this way he led them for about two miles farther on in the wood, and then told them to wait there till he came back from the next town, where he would go and get them some food. William took his sister Jane by the hand, and they walked in fear up and down in the wood.

"Will the strange man come with some cakes, Billy?" said little Jane.

"By and by, dear Jane," said William.

And soon after, "I wish I had some cakes, Billy," said she.

They then looked about with their little eyes to every part of the wood; and it would have melted a heart as hard as stone to see how sad they looked, and how they listened to every sound of wind in the trees. After they had waited a very long time, they tried to stay their hunger with blackberries; but they soon ate all that were within their reach.

Night was now coming on; and William, who had tried all

he could to comfort his little sister, at last wanted comfort himself; so when Jane said once more, "How hungry I am, Billy. I b-e-l-ieve — I cannot help crying — " William burst out a-crying too; and down they lay upon the cold earth; and putting their arms round each other's neck, there they starved, and there they died.

Thus were those two pretty harmless babes murdered; and as no one knew of their death, so there was no one to dig a grave and bury them. In the mean time the wicked uncle thought they had been killed as he ordered, so he told all the folks who asked about them an artful tale of their having died in London of the smallpox, and he then took all their fortune to himself, and lived upon it as if it had been his own by good right. But all this did him very little service; for soon after his wife died; and as he could not help being very unhappy, and was always thinking, too, that he saw the children before his eyes, he did not attend at all to his affairs; so that, instead of growing richer, he became poorer every day.

Besides this, his two sons had gone on board a ship to try their fortune abroad. They both were drowned at sea, and he became quite wretched, so that his life was a burden to him. When things had gone on in this manner for some years the ruffian who took pity on the children and would not kill them robbed some person in that very wood; and being pursued, he was caught and brought to prison, and soon after was tried before a judge and was found guilty; and sentenced to be hanged for the crime. As soon as he found what his death must be, he sent for the keeper of the prison, and told him all the crimes he had been guilty of.

Thus he made known the story of the two children; and at the same time told what part of the wood he had left them to starve in. The news of this matter soon reached the uncle's ears, who, already broken-hearted by many ills and worries, could not bear the load of public shame that must now fall on him, so he lay down upon his bed and died that very day.

As soon as the manner of the death of the two children was made public, proper persons were sent to search the wood for them; and after a great deal of trouble, the pretty babes were at last found stretched in each other's arms; with William's arm round the neck of Jane, his face turned close to hers, and his frock pulled over her body.

They were quite covered with leaves, which in all that time had not withered; and on a bush near this cold grave there sat a robin red-breast, watching and chirping: so that many gentle hearts still think it was this kind little bird that brought the leaves and covered the little babes over with them.

JACK AND THE BEAN-STALK

IN the days of King Alfred, there lived a poor woman, in a remote country village in England, a great many miles from London. She had been a widow some years, and had an only son named Jack, whom she indulged in every wish. The consequence of this was that Jack did not pay the least attention to anything she said, but was idle, careless, and wasteful. His follies were not owing to a bad disposition, but to the fact that his mother had never checked him. By degrees she spent all that she had — scarcely anything was left to her but a cow.

The poor woman one day met Jack with tears in her eyes. Her distress was great, and for the first time in her life she could not help scolding him, saying, " Oh! you cruel child; you have at last brought me to beggary and ruin. I have not money enough to purchase even a bit of bread for another day. Nothing now remains to sell but my poor cow. I am sorry to part with her. It grieves me sadly, but we must not starve! "

For a few minutes Jack felt sorry, but this feeling soon passed away, and he began teasing his mother to let him sell the cow at the next village, and at last she gave her consent. As he was going along he met a butcher, who inquired why he was driving the cow from home. Jack replied that he was going to sell it. Now the butcher held some curious beans in his hat. They were of various colors and attracted Jack's attention. This the butcher noticed, and, knowing Jack's easy temper, thought this was the time to take advantage of it. He could not let slip so good an opportunity, so he asked what was the price of the cow, offering at the same time all the beans in his hat for her.

The silly boy could not hide the joy he felt at what he supposed was so good an offer, and the bargain was struck at once. The cow was thus exchanged for a few paltry beans. Jack made the best of his way back, calling aloud to his mother before he reached home, thinking in this way to surprise her.

When she saw the beans and heard Jack's story, her patience quite forsook her. She was so angry that she threw the beans out of the window, and they were scattered in all directions, some falling into the garden. Then she threw her apron over her head and cried bitterly. Not having anything to eat, they both went supperless to bed.

Jack awoke early in the morning, and seeing something uncommon darkening the window of his bedchamber, ran downstairs into the garden. Here he found that some of the beans had taken root, and had sprung up in a wonderful manner. The stalks were of an immense thickness, and had so twined together that they formed a ladder like a chain. Looking up he could not see the top, it appeared to be lost in the clouds. He tried it, and found it firm and not to be shaken.

He quickly made up his mind to climb to the top, in order to seek his fortune, and ran to tell his mother what he meant to do, not doubting but she would be as pleased as he was. She declared he should not go; she said it would break her heart if he did. She begged and prayed him not to go, but all in vain, for Jack set out, and after climbing for some hours reached the top of the bean-stalk, tired and quite worn out. Looking around he found himself in a strange country; it appeared to be a barren desert, not a tree, shrub, house, or living creature was to be seen. Here and there were scattered fragments of stone, and at unequal distances small heaps of earth were loosely thrown together.

Jack seated himself sadly upon a block of stone and thought of his mother. He thought with sorrow upon his disobedience in climbing the bean-stalk against her will; and after a while began to fear that he must die of hunger. However, he walked on, hoping to find a house where he might beg something to eat and drink. Presently he saw in the distance a handsome young woman; as she approached, Jack could not help admiring her for her beauty. She was dressed in the most elegant style, and had a small white wand in her hand, on the top of which was a peacock of pure gold.

While Jack was looking with the greatest surprise at this charming person, she came up to him, and with a sweet smile asked how he came there. Jack told her all about the beanstalk. She asked him if he remembered his father. He replied that he did not; and added, there must be some mystery about him, because when he asked his mother about his father, she always would weep and would tell him nothing. He could not help noticing that she would never answer his questions, and she even seemed afraid of speaking, as if there was some secret connected with his father's history which she must not tell.

The young woman replied: "I will tell the whole story; your mother must not do so. But, before I begin, I require a solemn promise on your part to do what I tell you. I am a fairy, and if you do not perform exactly what I desire, you will be destroyed." Jack was frightened at her threats, but promised to do exactly as she bade him, and the fairy then said: —

"Your father was a rich man. He was very good to the poor and constantly helped them. He made it a rule never to let a day pass without doing good to some one. On one day in the week he kept open house and invited only those who

were poor but had once lived well. He always sat at the head
of the table himself, and did all in his power to make his guests
comfortable. The rich and the great, however, were not invited. The servants were all happy, and greatly loved their
master and mistress. Now a giant lived a great many miles off,
and he was altogether as wicked as your father was good. He
was in his heart envious, covetous, and cruel, but he had the art
of hiding those vices.

"He was poor, and wished to get rich no matter how.
Hearing your father spoken of, he thought it would be a good
thing to make friends with him and get into his good graces.
He removed quickly into your neighborhood, where he pretended that he was a gentleman who had just lost all he had
by an earthquake, and found it difficult to escape with his life.

"Your father believed his story, and pitied him. He gave
him handsome rooms in his own house, and caused him and his
wife to be treated like visitors of importance, little imagining
that the giant was planning to make him a horrid return for
all his kindness.

"Things went on in this way for some time, the giant becoming daily more impatient to carry out his plan. At last his
chance came. Your father's house was at some distance from
the seashore, but with a glass the coast could be seen distinctly.
The giant was one day using the telescope. The wind was very
high, and he saw a fleet of ships in distress off the rock. He
hastened to your father, mentioned the circumstance, and eagerly
begged him to send all the servants he could spare to help the
sufferers.

"Every one was at once sent off, except the porter and your
nurse. The giant then joined your father in the study, and
appeared to be delighted — he really was so. Your father
recommended to him a favorite book, and was handing it down,
when the giant took the opportunity, and stabbed him, killing

him instantly. The giant left the body, found the porter and nurse, and at once killed them, being determined to have no living witnesses of his crimes.

"You were then only three months old. Your mother had you in her arms in another part of the house, and did not know what was going on. She went into the study, but how was she shocked on finding your father a corpse! She was overcome with horror and grief, and could not move from the spot. The giant, who was seeking her, found her in that state, and was about to serve her and you as he had done your father, but she fell at his feet, and begged him to spare your life and hers.

"Remorse, for a moment, seemed to touch the villain's heart. He granted your lives, but first he made her take a most solemn oath never to tell you who your father was, or to answer any questions about him, assuring her that if she did he would certainly find it out, and put both of you to death in the most cruel manner.

"Your mother took you in her arms and fled as quickly as possible. She was scarcely gone when the giant repented that he had allowed her to escape. He would have pursued her instantly, but he had to look out for his own safety, as it was necessary he should be gone before the servants returned. Having gained your father's confidence, he knew where to find all his treasure. Therefore, he soon loaded himself and his wife with it, set the house on fire in several places, and when the servants came back the house was burned quite down to the ground.

"Your poor mother, forlorn, alone, and forsaken, wandered with you a great many miles from her home. At last she settled in the cottage where you were brought up, and it was entirely owing to her fear of the giant that she never spoke of your father to you. I became your father's guardian at his birth; but fairies have laws to which they are subject as well as mortals. A short time before the giant went to your father's house, I did something wrong; to punish me my power was taken away for a time — an unfortunate circumstance, as it totally prevented my helping him.

"The day on which you met the butcher, as you went to sell your mother's cow, my power was given me again. It was I who made you take the beans in exchange for the cow, though you did not know it. By my power the bean-stalk grew to so great a height and became a ladder. I need not add that I gave you the strong desire to climb up the ladder.

"Now, the giant lives in this country, and you are the person appointed to punish him for all his wickedness. You will have dangers and difficulties, but you must persevere in avenging the death of your father, or you will not prosper in anything you do, but will always be miserable. As to the giant's possessions, you may seize on all you can; for everything he has is yours because it belonged to your father, though now you are unjustly deprived of it. One thing I desire, — do not let your mother know you are acquainted with your father's history till you see me again. Go along the direct road, you will soon see the house where your cruel enemy lives. While you do as I order you, I will protect and guard you; but, remember, if you dare disobey my orders, a most dreadful punishment awaits you."

When the fairy had ended she disappeared, leaving Jack to pursue his journey. He walked on till after sunset, when, to his great joy, he saw a large mansion. This pleasant sight cheered him greatly; he walked as fast as he could and soon reached it.

A plain-looking woman was at the door; he spoke to her and begged that she would give him a morsel of bread and a night's lodging.

She expressed the greatest surprise at seeing him, and said

it was quite uncommon to see a human being near their house, for it was well known that her husband was a large and very powerful giant, and that he would never eat anything but human flesh if he could possibly get it. She said, also, that he did not think anything of walking fifty miles to get it, usually being out the whole day for that purpose.

This account greatly terrified Jack, but still he hoped to escape from the giant; and therefore again he begged the woman to take him in for one night only, and hide him where she thought he would be safe. The good woman was at last persuaded, for she was of a kindly and generous nature, and took him into the house.

First, they entered a fine large hall, magnificently furnished; they then passed through several spacious rooms, all in the same style of grandeur; but the rooms appeared to be quite forsaken and desolate. A long gallery was next; it was very dark — just light enough to show that instead of a wall on one side, there was a grating of iron, which parted off a dismal dungeon, from whence issued the groans of those poor victims whom the cruel giant kept in confinement.

Poor Jack was half dead with fear, and would have given the world to have been with his mother again, for he now began to fear that he should never see her more, and gave himself up for lost. He even did not trust the good woman, and thought she had let him into the house for no other purpose than to lock him up among the poor people in the dungeon.

At the farther end of the long gallery there was a very large kitchen, and a good fire was burning in the grate. The good woman told Jack to sit down, and gave him plenty to eat and drink. Jack, not seeing anything here to make him uncomfortable, soon forgot his fear, and was just beginning to enjoy himself when he was aroused by a loud knocking at the street door, which made the whole house shake. The giant's wife ran to hide him in the oven, and then went to let her husband in. Jack heard him accost her in a voice like thunder, saying, "Wife, I smell fresh meat."

"Oh! my dear," replied she, "it is nothing but the people in the dungeon."

The giant appeared to believe her, and walked into the very kitchen where poor Jack was hidden, who was more frightened than he had yet been.

At last the monster seated himself quietly by the fireside, while his wife made the supper. Little by little Jack got over his fright so far as to be able to look at the giant through a small crack, and he was quite astonished to see what an enormous quantity he ate; it seemed as if he never would have done eating and drinking.

When supper was ended, the giant desired his wife to bring him his hen. A very beautiful hen was then brought and placed on the table before him. Jack's desire to see what would happen was very great, and soon he saw that every time the giant said "Lay!" the hen laid an egg of solid gold. The giant amused himself a long time with his hen, and meanwhile his wife went to bed. At length the giant fell asleep by the fireside and snored like the roaring of a cannon.

At daybreak, Jack, finding the giant still asleep, and not likely to awaken soon, crept softly out of his hiding-place, seized the hen, and ran off with her. He met with some difficulty in finding his way out of the house, but at last he reached the road in safety. He easily found the way to the bean-stalk, and contrived to get down it better and quicker than he expected.

He found his mother crying bitterly over his hard fate, for she was certain he had come to some sad end through his rashness. Jack was impatient to show his hen, and inform his mother how valuable it was.

"And now, mother," said Jack, "I have brought home that

which will quickly make us rich; and I hope to make up for the sorrow I have caused you through my idleness, wastefulness, and folly."

The hen laid as many golden eggs as they wished; they sold them, and in a little time they became possessed of as much riches as they wanted.

For some months Jack and his mother lived very happily together; but he was very desirous of travelling; he remembered the fairy's commands, and he feared that if he delayed she would put her threats into execution. Jack longed also to climb the bean-stalk and pay the giant another visit, in order to carry away some more of his treasures. For during the time that Jack was in the giant's mansion, and while he lay concealed in the oven, he learned from the talk between the giant and his wife that he had many wonderful things in his house. Jack thought of his journey again and again, but still he could not make up his mind to speak of it to his mother, being quite sure that she would try to prevent his going.

However, one day he told her boldly that he must take a journey up the bean-stalk; but she begged and prayed him not to think of it, and tried all in her power to keep him from doing so. She told him that the giant's wife would certainly know him again, and that the giant would desire nothing better than to get him into his power, that he might put him to a cruel death in order to be revenged for the loss of his hen. Jack, finding that all he said was useless, pretended to give it up, though he made up his mind to go at all events. So he had a dress made which would disguise him, and found something to color his skin in such a way that he thought it would be impossible for any one to know him again.

A few mornings after this, he arose very early, colored the the skin of his face, and, unseen by any one, climbed the bean-stalk a second time. He was very tired when he reached the top, and very hungry. But after resting some time on one of the stones, he went on his way to the giant's mansion. He reached it late in the evening, and found the woman at the door as before. Jack told her a pitiful tale, and begged of her to give him some victuals and drink, and also a night's lodging.

She told him (what he knew before very well) what a powerful and cruel giant her husband was; and also that one night she took into her house a poor, hungry, friendless boy, who was half dead with travelling; but the little ungrateful fellow had stolen one of the giant's treasures, and ever since that her husband had been worse than before, using her very cruelly and continually scolding her for being the cause of his loss.

Jack at once knew that he was listening to a story in which he was the chief actor; he did his best to persuade the good woman to take him in, but he found it a very hard task. At last she consented; and as she led the way Jack saw that everything was just as he had found it before. She took him into the kitchen, and after he had done eating and drinking, she hid him in an old lumber closet. The giant returned at the usual time, and walked in so heavily that the house was shaken to its foundation.

He seated himself by the fire and soon after exclaimed, " Wife, I smell fresh meat! "

The wife replied it was the crows, who had brought a piece of raw meat and left it on the top of the house.

Whilst supper was preparing, the giant was very cross and impatient, frequently scolding his wife for the loss of his wonderful hen.

The giant at last having eaten till he was quite satisfied, said to his wife, " I must have something to amuse me: either my bags of money or my harp."

After a great deal of ill humor, and having teased his wife some time, he told her to bring down his bags of gold and silver. Jack, as before, peeped out of his hiding-place, and presently the giant's wife brought two very large bags into the room. One was filled with gold and the other with silver pieces. They were both placed before the giant, who began scolding his poor wife most severely for being so long away. She replied, trembling with fear, that the bags were so heavy that she could scarcely lift them, and ended by saying that she would never again bring them downstairs, adding that she had nearly fainted, owing to their weight. This so enraged the giant that he raised his hand to strike her, but she ran away and went to bed, leaving him to count his treasure by way of amusement.

The giant took his bags, and after turning them over and over to see that they were in the same state as he left them, began to count their contents. First, the bag which contained the silver was emptied, and the contents placed upon the table. Jack saw the glittering heaps with delight, and most heartily wished they were his own. The giant (little thinking he was so closely watched) counted the silver over several times; and then, having satisfied himself that all was safe, put it into the bag again, which he made very secure.

The other bag was opened next, and the golden pieces placed upon the table. If Jack was pleased at the sight of the silver, how much more delighted he felt when he saw such a heap of glittering gold! He even had the boldness to think of gaining both bags; but suddenly recollecting himself, he began to fear that the giant would sham sleep, the better to catch any one who might be hidden in the house. When the giant had counted over the gold till he was tired, he put it up more secure if possible than he had put up the silver before. Then he leaned back on his chair by the fireside and fell asleep. He snored so loud that Jack compared his noise to the roaring of the sea in a high wind, when the tide is coming in.

At last Jack, feeling sure the giant was asleep, stole out of his hiding-place and went near him, in order to carry off the two bags of money; but just as he laid his hand upon one of the bags, a little dog which he had not seen before started from under the giant's chair and barked at Jack most furiously. Jack now gave himself up for lost. Fear chained him to the spot. Instead of trying to escape, he stood still, though expecting the giant to wake every instant. Strange to say, however, the giant did not wake from his sound sleep, and the dog grew tired of barking.

Jack now began to have his wits about him, and on looking round he saw a large piece of meat. This he threw to the dog, which seized it at once and took it into the lumber closet which Jack had just left. Finding himself free from a noisy and troublesome enemy, and seeing the giant did not awake, Jack boldly seized the bags, and throwing them over his shoulders ran out of the kitchen. He reached the street door in safety and found it was quite daylight. On his way to the top of the bean-stalk he found it hard work to carry the heavy money-bags.

Jack was delighted when he found himself near the bean-stalk. When he reached it he soon went to the bottom, and at once ran to seek his mother. To his great surprise there was no one in the cottage. He ran from one room to another, but found no one. At last he ran into the village, hoping to see some of the neighbors, who might be able to tell him where he could find his mother. An old woman at last directed him to a house near by, where he found his mother ill of a fever. He was greatly shocked, for she seemed to be dying, and he could scarcely bear his own thoughts on knowing himself to be the cause of her sickness. But on being told of her son's safe return, his mother began to improve and at last became quite well again.

Jack at once gave her his two valuable bags, and with the money the cottage was rebuilt and well furnished, and they lived happily and comfortably for a long time after.

For three years Jack heard no more of the bean-stalk, but he could not forget it, although he would not mention it for he feared to make his mother unhappy. She, too, would not mention the hated bean-stalk, lest it should remind her son of taking another journey. In spite of the comforts Jack enjoyed at home, he often thought about the bean-stalk; for the fairy's threats, in case of his disobedience, were ever present to his mind, and prevented him from being happy. The idea grew upon him so that he could think of nothing else. He vainly tried to amuse himself; he became quiet and sullen, and would arise at the dawn of day and look at the bean-stalk for hours together. His mother saw that something lay heavy upon his mind, and tried to discover the cause; but Jack knew too well what the consequence would be, should she succeed. He did his utmost, therefore, to conquer the great desire he had for another journey up the bean-stalk.

Finding, however, that his desire grew too strong for him, he began to make secret preparations for his journey; and, on the longest day of the year, he arose as soon as it was light and climbed the bean-stalk, reaching the top with some little trouble. He found the road journey much as it was on the two former times. He arrived at the giant's mansion in the evening, and found his wife standing, as usual, at the door. Jack had disguised himself so completely that she did not appear to have the least recollection of him. However, when he told her of his hunger and poverty, in order to be allowed to enter the mansion, he found it very difficult indeed to persuade her. At last he succeeded, and was hidden in the copper again this time.

When the giant returned, he said, " I smell fresh meat."

But Jack felt quite easy in his mind, as the giant had said

so before, and had been soon satisfied. However, the giant started up all at once, and his wife could not prevent him from searching all round the room.

Whilst this was going on, Jack was exceedingly frightened, and wished himself at home a thousand times. When the giant came near the copper and put his hand upon the lid, Jack thought his death was certain. The giant ended his search there, though, without moving the lid, and seated himself quietly by the fireside. This fright nearly killed poor Jack; he was afraid to move or even to breathe, lest he should be discovered. The giant at last ate a hearty supper, and when he had finished he commanded his wife to fetch down his harp.

Jack peeped under the copper lid, and soon saw the most beautiful harp that could be thought of; it was placed on the table by the giant, who said, " Play! " and it instantly played of its own accord without being touched. The music was wonderfully fine.

Jack was delighted, and felt more anxious to get the harp into his possession than either of the former treasures; fortunately for him the music soon lulled the giant into a sound sleep. Now, therefore, was the time to carry off the harp, as the giant appeared to be in a deeper sleep than usual.

Jack soon made up his mind, got out of the copper, and seized the harp. But the harp, being enchanted by a fairy, called out loudly, " Master! master! "

The giant awoke, stood up, and tried to run after Jack; but he had drank so much that he could hardly stand.

Poor Jack ran as fast as he could, and in a little time the giant recovered sufficiently to walk slowly, or rather to reel after him. Had he been sober, he must have overtaken Jack instantly; but as he then was Jack contrived to be first at the top of the bean-stalk. The giant called after him in a voice like thunder, and sometimes was very near him.

The moment Jack got down the bean-stalk he called out for a hatchet, and one was brought him directly. Now, just at that instant, the giant was beginning to descend; but Jack cut the bean-stalk with his hatchet close off at the root, which made the giant fall headlong into the garden. The fall was so great that it killed him, thereby releasing the world from a barbarous enemy.

At this instant the fairy appeared, and first addressed Jack's mother, explaining every circumstance relating to the journeys up the bean-stalk. The fairy charged Jack to be dutiful to his mother, and to follow his father's good example, which was the only way to be happy. She then disappeared. Jack heartily begged his mother's pardon for all the sorrow and affliction he had caused her, promising most faithfully to be very dutiful and obedient to her for the future.

RED RIDING HOOD

Page 58

BABES IN THE WOOD

Page 61

THE SLEEPING BEAUTY IN THE WOOD

THERE were formerly a king and a queen who were so sorry that they had no children; so sorry that it cannot be expressed. They went to all the waters in the world; vows, pilgrimages, all ways were tried, and all to no purpose.

At last the queen had a daughter. There was a very fine christening, and the princess had for her godmother all the fairies they could find in the whole kingdom (they found seven), that every one of them might give her a gift, as was the custom of fairies in those days. By this means the princess had all the perfections imaginable.

After the ceremonies of the christening were over all the company returned to the king's palace, where was prepared a great feast for the fairies. There was placed before every one of them a magnificent cover with a case of massive gold, wherein were a spoon, knife, and fork, all of pure gold set with diamonds and rubies. But as they were all sitting down at table they saw come into the hall a very old fairy, whom they had not invited, because it was above fifty years since she had been out of a certain tower, and she was believed to be either dead or enchanted.

The king ordered her a cover, but could not furnish her with a case of gold as the others, because they had seven only made for the seven fairies. The old fairy fancied she was slighted and muttered some threats between her teeth. One of the young fairies who sat by her overheard how she grumbled, and judging that she might give the little princess some unlucky gift, went, as soon as they rose from the table, and hid herself behind the hangings, that she might speak last and repair, as much as she could, the evil which the old fairy might intend.

In the mean while all the fairies began to give their gifts to the princess. The youngest gave her for a gift that she should be the most beautiful person in the world; the next that she should have the wit of an angel; the third that she should have a wonderful grace in everything she did; the fourth that she should dance perfectly well; the fifth that she should sing like a nightingale; and the sixth that she should play all kinds of music to the utmost perfection. The old fairy's turn coming next, with a head shaking more with spite than age she said that the princess should have her hand pierced with a spindle and die of the wound. This terrible gift made the whole company tremble, and everybody fell a-crying.

At this very instant the young fairy came out from behind the hangings and spake these words aloud:

" Assure yourselves, O king and queen, that your daughter shall not die of this disaster. It is true, I have no power to undo entirely what my elder has done. The princess shall indeed pierce her hand with a spindle, but instead of dying she shall only fall into a profound sleep, which shall last a hundred years, at the expiration of which a king's son shall come and awake her."

The king, to avoid the misfortune foretold by the old fairy, caused an immediate proclamation to be made, whereby everybody was forbidden, on pain of death, to spin with a distaff and spindle or to have so much as a spindle in their houses. About fifteen or sixteen years after, the king and queen being gone to one of their houses of pleasure, the young princess happened one day to divert herself by running up and down the palace, when, going up from one apartment to another, she came into a little room on the top of the tower, where a good old woman, alone, was spinning with her spindle. This good woman had never heard of the king's proclamation against spindles.

"What are you doing there, goody?" said the princess.

"I am spinning, my pretty child," said the old woman, who did not know who she was.

"Ha!" said the princess, "this is very pretty. How do you do it? Give it to me, that I may see if I can do so."

She had no sooner taken it into her hand than, whether being very hasty at it, somewhat unhandy, or that the decree of the fairy had so ordained it, it ran into her hand and she fell down in a swoon.

The good old woman, not knowing very well what to do in this affair, cried out for help. People came in from every quarter in great numbers. They threw water upon the princess' face, unlaced her, struck her on the palms of her hands, and rubbed her temples with Hungary water; but nothing would bring her to herself.

And now the king, who came up at the noise, bethought himself of the prediction of the fairies, and judging very well that this must necessarily come to pass, since the fairies had said it, caused the princess to be carried into the finest apartment in his palace and to be laid upon a bed all embroidered with gold and silver.

One would have taken her for a little angel, she was so very beautiful, for her swooning away had not diminished one bit of her complexion: her cheeks were carnation and her lips were coral. Indeed, her eyes were shut, but she was heard to breathe softly, which satisfied those about her that she was not dead. The king commanded that they should not disturb her, but let her sleep quietly till her hour of awaking was come.

The good fairy who had saved her life by condemning her to sleep a hundred years was in the kingdom of Matakin, twelve thousand leagues off, when this accident befell the princess; but she was instantly informed of it by a little dwarf, who had boots of seven leagues — that is, boots with which he could tread over seven leagues of ground in one stride. The fairy came away immediately, and she arrived about an hour after, in a fiery chariot drawn by dragons.

The king handed her out of the chariot, and she approved everything he had done; but as she had very great foresight, she thought when the princess should awake she might not know what to do with herself, being all alone in this old palace; and this was what she did: she touched with her wand everything in the palace (except the king and the queen) — governesses, maids of honor, ladies of the bedchamber, gentlemen, officers, stewards, cooks, under cooks, scullions, guards, with their beefeaters, pages, footmen; she likewise touched all the horses which were in the stables, as well pads as others, the great dogs in the outward court and pretty little Mopsey too, the princess' little spaniel, which lay by her on the bed.

Immediately upon her touching them they all fell asleep, that they might not awake before their mistress and that they might be ready to wait upon her when she wanted them. The very spits at the fire, as full as they could hold of partridges and pheasants, did fall asleep also. All this was done in a moment. Fairies are not long in doing their business.

And now the king and the queen, having kissed their dear child without waking her, went out of the palace and put forth a proclamation that nobody should dare to come near it.

This, however, was not necessary, for in a quarter of an hour's time there grew up all round about the park such a vast number of trees, great and small, bushes and brambles, twining one within another, that neither man nor beast could pass through; so that nothing could be seen but the very top of the towers of the palace, and that, too, not unless it was a good way off. Nobody doubted but the fairy gave herein a very extraordinary sample of her art, that the princess, while she continued sleeping, might have nothing to fear from any curious people.

When a hundred years were gone and passed the son of the king then reigning, and who was of another family from that of the sleeping princess, being gone a-hunting on that side of the country, asked what those towers were which he saw in the middle of a great thick wood.

Every one answered according as they had heard. Some said that it was a ruinous old castle haunted by spirits; others that all the sorcerers and witches of the country kept there their sabbath or night's meeting.

The common opinion was that an ogre lived there, and that he carried thither all the little children he could catch, that he might eat them up at his leisure, without anybody being able to follow him, as having himself only the power to pass through the wood.

The prince was at a stand, not knowing what to believe, when a very aged countryman spake to him thus:

"May it please your royal highness, it is now about fifty years since I heard from my father, who heard my grandfather say, that there was then in this castle a princess, the most beautiful was ever seen; that she must sleep there a hundred years and should be waked by a king's son, for whom she was reserved."

The young prince was all on fire at these words, believing, without weighing the matter, that he could put an end to this rare adventure; and pushed on by love and honor he resolved that moment to look into it.

Scarce had he advanced toward the wood when all the great trees, the bushes, and brambles gave way of themselves to let him pass through. He walked up to the castle which he saw at the end of a large avenue which he went into, and what a little surprised him was that he saw none of his people could follow him, because the trees closed again as soon as he had passed through them. But he did not cease from continuing his way; a young and amorous prince is always valiant.

He came into a spacious outward court, where everything he saw might have frozen up the most fearless person with horror. There reigned over all a most frightful silence; the image of death everywhere showed itself, and there was nothing to be seen but stretched-out bodies of men and animals, all seeming to be dead. He very well knew, by the ruby faces and pimpled noses of the beef-eaters, that they were only asleep; and their goblets, wherein still remained some drops of wine, showed plainly that they fell asleep in their cups.

He then crossed a court paved with marble, went up the stairs, and came into the guard-chamber, where guards were standing in their ranks, with their muskets upon their shoulders, and snoring as loud as they could. After that he went through several rooms full of gentlemen and ladies, all asleep, some standing, others sitting. At last he came into a chamber all gilded with gold, where he saw upon a bed, the curtains of which were all open, the finest sight was ever beheld — a princess, who appeared to be about fifteen or sixteen years of age and whose bright and, in a manner, resplendent beauty had somewhat in it divine. He approached with trembling and admiration and fell down before her upon his knees.

And now, as the enchantment was at an end, the princess awaked, and looking on him with eyes more tender than the first view might seem to admit of, said:

" Is it you, my prince? You have waited a long while."

The prince, charmed with these words, and much more with the manner in which they were spoken, knew not how to show his joy and gratitude. He assured her that he loved her better than he did himself. Their discourse was not well connected, they did weep more than talk — little eloquence, a great deal of love. He was more at a loss than she, and we need not wonder at it. She had had time to think on what to say to him; for it is very probable (though history mentions nothing of it) that the good fairy, during so long a sleep, had given her very agreeable dreams. In short, they talked four hours together, and yet they said not half what they had to say.

In the mean while all the palace awaked. Every one thought upon their particular business, and as all of them were not in love they were ready to die for hunger. The chief lady of honor, being as sharp set as other folks, grew very impatient, and told the princess aloud that supper was served up. The prince helped the princess to rise. She was entirely dressed, and very magnificently, but his royal highness took care not to tell her that she was dressed like his great-grandmother, and had a point band peeping over a high collar; she looked not a bit the less charming and beautiful for all that.

They went into the great hall of looking-glasses, where they supped and were served by the princess' officers; the violins and hautboys played old tunes, but very excellent, though it was now above a hundred years since they had played; and after supper, without losing any time, the lord almoner married them in the chapel of the castle, and the chief lady of honor drew the curtains. They had but very little sleep — the princess had no occasion; and the prince left her next morning to return into the city, where his father must needs have been in pain for him. The prince told him that he lost his way in the forest as he was hunting, and that he had lain in the cottage of a charcoal-burner, who gave him cheese and brown bread.

The king his father, who was a good man, believed him, but his mother could not be persuaded it was true; and seeing that he went almost every day a-hunting, and that he always had some excuse ready for so doing, though he had lain out three or four nights together, she began to suspect that he was married, for he lived with the princess above two whole years, and had by her two children, the eldest of which, who was a daughter, was named Morning, and the youngest, who was a son, they called Day, because he was a great deal handsomer and more beautiful than his sister.

The queen spoke several times to her son, to inform herself after what manner he did pass his time, and that in this he ought in duty to satisfy her. But he never dared to trust her with his secret. He feared her, though he loved her, for she was of the race of the ogres, and the king would never have married her had it not been for her vast riches. It was even whispered about the court that she had ogreish inclinations, and that whenever she saw little children passing by she had all the difficulty in the world to avoid falling upon them. And so the prince would never tell her one word.

But when the king was dead, which happened about two years afterward, and he saw himself lord and master, he openly declared his marriage, and he went in great ceremony to conduct his queen to the palace. They made a magnificent entry into the capital city, she riding between her two children.

Soon after the king went to make war with the Emperor Contalabutte, his neighbor. He left the government of the kingdom to the queen his mother, and earnestly recommended to her care his wife and children. He was obliged to continue his expedition all the summer, and as soon as he departed the queen-mother sent her daughter-in-law to a country house among the woods, that she might with the more ease gratify her horrible longing.

Some few days afterward she went thither herself and said to her clerk of the kitchen:

"I have a mind to eat little Morning for my dinner to-morrow."

"Ah! madam," cried the clerk of the kitchen.

"I will have it so," replied the queen (and this she spoke in the tone of an ogress who had a strong desire to eat fresh meat), "and will eat her with a sauce, Robert."

The poor man, knowing very well that he must not play tricks with ogresses, took his great knife and went up into little Morning's chamber. She was then four years old, and came up to him jumping and laughing, to take him about the neck and ask him for some sugar-candy. Upon which he began to weep, the great knife fell out of his hand, and he went into the back yard and killed a little lamb, and dressed it with such good sauce that his mistress assured him she had never eaten anything so good in her life. He had at the same time taken up little Morning and carried her to his wife, to conceal her in the lodging he had at the bottom of the court-yard.

About eight days afterward the wicked queen said to the clerk of the kitchen: "I will sup upon little Day."

He answered not a word, being resolved to cheat her as he had done before. He went to find little Day, and saw him with a little foil in his hand, with which he was fencing with a great monkey, the child being then only three years of age. He took him up in his arms and carried him to his wife, that she might conceal him in her chamber along with his sister, and in place of little Day cooked up a young kid, very tender, which the ogress found to be wonderfully good.

This was hitherto all mighty well; but one evening this wicked queen said to her clerk of the kitchen:

"I will eat the queen with the same sauce I had with her children."

It was now that the poor clerk of the kitchen despaired of being able to deceive her. The young queen was turned of twenty, not reckoning the hundred years she had been asleep; and how to find in the yard a beast so firm was what puzzled him. He took then a resolution, that he might save his own life, to cut the queen's throat; and going up into her chamber, with intent to do it at once, he put himself into as great fury as he could possibly, and came into the young queen's room with his dagger in his hand. He would not surprise her, but told her, with a great deal of respect, the orders he had received from the queen-mother.

"Do it; do it," said she, stretching out her neck. "Execute your orders, and then I shall go and see my children, my poor children, whom I so much and so tenderly loved."

For she thought them dead ever since they had been taken away without her knowledge.

"No, no, madam," cried the poor clerk of the kitchen, all in tears. "You shall not die, and yet you shall see your children again; but then you must go home with me to my lodgings, where I have concealed them, and I shall deceive the queen once more by giving her in your stead a young hind."

Upon this he forthwith conducted her to his chamber, where, leaving her to embrace her children and cry along with them, he went and dressed a young hind, which the queen had for her supper, and devoured it with the same appetite as if it had been the young queen. Exceedingly was she delighted with her cruelty, and she had invented a story to tell the king, at his return, how the mad wolves had eaten up the queen his wife and her two children.

One evening, as she was, according to her custom, rambling round about the courts and yards of the palace to see if she could smell any fresh meat, she heard, in a ground room, little Day crying, for his mamma was going to whip him because he had been naughty; and she heard, at the same time, little Morning begging pardon for her brother.

The ogress presently knew the voice of the queen and her children, and being quite mad that she had been thus deceived, she commanded next morning, by break of day (with a most horrible voice, which made everybody tremble), that they should bring into the middle of the great court a large tub, which she caused to be filled with toads, vipers, snakes, and all sorts of serpents, in order to have thrown into it the queen and her children, the clerk of the kitchen, his wife and maid; all whom she had given orders should be brought thither with their hands tied behind them.

They were brought out accordingly, and the executioners were just going to throw them into the tub, when the king (who was not so soon expected) entered the court on horseback (for he came post) and asked, with the utmost astonishment, the meaning of that horrible spectacle.

No one dared to tell him, when the ogress, all enraged to see what had happened, threw herself head foremost into the tub, and was instantly devoured by the ugly creatures she had ordered to be thrown into it for others. The king could not but be very sorry, for she was his mother; but he soon comforted himself with his beautiful wife and his pretty children.

THE BRAVE TIN SOLDIER

THERE were once five-and-twenty tin soldiers, who were all brothers, for they had been made out of the same old tin spoon. They shouldered arms and looked straight before them. They wore splendid red and blue uniforms. The first thing in the world they ever heard were the words, "Tin soldiers!" uttered by a little boy, who clapped his hands with delight when the lid of the box in which they lay was taken off. They were given him for a birthday present, and he stood at the table to set them up. The soldiers were all exactly alike, except one, who had only one leg; he had been left till the last, and then there was not enough of the melted tin to finish him; but he stood just as firmly on one leg as the others did on two, and on that account he was very noticeable.

The table on which the tin soldiers stood was covered with other playthings, but the most attractive one was a pretty little paper castle. Through the small windows, the rooms could be seen. In front of the castle, a number of little trees surrounded a piece of looking-glass, which was intended to represent a transparent lake. Swans, made of wax, swam on the lake, and were reflected in it. All this was very pretty, but the prettiest of all was a tiny little lady, who stood at the open door of the castle. She, also, was made of paper, and she wore a dress of the thinnest muslin, with a narrow blue ribbon over her shoulders just like a scarf. In the middle of this was fixed a glittering tinsel rose, as large as her whole face.

94

THE BRAVE TIN SOLDIER

The little lady was a dancer, and she stretched out both her arms, and raised one of her legs so high that the tin soldier could not see it at all, and he thought that she, like himself, had only one leg. "That is the wife for me," he thought; "yet she is too grand, and lives in a castle, while I have only a box to live in, five-and-twenty of us all together; that is no place for her. Still I must try to make her acquaintance." Then he laid himself at full length on the table behind a snuff-box that stood upon it, so that he could peep at the delicate little lady who continued to stand on one leg without losing her balance.

When evening came, the other tin soldiers were all placed in the box, and the people of the house went to bed. Then the playthings began to have their own games together, to pay visits, to have sham fights, and to give balls. The tin soldiers rattled in their box; they wanted to get out and join the amusements, but they could not open the lid. The nut-crackers played at leap-frog, and the pencil jumped about the table. There was such a noise that the canary woke up and began to talk, and in poetry too. Only the tin soldier and the dancer remained in their places. She stood on the tip of one toe, with her arms stretched out, as firmly as he did on his one leg. He never took his eyes from her even for a moment. The clock struck twelve, and, with a bounce, up sprang the lid of the snuff-box; but, instead of snuff, there jumped up a little black goblin; for the snuff-box was a toy puzzle.

"Tin soldier," said the goblin, "don't wish for what does not belong to you."

But the tin soldier pretended not to hear. "Very well; wait till to-morrow, then," said the goblin.

When the children came in the next morning, they placed the tin soldier in the window. Now, whether it was the goblin that did it, or draught, at all events the window flew open, and out fell the tin soldier, heels over head, from the third story, into the street beneath. It was a terrible fall; for he came head downwards, his helmet and his bayonet stuck in between the flagstones, and his one leg up in the air. The servant-maid and the little boy went downstairs directly to look for him; but, although once they nearly trod upon him, they did not see him. If he had called out, "Here I am," it would have been all right; but he was too proud to cry out for help while he wore a uniform.

Presently it began to rain, and the drops fell faster, till there was a heavy shower. When it was over, two boys happened to pass by, and one of them said, "Look, there is a tin soldier! He ought to have a boat to sail in."

So they made a boat out of a newspaper, and placed the tin soldier in it, and sent him sailing down the gutter, while the two boys ran by the side of it, and clapped their hands. Good gracious, what large waves arose in that gutter! and how fast the stream rolled on! The rain had been very heavy.

The paper boat rocked up and down, and turned itself round sometimes so quickly that the tin soldier trembled; yet he remained firm; his countenance did not change; he looked straight before him, and shouldered his musket. Suddenly the boat shot under a bridge which crossed the drain, and then it was as dark as the tin soldier's box.

"Where am I going now?" thought he. "This is the black goblin's fault, I am sure. Ah, well, if the little lady were only here with me in the boat, I should not care for any darkness."

Suddenly there appeared a great water-rat, which lived in the drain.

"Have you a passport?" asked the rat; "give it to me at once." But the tin soldier remained silent, and held his musket tighter than ever.

The boat sailed on, and the rat followed it. How he did gnash his teeth and cry out to the bits of wood and straw,

"Stop him, stop him; he has not paid his toll, and has not shown his pass."

But the stream rushed on stronger and stronger. The tin soldier could already see daylight where the arch ended. Then he heard a roaring sound quite terrible enough to frighten the bravest man. It was only that, at the end of the tunnel, the gutter emptied into a large drain; but that was as dangerous to him as a high water-fall would be to us.

He was too close to it to stop. The boat rushed on, and the poor tin soldier could only hold himself as stiffly as possible, without moving an eyelid, to show that he was not afraid. The boat whirled round three or four times, and then filled with water to the very edge; nothing could save it from sinking. He now stood up to his neck in water, while deeper and deeper sank the boat, and the paper became soft and loose with the wet. At last the water closed over the soldier's head. He thought of the pretty little dancer whom he should never see again, and the words of the song sounded in his ears —

> "Farewell warrior! ever brave,
> Drifting onward to thy grave."

Then the paper boat fell to pieces, and the soldier sank into the water, and was immediately swallowed by a great fish.

Oh, how dark it was inside the fish! a great deal darker than in the drain, and narrower too, but the tin soldier continued firm, and lay at full length, shouldering his musket. The fish swam to and fro, making the most fearful movements, but at last he became quite still. Presently a flash of lightning seemed to pass through him, and then the daylight appeared, and a voice cried out, "I declare, here is the tin soldier!" The fish had been caught, taken to the market and sold to the cook, who took it into the kitchen and cut it open with a knife. She picked up the soldier and held him by the waist between her finger and thumb, and carried him into another room, where the people were all anxious to see this wonderful soldier who had travelled about inside a fish; but he was not at all proud. They placed him on the table, and — how many curious things do happen in the world! — there he was in the very same room from the window of which he had fallen; there were the same children, the same playthings standing on the table, and the fine castle with the little dancer at the door. She still balanced herself on one leg and held up the other: she was as firm as himself. It touched the tin soldier so much to see her that he almost wept tin tears, but he kept them back. He looked at her, but she said nothing.

Presently one of the little boys took up the tin soldier, and threw him into the stove. He had no reason for doing so, therefore it must have been the fault of the black goblin who lived in the snuff-box. The flames lighted up the tin soldier as he stood; the heat was terrible, but whether it proceeded from the real fire or from the fire of love he could not tell. The bright colors of his uniform were faded, but whether they had been washed off during his journey, or from the effects of his sorrow, no one could say. He looked at the little lady, and she looked at him. He felt himself melting away, but he still remained firm with his gun on his shoulder. Suddenly the door of the room flew open, and the draught of air caught up the little dancer. She fluttered like a sylph right into the stove by the side of the tin soldier, was instantly in flames and was gone. The tin soldier melted down into a lump, and the next morning, when the servant took the ashes out of the stove, she found him in the shape of a little tin heart. Of the little dancer nothing remained but the tinsel rose, which was burnt black as a cinder.

THE ENCHANTED HIND

A QUEEN was one day sitting by a fountain weeping. She wished very much to have a child of her own, and she thought it sad that she had none. As she wept, she saw a craw-fish rise on the water, and she started as she heard it speak. "Great Queen," it said, "you will soon have a child. Near this spot is a palace of the fairies, my sisters; I will take you there, if you like to go." The Queen said that she would like. Then the craw-fish turned into a pretty little old lady, who led the Queen to a beautiful palace, where six fairies came out to meet them. They said that they were glad to see the Queen, and they gave her a bouquet of jewels, a rose, a tulip, an anemone, a hyacinth, a pink, and an auricula. "Madam," said one of them, "we are glad to tell you that you will soon have a little girl baby. You must call her 'Welcome.' As soon as she is born call us. You have only to take the bouquet we have given in your hands, and name each of the six flowers, and we will be with you to offer our gifts to little Welcome." The Queen stayed some hours with the fairies after the old lady had left them. She then went home very happy, and, as the fairies had said, a baby was soon after born, whom she said should be called Welcome. Then she took the bouquet and named the flowers. As she spoke, the six fairies came into the room. They kissed the baby, and all gave it gifts. One said it should have a good temper, the second said that she should be clever, the third that she should be beautiful, the fourth that she should have good fortune, the fifth gave her health, the last said that whatever she tried to do would be well done. At that moment a great craw-fish came into the room. "Oh," it said, "you ungrateful Queen! you never once thought of me! Yet I took you to my sisters' palace."

The Queen was very sorry that she had not asked the craw-fish to come and see her, and she begged her pardon with tears, asking her to forgive her, and not to hurt the baby. The other fairies also begged the old fairy to be kind to the child; and at last she said, "Well, I forgive the Queen, but if that baby sees the light of day before she is fifteen years old, she will have to suffer." And she went away still as a craw-fish. The Queen in great fear asked the fairies what she should do. They advised her to build a palace with no doors or window in it, the entrance being far down under the ground, and to shut the Princess up in it till she was fifteen years old.

The King and Queen did so; the baby was not let see the light of day, and when the palace was built she and her nurses were put in it. There she grew up, and was taught everything that a Princess ought to know. The fairies often came to see the Queen, and begged her to take great care not to let the Princess see the light. As she grew up to nearly fifteen, the Queen, who was proud of her beauty, had her likeness painted, and sent copies of the pictures to all the kings and queens, her friends. One young Prince, named Valiant, was so struck by its beauty, that he begged his father to ask the Princess's father to give her to him for his wife. The King consented, and an ambassador was sent to Welcome's father to ask for the hand of the Princess. He was the friend of Prince Valiant, and his name was Becafica. Just before he arrived the Fairy Tulip came to see the Queen, and begged her not to let the ambassador see Welcome, and above all, not to let her leave the tower till she was quite fifteen. So the King and Queen would not let Becafica see the Princess, but they consented to let her see the portrait of the young Prince that he had brought. Welcome was delighted with it, and kept it in her room; and the King told Becafica about the fairies, but promised that in three months' time he would bring his daughter to the court of Valiant's father to become the bride of his son.

But when Prince Valiant heard this message, he doubted whether the King would keep his word, and grew so ill that the doctors said he would die unless the Princess were sent to him at once. The King, his father, was miserable, in fear of the death of his only son. He sent Becafica again to Welcome's father with such a sad letter, saying that they would be cruel not to let the Princess come, as it would kill his only son, that they felt they must consent.

So they had a carriage made into which no ray of light could come, and sent Welcome away in it, accompanied by the Mistress of the Robes, her daughter Narcissa, and a maid of honor named Flora. Flora loved Welcome, but Narcissa hated her and loved Valiant; so she and her mother laid a plot that Narcissa should pretend to be the Princess, and, in order to gain their end, they would let Welcome see the light, so that it might kill her. At noon the next day the old mother cut a large hole in the side of the carriage, and the Princess, seeing the light, was changed into a white hind. The door was thrown open, and she at once sprang out and ran into the forest, afterwards seeking shelter at a cottage near by. Flora immediately followed her.

When the wicked Mistress of the Robes and Narcissa reached the kingdom of Prince Valiant, he and his father came to meet them; but when they saw Narcissa, they cried out at once that some wicked deed had been done, for that she was not the Princess. In vain Narcissa declared that she was Welcome; she and her mother were taken to the town and lodged in a dungeon.

Then Prince Valiant declared that he could not live at court, and he and Becafica left the palace secretly, and went to stay in the forest. As it chanced, it was the one in which the White Hind lived. Flora had found her, and taken her with her to a shepherd's cot, where she hired a bedroom; and then, to their joy, they found that Welcome was a hind only by day, and at night she took her own form. Prince Valiant's only amusement was hunting, and, seeing a White Hind the next day in the wood, he chased it and shot several arrows at it, but did not wound it, and Welcome came home safely, but very tired from her chase. The next day the Prince again chased the White Hind, but, feeling tired, lay down under a tree at noon and fell asleep, where the White Hind found him, and saw, to her grief, that she was chased by none other than her beloved Valiant. Presently the Prince awoke, and the chase was continued, and at last Valiant shot the White Hind. He ran to the spot as she fell, and was sorry to have hurt the pretty deer. He thought that he would keep her for a pet, and tied her to a tree, where Flora found her, and of course set her free. But Becafica had seen Flora, and recollected her at the court of Welcome's father. So he watched in the garden of the cottage that night, and there by moonlight he saw the Princess herself. He ran to tell the Prince, who at once hastened to the same spot, and threw himself on his knees before the Princess. From that moment the spell was broken, and Welcome did not again become a hind.

Valiant now took Welcome to the old King, his father, who was charmed with her, and told him the whole story.

The Prince and Princess were married, and Becafica was wedded the same day to Flora. The two wicked prisoners were set free, but sent out of the kingdom. The fairies came to the marriage feast, and were glad to wish all happiness to the White Hind.

LITTLE THUMB

THERE was, once upon a time, a man and his wife, fagot-makers by trade, who had seven children, all boys. The eldest was but ten years old and the youngest only seven.

They were very poor, and their seven children incommoded them greatly, because not one of them was able to earn his bread. That which gave them yet more uneasiness was that the youngest was of a very puny constitution and scarce ever spoke a word, which made them take that for stupidity which was a sign of good sense. He was very little, and, when born no bigger than one's thumb, which made him be called Little Thumb.

The poor child bore the blame of whatsoever was done amiss in the house, and guilty or not, was always in the wrong; he was, notwithstanding, more cunning and had a far greater share of wisdom than all his brothers put together; and if he spoke little, he heard and thought the more.

There happened now to come a very bad year, and the famine was so great that these poor people resolved to rid themselves of their children. One evening, when they were all in bed and the fagot-maker was sitting with his wife at the fire, he said to her, with his heart ready to burst with grief:

" Thou seest plainly that we are not able to keep our children, and I cannot see them starve to death before my face. I am resolved to lose them in the wood to-morrow, which may very easily be done; for while they are busy in tying up the fagots,

103

we may run away and leave them, without their taking any notice."

"Ah!" cried out his wife; "and canst thou thyself have the heart to take thy children out along with thee on purpose to lose them?"

In vain did her husband represent to her their extreme poverty: she would not consent to it; she was indeed poor, but she was their mother. However, having considered what a grief it would be to her to see them perish with hunger, she at last consented, and went to bed all in tears.

Little Thumb heard every word that had been spoken; for observing, as he lay in his bed, that they were talking very busily, he got up softly and hid himself under his father's stool, that he might hear what they said without being seen. He went to bed again, but did not sleep a wink all the rest of the night, thinking on what he had to do. He got up early in the morning and went to the river side, where he filled his pockets full of small white pebbles, and then returned home.

They all went abroad, but Little Thumb never told his brothers one syllable of what he knew. They went into a very thick forest, where they could not see one another at ten paces distance. The fagot-maker began to cut wood and the children to gather up the sticks and make fagots. Their father and mother, seeing them busy at their work, got away from them insensibly and ran away from them all at once along a by-way through the winding bushes.

When the children saw they were left alone, they began to cry as loud as they could. Little Thumb let them cry on, knowing very well how to get home again, for as he came he took care to drop all along the way the little white pebbles he had in his pockets. Then he said to them:

"Be not afraid, brothers: father and mother have left us here, but I will lead you home again; only follow me."

They did so, and he brought them home by the very same way they came into the forest. They dared not go in, but sat themselves down at the door, listening to what their father and mother were talking.

The very moment the fagot-maker and his wife were got home the lord of the manor sent them 10 crowns, which he had owed them a long while, and which they never expected. This gave them new life, for the poor people were almost famished. The fagot-maker sent his wife immediately to the butcher's. As it was a long while since they had eaten a bit, she bought thrice as much meat as would sup two people. When they had eaten the woman said:

"Alas! where are now our poor children? They would make a good feast of what we have left here; but it was you, William, who had a mind to lose them: I told you we should repent of it. What are they now doing in the forest? Alas! dear God, the wolves have perhaps already eaten them up: thou art very inhuman thus to have lost thy children."

The fagot-maker grew at last quite out of patience, for she repeated it above twenty times that they should repent of it and that she was in the right of it for so saying. He threatened to beat her if she did not hold her tongue. It was not that the fagot-maker was not, perhaps, more vexed than his wife, but that she teased him, and that he was of the humor of a great many others, who love wives who speak well, but think those very importunate who are continually doing so. She was half-drowned in tears, crying out:

"Alas! where are now my children, my poor children?"

She spoke this so very loud that the children, who were at the gate, began to cry out all together:

"Here we are! Here we are!"

She ran immediately to open the door, and said, hugging them:

"I am glad to see you, my dear children; you are very hungry and weary; and, my poor Peter, thou art horribly be-mired; come in and let me clean thee."

Now, you must know that Peter was her eldest son, whom she loved above all the rest, because he was somewhat carroty, as she herself was. They sat down to supper, and ate with such a good appetite as pleased both father and mother, whom they acquainted how frightened they were in the forest, speaking almost always all together. The good folks were extremely glad to see their children once more at home, and this joy continued while the 10 crowns lasted; but when the money was all gone they fell again into their former uneasiness and re-solved to lose them again; and that they might be the surer of doing it, to carry them to a much greater distance than before.

They could not talk of this so secretly but they were over-heard by Little Thumb, who made account to get out of this difficulty as well as the former; but though he got up very be-times in the morning to go and pick up some little pebbles, he was disappointed, for he found the house door double-locked, and was at a stand what to do. When their father had given each of them a piece of bread for their breakfast, he fancied he might make use of this instead of the pebbles, by throwing it in little bits all along the way they should pass; and so he put it in his pocket.

Their father and mother brought them into the thickest and most obscure part of the forest, when, stealing away into a by-path, they there left them. Little Thumb was not very uneasy at it, for he thought he could easily find the way again by means of his bread, which he had scattered all along as he came; but he was very much surprised when he could not find so much as one crumb: the birds had come and had eaten it up, every bit. They were now in great affliction, for the further they went the more they were out of their way and were more and more bewildered in the forest.

Night now came on, and there arose a terrible high wind, which made them dreadfully afraid. They fancied they heard on every side of them the howling of wolves coming to eat them up. They scarce dared to speak or turn their heads. After this it rained very hard, which wetted them to the skin; their feet slipped at every step they took, and they fell into the mire, whence they got up in a very dirty pickle; their hands were quite benumbed.

Little Thumb climbed up to the top of a tree to see if he could discover anything; and having turned his head about on every side, he saw at last a glimmering light, like that of a candle, but a long way from the forest. He came down, and when upon the ground he could see it no more, which grieved him sadly. However, having walked for some time with his brothers toward that side on which he had seen the light, he perceived it again as he came out of the wood.

They came at last to the house where this candle was, not without an abundance of fear: for very often they lost sight of it, which happened every time they came into a bottom. They knocked at the door, and a good woman came and opened it; she asked them what they would have.

Little Thumb told her they were poor children who had been lost in the forest, and desired to lodge there.

The woman, seeing them so very pretty, began to weep and said to them:

"Alas! poor babies; whither are ye come? Do ye know that this house belongs to a cruel ogre who eats up little children?"

"Ah! dear madam," answered Little Thumb (who trembled every joint of him, as well as his brothers), "what shall we do? To be sure the wolves of the forest will devour us to-night if you refuse us to lie here; and so we would rather the gentleman should eat us; and perhaps he may take pity upon us, especially if you please to beg it of him."

The ogre's wife, who believed she could conceal them from her husband till morning, let them come in, and brought them to warm themselves at a very good fire; for there was a whole sheep upon the spit, roasting for the ogre's supper.

As they began to be a little warm they heard three or four great raps at the door; this was the ogre, who was come home. Upon this she hid them under the bed and went to open the door. The ogre presently asked if supper was ready and the wine drawn, and then sat himself down to table. The sheep was as yet all raw and bloody; but he liked it the better for that. He sniffed about to the right and left, saying:

" I smell fresh meat."

" What you smell so," said his wife, " must be the calf which I have just now killed and flayed."

" I smell fresh meat, I tell thee once more," replied the ogre, looking crossly at his wife; " and there is something here which I do not understand."

As he spoke these words he got up from the table and went directly to the bed.

" Ah! ah!" said he; " I see then how thou wouldst cheat me, thou cursed woman; I know not why I do not eat thee up too, but it is well for thee that thou art a tough old carrion. Here is a good game, which comes very luckily to entertain three ogres of my acquaintance who are to pay me a visit in a day or two."

With that he dragged them out from under the bed one by one. The poor children fell upon their knees and begged his pardon; but they had to do with one of the most cruel ogres in the world, who, far from having any pity on them, had already devoured them with his eyes, and told his wife they would be delicate eating when tossed up with good savory sauce. He then took a great knife, and coming up to these poor children, whetted it upon a great whetstone which he held in his left hand. He had already taken hold of one of them when his wife said to him:

"What need you do it now? Is it not time enough to-morrow?"

"Hold your prating," said the ogre; "they will eat the tenderer."

"But you have so much meat already," replied his wife, "you have no occasion; here are a calf, two sheep, and half a hog."

"That is true," said the ogre; "give them their belly full that they may not fall away, and put them to bed."

The good woman was overjoyed at this, and gave them a good supper; but they were so much afraid they could not eat a bit. As for the ogre, he sat down again to drink, being highly pleased that he had got wherewithal to treat his friends. He drank a dozen glasses more than ordinary, which got up into his head and obliged him to go to bed.

The ogre had seven daughters, all little children, and these young ogresses had all of them very fine complexions, because they used to eat fresh meat like their father; but they had little gray eyes, quite round, hooked noses, and very long sharp teeth, standing at a good distance from each other. They were not as yet over and above mischievous, but they promised very fair for it, for they had already bitten little children, that they might suck their blood.

They had been put to bed early, with every one a crown of gold upon her head. There was in the same chamber a bed of the like bigness, and it was into this bed the ogre's wife put the seven little boys, after which she went to bed to her husband.

Little Thumb, who had observed that the ogre's daughters had crowns of gold upon their heads, and was afraid lest the ogre should repent his not killing them, got up about midnight, and taking his brothers' bonnets and his own, went very softly and put them upon the heads of the seven little ogresses, after having taken off their crowns of gold, which he put upon his own head and his brothers', that the ogre might take them for his daughters, and his daughters for the little boys whom he wanted to kill.

All this succeeded according to his desire; for, the ogre waking about midnight, and sorry that he deferred to do that till morning which he might have done overnight, threw himself hastily out of bed, and taking his great knife —

"Let us see," said he, "how our little rogues do, and not make two jobs of the matter."

He then went up, groping all the way, into his daughters' chamber, and coming to the bed where the little boys lay, and who were every soul of them fast asleep, except Little Thumb, who was terribly afraid when he found the ogre fumbling about his head as he had done about his brothers', the ogre, feeling the golden crowns, said:

"I should have made a fine piece of work of it, truly. I find I drank too much last night."

Then he went to the bed where the girls lay; and having found the boys' little bonnets —

"Ah!" said he, "my merry lads, are you there? Let us work as we ought."

And saying these words, without more ado, he cut the throats of all his seven daughters.

Well pleased with what he had done, he went to bed again to his wife. So soon as Little Thumb heard the ogre snore, he waked his brothers and bade them put on their clothes presently and follow him. They stole down softly into the garden and got over the wall. They kept running about all night, and trembled all the while, without knowing which way they went.

The ogre, when he awoke, said to his wife: "Go upstairs and dress those young rascals who came here last night."

The ogress was very much surprised at this goodness of her husband not dreaming after what manner she should dress them; but thinking that he had ordered her to go and put on their clothes, she went up, and was strangely astonished when she perceived her seven daughters killed and weltering in their blood.

She fainted away, for this is the first expedient almost all women find in such cases. The ogre, fearing his wife would be too long in doing what he had ordered, went up himself to help her. He was no less amazed than his wife at this frightful spectacle.

"Ah! what have I done?" cried he. "The wretches shall pay for it, and that instantly."

He threw a pitcher of water upon his wife's face, and having brought her to herself —

"Give me quickly," cried he, "my boots of seven leagues, that I may go and catch them." He went out, and having run over a vast deal of ground, both on this side and that, he came at last into the very road where the poor children were, and not above a hundred paces from their father's house. They espied the ogre, who went at one step from mountain to mountain and over rivers as easily as the narrowest kennels. Little Thumb, seeing a hollow rock near the place where they were, made his brothers hide themselves in it, and crowded into it himself, minding always what would become of the ogre. The ogre, who found himself much tired with his long and fruitless journey (for these boots of seven leagues greatly fatigued the wearer), had a great mind to rest himself, and by chance went to sit down upon the rock where the little boys had hid themselves. As it was impossible he could be more weary than he was he fell asleep, and after reposing himself some time began to snore so frightfully that the poor children were no less afraid of him than when he held up his great knife and was going to cut their throats. Little Thumb was not so much frightened as his brothers, and told them that they should run away immediately toward home while the ogre was asleep so soundly, and that they should not be in any pain about him. They took his advice and got home presently. Little Thumb came up to the ogre, pulled off his boots gently, and put them on his own legs. The boots were very long and large, but as they were fairies they had the gift of becoming big and little, according to the legs of those who wore them; so that they fitted his feet and legs as well as if they had been made on purpose for him. He went immediately to the ogre's house, where he saw his wife crying bitterly for the loss of her murdered daughters.

"Your husband," said Little Thumb, "is in very great danger, being taken by a gang of thieves, who have sworn to kill him if he does not give them all his gold and silver. The very moment they held their daggers at his throat he perceived me, and desired me to come and tell you the condition he is in, and that you should give me whatsoever he has of value, without retaining any one thing; for otherwise they will kill him without mercy; and as his case is very pressing, he desired me to make use (you see I have them on) of his boots, that I might make the more haste and to show you that I do not impose upon you."

The good woman, being sadly frightened, gave him all she had: for this ogre was a very good husband, though he used to eat up little children. Little Thumb, having thus got all the ogre's money, came home to his father's house, where he was received with abundance of joy.

There are many people who do not agree in this circumstance, and pretend that Little Thumb never robbed the ogre at all, and that he only thought he might very justly, and with a safe conscience, take off his boots of seven leagues, because he made no other use of them but to run after little children. These folks affirm that they are very well assured of this, and the more as having drunk and eaten often at the fagot-maker's house. They aver that when Little Thumb had taken off the ogre's boots he went to court, where he was informed that they were very much in pain about a certain army, which was two hundred leagues off, and the success of a battle. He went, say they, to the king, and told him that if he desired it he would bring him news from the army before night.

The king promised him a great sum of money upon that condition. Little Thumb was as good as his word, and returned that very same night with the news; and this first expedition causing him to be known, he got whatever he pleased, for the king paid him very well for carrying his orders to the army. After having for some time carried on the business of a messenger and gained thereby great wealth, he went home to his father, where it was impossible to express the joy they were all in at his return. He made the whole family very easy, bought places for his father and brothers, and by that means settled them very handsomely in the world, and in the mean time made his court to perfection.

THE HISTORY OF LITTLE GOLDEN HOOD

YOU know the tale of poor Little Red Riding Hood, that the wolf deceived and devoured, with her cake, her little butter can, and her grandmother; well, the true story happened quite differently, as we know now. And first of all, the little girl was called and is still called Little Golden Hood; secondly, it was not she, nor the good granddame, but the wicked wolf who was, in the end, caught and devoured.

Only listen.

The story begins something like the tale.

There was once a little peasant girl, pretty and nice as a star in its season. Her real name was Blanchette, but she was more often called Little Golden Hood, on account of a wonderful little cloak with a hood, gold and fire colored, which she always had on. This little hood was given her by her grandmother, who was so old that she did not know her age; it ought to bring her good luck, for it was made of a ray of sunshine, she said. And as the good old woman was considered something of a witch, everyone thought the little hood rather bewitched too.

And so it was, as you will see.

One day the mother said to the child: " Let us see, my little Golden Hood, if you know how to find your way by yourself. You shall take this good piece of cake to your grandmother for a Sunday treat to-morrow. You will ask her how she is, and

114

JACK AND THE BEAN-STALK

Page 69

SNOW-DROP AND THE SEVEN LITTLE DWARFS

Page 454

come back at once, without stopping to chatter on the way with people you don't know. Do you quite understand?"

"Yes, mother," replied Blanchette gayly. And off she went with the cake, quite proud of her errand.

But the grandmother lived in another village and there was a big wood to cross before getting there. At a turn of the road under the trees, suddenly "Who goes there?"

"Friend Wolf."

He had seen the child start alone, and the villain was waiting to devour her, when at the same moment he saw some wood-cutters who might observe him, and he changed his mind. Instead of falling upon Blanchette he came frisking up to her like a good dog.

"'T is you! my nice Little Golden Hood," said he. So the little girl stops to talk with the wolf, who, for all that, she did not know in the least.

"You know me, then!" said she; "what is your name?"

"My name is Friend Wolf. And where are you going thus, my pretty one, with your little basket on your arm?"

"I am going to my grandmother, to take her a good piece of cake for her Sunday treat to-morrow."

"And where does she live, your grandmother?"

"She lives at the other side of the wood, in the first house in the village, near the windmill, you know."

"Ah! yes! I know now," said the wolf. "Well, that's just where I'm going; I shall get there before you, no doubt, with your little bits of legs, and I'll tell her you're coming to see her; then she'll wait for you."

Thereupon the wolf cuts across the wood, and in five minutes arrives at the grandmother's house.

He knocked at the door: toc, toc.

No answer.

He knocks louder.

Nobody answers.

Then he stands upon end, puts his two fore paws on the latch, and the door opens.

Not a soul in the house.

The old woman had risen early to sell herbs in the town, and she had gone off in such haste that she had left her bed unmade, with her great night-cap on the pillow.

"Good!" says the wolf to himself, "I know what I'll do."

He shuts the door, pulls on the grandmother's night-cap down to his eyes, then he lies down all his length in the bed and draws the curtains.

In the meantime the good Blanchette went quietly on her way, as little girls do, amusing herself here and there by picking Easter daisies, watching the little birds making their nests, and running after the butterflies which fluttered in the sunshine.

At last she arrives at the door.

Knock, knock.

"Who is there?" says the wolf, softening his rough voice as best he can.

"It's me, granny, your Little Golden Hood. I'm bringing you a big piece of cake for your Sunday treat to-morrow."

"Press your finger on the latch, then push and the door opens."

"Why, you've got a cold, granny," said she, coming in.

"Ahem! a little, my dear, a little," replied the wolf, pretending to cough. "Shut the door well, my little lamb. Put your basket on the table, and then take off your frock and come and lie down by me; you shall rest a little."

The good child undresses, but observe this: She kept her little hood upon her head. When she saw what a figure her granny cut in bed, the poor little thing was much surprised.

"Oh!" cried she, "how like you are to Friend Wolf, grandmother!"

"That's on account of my night-cap, child," replies the wolf.

"Oh! what hairy arms you've got, grandmother!"

"All the better to hug you, my child."

"Oh! what a big tongue you've got, grandmother!"

"All the better for answering, child."

"Oh! what a mouthful of great white teeth you have, grandmother!"

"That's for crunching little children with!" And the wolf opened his jaws wide to swallow Blanchette.

But she put down her head, crying:

"Mamma! mamma!" and the wolf only caught her little hood.

Thereupon, oh, dear! oh, dear! he draws back, crying and shaking his jaw as if he had swallowed red-hot coals.

It was the little fire-colored hood that had burnt his tongue right down his throat.

The little hood, you see, was one of those magic caps that they used to have in former times, in the stories, for making one's self invisible or invulnerable.

So there was the wolf with his throat burned, jumping off the bed and trying to find the door, howling and howling as if all the dogs in the country were at his heels.

Just at this moment the grandmother arrives, returning from the town with her long sack empty on her shoulder.

"Ah, brigand!" she cries, "wait a bit!" Quickly she opens her sack wide across the door, and the maddened wolf springs in head downward.

It is he now that is caught, swallowed like a letter in the post.

For the brave old dame shuts her sack, so; and she runs and empties it in the well, where the vagabond, still howling, tumbles in and is drowned.

"Ah, scoundrel! you thought you would crunch my little grandchild! Well, to-morrow we will make her a muff of your skin, and you yourself shall be crunched, for we will give your carcass to the dogs."

Thereupon the grandmother hastened to dress poor Blanchette, who was still trembling with fear in the bed.

" Well," she said to her, " without my little hood where would you be now, darling?" And, to restore heart and legs to the child, she made her eat a good piece of her cake, and drink a good draught of wine, after which she took her by the hand and led her back to the house.

And then, who was it scolded her when she knew all that had happened?

It was the mother.

But Blanchette promised over and over again that she would never more stop to listen to a wolf, so that at last the mother forgave her.

And Blanchette, the Little Golden Hood, kept her word. And in fine weather she may still be seen in the fields with her pretty little hood, the color of the sun.

But to see her you *must rise* early.

THE STORY OF PRETTY GOLDILOCKS

O NCE upon a time there was a princess who was the prettiest creature in the world. And because she was so beautiful, and because her hair was like the finest gold and waved and rippled nearly to the ground, she was called Pretty Goldilocks. She always wore a crown of flowers, and her dresses were embroidered with diamonds and pearls, and everybody who saw her fell in love with her.

Now, one of her neighbors was a young king who was not married. He was very rich and handsome, and when he heard all that was said about Pretty Goldilocks, though he had never seen her, he fell so deeply in love with her that he could neither eat nor drink. So he resolved to send an ambassador to ask her in marriage. He had a splendid carriage made for his ambassador, and gave him more than a hundred horses and a hundred servants, and told him to be sure to bring the princess back with him. After he had started nothing else was talked of at court, and the king felt so sure that the princess would consent that he set his people to work at pretty dresses and splendid furniture, that they might be ready by the time she came. Meanwhile the ambassador arrived at the princess' palace and delivered his little message, but whether she happened to be cross that day, or whether the compliment did not please her, is not known. She only answered that she was very much obliged to the king, but she had no wish to be married. The ambassador set off sadly on his homeward way, bringing all the king's presents back with him, for the princess was too well brought up to accept the pearls and diamonds when she would not accept the king, so she had only kept twenty-five English pins that he might not be vexed.

When the ambassador reached the city, where the king was waiting impatiently, everybody was very much annoyed with him for not bringing the princess, and the king cried like a baby, and nobody could console him. Now, there was at the court a young man, who was more clever and handsome than any one else. He was called Charming, and every one loved him, excepting a few envious people who were angry at his being the king's favorite and knowing all the state secrets. He happened one day to be with some people who were speaking of the ambassador's return and saying that his going to the princess had not done much good, when Charming said rashly:

"If the king had sent me to the Princess Goldilocks I am sure she would have come back with me."

His enemies at once went to the king and said:

"You will hardly believe, sire, what Charming has the audacity to say — that if he had been sent to the Princess Goldilocks she would certainly have come back with him. He seems to think that he is so much handsomer than you that the princess would have fallen in love with him and followed him willingly." The king was very angry when he heard this.

"Ha! ha!" said he; "does he laugh at my unhappiness and think himself more fascinating than I am? Go, and let him be shut up in my great tower to die of hunger."

So the king's guards went to fetch Charming, who had thought no more of his rash speech, and carried him off to prison with great cruelty. The poor prisoner had only a little straw for his bed, and but for a little stream of water which flowed through the tower he would have died of thirst.

One day when he was in despair he said to himself:

"How can I have offended the king? I am his most faithful subject and have done nothing against him."

The king chanced to be passing the tower and recognized the voice of his former favorite. He stopped to listen in spite of Charming's enemies, who tried to persuade him to have nothing more to do with the traitor. But the king said:

"Be quiet. I wish to hear what he says."

And then he opened the tower door and called to Charming, who came very sadly and kissed the king's hand, saying:

"What have I done, sire, to deserve this cruel treatment?"

"You mocked me and my ambassador," said the king, "and you said that if I had sent you for the Princess Goldilocks you would certainly have brought her back."

"It is quite true, sire," replied Charming. "I should have drawn such a picture of you, and represented your good qualities in such a way, that I am certain the princess would have found you irresistible. But I cannot see what there is in that to make you angry."

The king could not see any cause for anger either when the matter was presented to him in this light, and he began to frown very fiercely at the courtiers who had so misrepresented his favorite.

So he took Charming back to the palace with him, and after seeing that he had a very good supper he said to him:

"You know that I love Pretty Goldilocks as much as ever. Her refusal has not made any difference to me; but I don't know how to make her change her mind. I really should like to send you, to see if you can persuade her to marry me."

Charming replied that he was perfectly willing to go, and would set out the very next day.

"But you must wait till I can get a grand escort for you," said the king. But Charming said that he only wanted a good horse to ride, and the king, who was delighted at his being ready to start so promptly, gave him letters to the princess and bade him good speed. It was on a Monday morning that he set out all alone upon his errand, thinking of nothing but how he could persuade the Princess Goldilocks to marry the king. He had a writing-book in his pocket, and whenever any happy thought struck him he dismounted from his horse and sat down under the trees to put it into the harangue, which he was preparing for the princess before he forgot it.

One day when he had started at the very earliest dawn and was riding over a great meadow, he suddenly had a capital idea, and springing from his horse, he sat down under a willow tree which grew by a little river. When he had written it down he was looking round him, pleased to find himself in such a pretty place, when all at once he saw a great golden carp lying gasping and exhausted upon the grass. In leaping after little flies she had thrown herself high upon the bank, where she had lain till she was nearly dead. Charming had pity upon her, and though he could n't help thinking that she would have been very nice for dinner, he picked her up gently and put her back into the water. As soon as Dame Carp felt the refreshing coolness of the water she sank down joyfully to the bottom of the river, then swimming up to the bank quite boldly she said:

" I thank you, Charming, for the kindness you have done me. You have saved my life; one day I will repay you." So saying, she sank down into the water again, leaving Charming greatly astonished at her politeness.

Another day, as he journeyed on, he saw a raven in great distress. The poor bird was closely pursued by an eagle, which would soon have eaten it up had not Charming quickly fitted an arrow to his bow and shot the eagle dead. The raven perched upon a tree very joyfully.

" Charming," said he, " it was very generous of you to rescue a poor raven. I am not ungrateful and some day I will repay you."

Charming thought it was very nice of the raven to say so, and went on his way.

Before the sun rose he found himself in a thick wood, where it was too dark for him to see his path, and here he heard an owl crying as if it were in despair.

"Hark!" said he; "that must be an owl in great trouble. I am sure it has got into a snare." And he began to hunt about, and presently found a great net which some bird-catchers had spread the night before.

"What a pity it is that men do nothing but torment and persecute poor creatures which never do them any harm!" said he, and he took out his knife and cut the cords of the net, and the owl flitted away into the darkness, but then turning, with one flicker of her wings, she came back to Charming and said:

"It does not need many words to tell you how great a service you have done me. I was caught; in a few minutes the fowlers would have been here — without your help I should have been killed. I am grateful, and one day I will repay you."

These three adventures were the only ones of any consequence that befell Charming upon his journey, and he made all the haste he could to reach the palace of the Princess Goldilocks.

When he arrived he thought everything he saw delightful and magnificent. Diamonds were as plentiful as pebbles and the gold and silver, the beautiful dresses, the sweetmeats and pretty things that were everywhere quite amazed him. He thought to himself, "If the princess consents to leave all this and come with me to marry the king, he may think himself lucky!"

Then he dressed himself carefully in rich brocade, with scarlet and white plumes, and threw a splendid embroidered scarf over his shoulder, and looking as gay and as graceful as possible, he presented himself at the door of the palace, carrying in his arm a tiny pretty dog which he had bought on the way. The guards saluted him respectfully, and a messenger was sent to the princess to announce the arrival of Charming as ambassador of her neighbor the king.

" ' Charming,' " said the princess; " the name promises well. I have no doubt that he is good-looking and fascinates everybody."

" Indeed he does, madam," said all her maids of honor in one breath. " We saw him from the window of the garret where we were spinning flax, and we could do nothing but look at him as long as he was in sight."

" Well, to be sure! " said the princess; " that 's how you amuse yourselves, is it? Looking at strangers out of the window! Be quick and give me my blue satin embroidered dress, and comb out my golden hair. Let somebody make me fresh garlands of flowers, and give me my high-heeled shoes and my fan, and tell them to sweep my great hall and my throne, for I want every one to say I am really 'Pretty Goldilocks.' "

You can imagine how all her maids scurried this way and that to make the princess ready, and how in their haste they knocked their heads together and hindered each other, till she thought they would never have done. However, at last they led her into the gallery of mirrors, that she might assure herself that nothing was lacking in her appearance, and then she mounted her throne of gold, ebony, and ivory, while her ladies took their guitars and began to sing softly. Then Charming was led in, and was so struck with astonishment and admiration that at first not a word could he say. But presently he took courage and delivered his harangue, bravely ending by begging the princess to spare him the disappointment of going back without her.

" Sir Charming," answered she, " all the reasons you have given me are very good ones, and I assure you that I should have more pleasure in obliging you than any one else, but you must know that a month ago as I was walking by the river with my ladies I took off my glove, and as I did so a ring that I was wearing slipped off my finger and rolled into the water. As I valued it more than my kingdom, you may imagine how vexed I was at losing it, and I vowed never to listen to any proposal of marriage unless the ambassador first brought me back my ring. So now you know what is expected of you, for if you talked for fifteen days and fifteen nights you could not make me change my mind."

Charming was very much surprised by this answer, but he bowed low to the princess and begged her to accept the embroidered scarf and the tiny dog he had brought with him. But she answered that she did not want any presents, and that he was to remember what she had just told him. When he got back to his lodging he went to bed without eating any supper, and his little dog, who was called Frisk, could n't eat any either, but came and lay down close to him. All night long Charming sighed and lamented.

"How am I to find a ring that fell into the river a month ago?" said he. "It is useless to try; the princess must have told me to do it on purpose, knowing it was impossible." And then he sighed again.

Frisk heard him and said:

"My dear master, don't despair; the luck may change. You are too good not to be happy. Let us go down to the river as soon as it is light."

But Charming only gave him two little pats and said nothing, and very soon he fell asleep.

At the first glimmer of dawn Frisk began to jump about, and when he had waked Charming they went out together, first into the garden, and then down to the river's brink, where they wandered up and down. Charming was thinking sadly of having to go back unsuccessful, when he heard some one calling: "Charming! Charming!" He looked all about him and thought he must be dreaming, as he could not see anybody. Then he walked on and the voice called again: "Charming! Charming!"

"Who calls me?" said he. Frisk, who was very small and could look closely into the water, cried out: "I see a golden carp coming." And sure enough there was the great carp, who said to Charming:

"You saved my life in the meadow by the willow tree, and I promised that I would repay you. Take this; it is Princess Goldilock's ring." Charming took the ring out of Dame Carp's mouth, thanking her a thousand times, and he and tiny Frisk went straight to the palace, where some one told the princess that he was asking to see her.

"Ah! poor fellow," said she, "he must have come to say good-bye, finding it impossible to do as I asked."

So in came Charming, who presented her with the ring and said:

"Madam, I have done your bidding. Will it please you to marry my master?" When the princess saw her ring brought back to her unhurt she was so astonished that she thought she must be dreaming.

"Truly, Charming," said she, "you must be the favorite of some fairy, or you could never have found it."

"Madam," answered he, "I was helped by nothing but my desire to obey your wishes."

"Since you are so kind," said she, "perhaps you will do me another service, for till it is done I will never be married. There is a prince not far from here whose name is Galifron, who once wanted to marry me, but when I refused he uttered the most terrible threats against me, and vowed that he would lay waste my country. But what could I do? I could not marry a frightful giant as tall as a tower, who eats up people as a monkey eats chestnuts, and who talks so loud that anybody who has to listen to him becomes quite deaf. Nevertheless, he does not cease to persecute me and to kill my subjects. So before I can listen to your proposal you must kill him and bring me his head."

Charming was rather dismayed at this command, but he answered:

"Very well, princess, I will fight this Galifron. I believe that he will kill me, but at any rate I shall die in your defense."

Then the princess was frightened and said everything she could think of to prevent Charming from fighting the giant, but it was of no use, and he went out to arm himself suitably, and then, taking little Frisk with him, he mounted his horse and set out for Galifron's country. Every one he met told him what a terrible giant Galifron was, and that nobody dared go near him; and the more he heard the more frightened he grew. Frisk tried to encourage him by saying:

"While you are fighting the giant, dear master, I will go and bite his heels, and when he stoops down to look at me you can kill him."

Charming praised his little dog's plan, but knew that his help would not do much good.

At last he drew near the giant's castle, and saw to his horror that every path that led to it was strewn with bones. Before long he saw Galifron coming. His head was higher than the tallest trees, and he sang in a terrible voice:

"Bring out your little boys and girls,
Pray do not stay to do their curls,
For I shall eat so very many,
I shall not know if they have any."

Thereupon Charming sang out as loud as he could to the same tune:

"Come out and meet the valiant Charming,
Who finds you not at all alarming;
Although he is not very tall,
He's big enough to make you fall."

The rhymes were not very correct, but you see he had made them up so quickly that it is a miracle that they were not worse; especially as he was horribly frightened all the time. When Galifron heard these words he looked all about him, and saw Charming standing, sword in hand; this put the giant into a terrible rage, and he aimed a blow at Charming with his huge iron club which would certainly have killed him if it had reached him, but at that instant a raven perched upon the giant's head, and pecking with its strong beak and beating with its great wings, so confused and blinded him that all his blows fell harmlessly upon the air, and Charming, rushing in, gave him several strokes with his sharp sword so that he fell to the ground. Whereupon Charming cut off his head before he knew anything about it, and the raven from a tree close by croaked out:

"You see, I have not forgotten the good turn you did me in killing the eagle. To-day I think I have fulfilled my promise of repaying you."

"Indeed, I owe you more gratitude than you ever owed me," replied Charming.

And then he mounted his horse and rode off with Galifron's head.

When he reached the city the people ran after him in crowds, crying:

"Behold the brave Charming, who has killed the giant!"

And their shouts reached the princess' ear, but she dared not ask what was happening, for fear she should hear that Charming had been killed. But very soon he arrived at the palace with the giant's head, of which she was still terrified, though it could no longer do her any harm.

"Princess," said Charming, "I have killed your enemy. I hope you will now consent to marry the king my master."

"Oh, dear! no," said the princess, "not until you have brought me some water from the gloomy cavern. Not far from here there is a deep cave, the entrance to which is guarded by two dragons with fiery eyes, who will not allow any one to pass them. When you get into the cavern you will find an immense hole, which you must go down, and it is full of toads and snakes; at the bottom of this hole there is another little cave, in which rises the fountain of health and beauty. It is some of this water that I really must have; everything it touches becomes wonderful. The beautiful things will always remain beautiful and the ugly things become lovely. If one is young one never grows old, and if one is old one becomes young. You see, Charming, I could not leave my kingdom without taking some of it with me."

"Princess," said he, "you at least can never need this water, but I am an unhappy ambassador, whose death you desire. Where you send me I will go, though I shall never return."

And as the Princess Goldilocks showed no sign of relenting, he started with his little dog for the gloomy cavern. Every one he met on the way said:

"What a pity that a handsome young man should throw away his life so carelessly! He is going to the cavern alone, though if he had a hundred men with him he could not succeed. Why does the princess ask impossibilities?"

Charming said nothing, but he was very sad. When he was near the top of a hill he dismounted to let his horse graze, while Frisk amused himself by chasing flies. Charming knew he could not be far from the gloomy cavern, and on looking about him he saw a black hideous rock from which came a thick smoke, followed in a moment by one of the dragons with fire blazing from his mouth and eyes. His body was yellow and green and his claws scarlet, and his tail was so long that it lay in a hundred coils. Frisk was so terrified at the sight of it that he did not know where to hide. Charming, quite determined to get the water or die, now drew his sword, and taking the crystal flask which Pretty Goldilocks had given him to fill, said to Frisk:

"I feel sure that I shall never come back from this expedition. When I am dead, go to the princess and tell her that her errand has cost me my life. Then find the king my master and relate all my adventures to him."

As he spoke he heard a voice calling: "Charming! Charming!"

"Who calls me?" said he; then he saw an owl sitting in a hollow tree, who said to him:

"You saved my life when I was caught in the net; now I can repay you. Trust me with the flask, for I know all the ways of the gloomy cavern and can fill it from the fountain of beauty." Charming was only too glad to give her the flask, and she flitted into the cavern quite unnoticed by the dragon, and after some time returned with the flask, filled to the very brim with sparkling water. Charming thanked her with all his heart and joyfully hastened back to the town.

He went straight to the palace and gave the flask to the princess, who had no further objection to make. So she thanked Charming and ordered that preparations should be made for her departure, and they soon set out together. The princess found Charming such an agreeable companion that she sometimes said to him:

"Why did n't we stay where we were? I could have made you king and we should have been so happy!"

But Charming only answered:

"I could not have done anything that would have vexed my master so much, even for a kingdom, or to please you, though I think you are as beautiful as the sun."

At last they reached the king's great city, and he came out to meet the princess, bringing magnificent presents, and the marriage was celebrated with great rejoicings. But Goldilocks was so fond of Charming that she could not be happy unless he was near her, and she was always singing his praises.

"If it hadn't been for Charming," she said to the king, "I should never have come here. You ought to be very much obliged to him, for he did the most impossible things and got me water from the fountain of beauty, so I can never grow old and shall get prettier every year."

Then Charming's enemies said to the king:

"It is a wonder that you are not jealous; the queen thinks there is nobody in the world like Charming. As if anybody you had sent could not have done just as much!"

"It is quite true, now I come to think of it," said the king. "Let him be chained hand and foot and thrown into the tower."

So they took Charming, and as a reward for having served the king so faithfully he was shut up in the tower, where he only saw the jailor, who brought him a piece of black bread and a pitcher of water every day.

However, little Frisk came to console him and told him all the news.

When Pretty Goldilocks heard what had happened she threw herself at the king's feet and begged him to set Charming free, but the more she cried the more angry he was, and at last she saw that it was useless to say any more; but it made her very sad. Then the king took it in his head that perhaps he was not handsome enough to please the Princess Goldilocks, and he thought he would bathe his face with the water from the fountain of beauty, which was in the flask on a shelf in the princess' room, where she had placed it that she might see it often. Now, it happened that one of the princess' ladies in chasing a spider had knocked the flask off the shelf and broken it, and every drop of the water had been spilled. Not knowing what to do, she had hastily swept away the pieces of crystal, and then remembered that in the king's room she had seen a flask of exactly the same shape, also filled with sparkling water. So, without saying a word, she fetched it and stood it upon the queen's shelf.

Now, the water in this flask was what was used in the kingdom for getting rid of troublesome people. Instead of having their heads cut off in the usual way, their faces were bathed with the water, and they instantly fell asleep and never woke up any more.

So when the king, thinking to improve his beauty, took the flask and sprinkled the water upon his face, he fell asleep and nobody could wake him.

Little Frisk was the first to hear the news, and he ran to tell Charming, who sent him to beg the princess not to forget the poor prisoner. All the palace was in confusion on account of the king's death, but tiny Frisk made his way through the crowd to the princess' side and said:

" Madam, do not forget poor Charming! "

Then she remembered all he had done for her, and without saying a word to any one went straight to the tower, and with her own hands took off Charming's chains. Then, putting a golden crown upon his head and the royal mantle upon his shoulders, she said:

" Come, faithful Charming: I make you king and will take you for my husband."

Charming, once more free and happy, fell at her feet and thanked her for her gracious words.

Everybody was delighted that he should be king, and the wedding, which took place at once, was the prettiest that can be imagined, and Prince Charming and Princess Goldilocks lived happily ever after.

THE PRINCESS ON THE GLASS HILL

ONCE upon a time there was a man who had a meadow which lay on the side of a mountain, and in the meadow there was a barn in which he stored hay. But there had not been much hay in the barn for the last two years, for every St. John's eve, when the grass was in the height of its vigor, it was all eaten clean up, just as if a whole flock of sheep had gnawed it down to the ground during the night. This happened once and it happened twice, but then the man got tired of losing his crop and said to his sons — he had three of them, and the third was called Cinderlad — that one of them must go and sleep in the barn on St. John's night, for it was absurd to let the grass be eaten up again, blade and stalk, as it had been the last two years, and the one who went to watch must keep a sharp lookout, the man said.

The eldest was quite willing to go to the meadow. He would watch the grass, he said, and he would do it so well that neither man nor beast, nor even the devil himself should have any of it. So when evening came he went to the barn and lay down to sleep, but when night was drawing near there was such a rumbling and such an earthquake that the walls and roof shook again, and the lad jumped up and took to his heels as fast as he could, and never even looked back, and the barn remained empty that year just as it had been for the last two.

Next St. John's eve the man again said he could not go on in this way losing all the grass in the outlying field year after year, and that one of his sons must just go there and watch it, and watch well too. So the next oldest son was willing to show what he could do. He went to the barn and lay down to sleep, as his brother had done; but when night was drawing near there was a great rumbling, and then an earthquake, which was even worse than that on the former St. John's night, and when the youth heard it he was terrified, and went off, running as if for a wager.

The year after it was Cinderlad's turn, but when he made ready to go the others laughed at him and mocked him. "Well, you are just the right one to watch the hay, you who have never learned anything but how to sit among the ashes and bake yourself!" they said. Cinderlad did not trouble himself about what they said, but when evening drew near rambled away to the outlying field. When he got there he went into the barn and lay down, but in about an hour's time the rumbling and creaking began, and it was frightful to hear it. "Well, if it gets no worse than that I can manage to stand it," thought Cinderlad. In a little time the creaking began again, and the earth quaked so that all the hay flew about the boy. "Oh! if it gets no worse than that I can manage to stand it," thought Cinderlad. But then came a third rumbling and a third earthquake, so violent that the boy thought the walls and roof had fallen down, but when that was over everything suddenly grew as still as death around him. "I am pretty sure that it will come again," thought Cinderlad; but no, it did not. Everything was quiet and everything stayed quiet, and when he had lain still a short time he heard something that sounded as if a horse were standing chewing just outside the barn door. He stole away to the door, which was ajar, to see what was there, and a horse was standing eating. It was so big and fat and fine a horse that Cinderlad had never seen one like it before, and a saddle and bridle lay upon it, and a complete suit of armor for a knight, and everything was of copper and so bright that it shone again. "Ha! ha! it is thou who eatest up our hay, then," thought the boy; " but I will stop that." So he made haste and took out his steel for striking fire and threw it over the horse, and then it had no power to stir from the spot, and became so tame that the boy could do what he liked with it. So he mounted it and rode away to a place which no one knew of but himself, and there he tied it up. When he went home again his brothers laughed and asked how he had got on.

" You did n't lie long in the barn, if even you have been so far as the field! " said they.

" I lay in the barn till the sun rose, but I saw nothing and heard nothing, not I," said the boy. " God knows what there was to make you two so frightened."

" Well, we shall soon see whether you have watched the meadow or not," answered the brothers, but when they got there the grass was all standing just as long and as thick as it had been the night before.

The next St. John's eve it was the same thing once again. Neither of the two brothers dared to go to the outlying field to watch the crop, but Cinderlad went, and everything happened exactly the same as on the previous St. John's eve. First there was a rumbling and an earthquake, and then there was another, and then a third; but all three earthquakes were much, very much more violent than they had been the year before. Then everything became still as death again, and the boy heard something chewing outside the barn door, so he stole as softly as he could to the door, which was slightly ajar, and again there was a horse standing close by the wall of the house, eating and chewing, and it was far larger and fatter than the first horse, and it had a saddle on its back, and a bridle was on it too, and a full suit of armor for a knight, all of bright silver, and as beautiful as any one could wish to see. " Ho! ho! " thought the boy, " is it thou who eatest up our hay in the night? But I will put a stop to that." So he took out his steel for striking fire and threw it over the horse's mane, and the beast stood there as quiet as a lamb. Then the boy rode this horse, too, away to the place where he kept the other, and then went home again.

"I suppose you will tell us that you have watched well again this time," said the brothers.

"Well, so I have," said Cinderlad. So they went there again, and there the grass was, standing as high and as thick as it had been before, but that did not make them any kinder to Cinderlad.

When the third St. John's night came neither of the two elder brothers dared to lie in the outlying barn to watch the grass, for they had been so heartily frightened the night that they slept there that they could not get over it, but Cinderlad dared to go, and everything happened just the same as on the two former nights. There were three earthquakes, each worse than the other, and the last flung the boy from one wall of the barn to the other, but then everything suddenly became still as death. When he had lain quietly a short time he heard something chewing outside the barn door. Then he once more stole to the door, which was slightly ajar, and behold! a horse was standing just outside it, which was much larger and fatter than the two others he had caught. "Ho! ho! it is thou, then, who art eating up our hay this time," thought the boy; "but I will put a stop to that." So he pulled out his steel for striking fire and threw it over the horse, and it stood as still as if it had been nailed to the field, and the boy could do just what he liked with it. Then he mounted it and rode away to the place where he had the two others, and then he went home again. Then the two brothers mocked him just as they had done before, and told him that they could see that he must have watched the grass very carefully that night, for he looked just as if he were walking in his sleep; but Cinderlad did not trouble himself about that, but just bade them go to the field and see. They did go, and this time too the grass was standing, looking as fine and as thick as ever.

PRINCESS ON THE GLASS HILL

The king of the country in which Cinderlad's father dwelt had a daughter whom he would give to no one who could not ride up to the top of the glass hill, for there was a high, high hill of glass, slippery as ice, and it was close to the king's palace. Upon the very top of this the king's daughter was to sit with three gold apples in her lap, and the man who could ride up and take the three golden apples should marry her and have half the kingdom. The king had this proclaimed in every church in the whole kingdom and in many other kingdoms too. The princess was very beautiful, and all who saw her fell violently in love with her, even in spite of themselves. So it is needless to say that all the princes and knights were eager to win her and half the kingdom besides, and that for this cause they came riding thither from the very end of the world, dressed so splendidly that their raiments gleamed in the sunshine, and riding on horses which seemed to dance as they went, and there was not one of these princes did not think that he was sure to win the princess.

When the day appointed by the king had come, there was such a host of knights and princes under the glass hill that they seemed to swarm, and every one who could walk or even creep was there too, to see who won the king's daughter. Cinderlad's two brothers were there, but they would not hear of letting him go with them, for he was so dirty and black with sleeping and grubbing among the ashes that they said every one would laugh at them if they were seen in the company of such an oaf.

" Well, then, I will go all alone by myself," said Cinderlad.

When the two brothers got to the glass hill all the princes and knights were trying to ride up it, and their horses were in a foam; but it was all in vain, for no sooner did the horses set foot upon the hill than down they slipped, and there was not one which could get even so much as a couple of yards up. Nor was this strange, for the hill was as smooth as glass window-panes and as steep as the side of a house. But they were all eager to win the king's daughter and half the kingdom, so they rode and they slipped, and thus it went on. At length all the horses were so tired that they could do no more and so hot that the foam dropped from them, and the riders were forced to give up the attempt.

The king was just thinking that he would cause it to be proclaimed that the riding should begin afresh on the following day, when perhaps it might go better, when suddenly a knight came riding up on so fine a horse that no one had ever seen the like of it before, and the knight had armor of copper, and his bridle was of copper too, and all his accouterments were so bright that they shone again. The other knights all called out to him that he might just as well spare himself the trouble of trying to ride up the glass hill, for it was of no use to try; but he did not heed them, and rode straight off to it and went up as if it were nothing at all. Thus he rode for a long way — it may have been a third part of the way up — but when he had got so far he turned his horse round and rode down again. But the princess thought that she had never yet seen so handsome a knight, and while he was riding up she was sitting thinking, " Oh! how I hope he may be able to come up to the top! " And when she saw that he was turning his horse back she threw one of the golden apples down after him, and it rolled into his shoe. But when he had come down from off the hill he rode away, and that so fast that no one knew what had become of him.

So all the princes and knights were bidden to present themselves before the king that night, so that he who had ridden so far up the glass hill might show the golden apple which the king's daughter had thrown down. But no one had anything to show. One knight presented himself after the other, and none could show the apple.

At night, too, Cinderlad's brothers came home again and had a long story to tell about the riding up the glass hill. At first they said, there was not one who was able to get even so much as one step up, but then came a knight who had armor of copper and a bridle of copper, and his armor and trappings were so bright that they shone to a great distance, and it was something like a sight to see him riding. He rode one-third of the way up the glass hill, and he could easily have ridden the whole of it if he had liked; but he had turned back, for he had made up his mind that that was enough for once. "Oh! I should have liked to see him too, that I should," said Cinderlad, who was as usual sitting by the chimney among the cinders. "You indeed!" said the brothers. "You look as if you were fit to be among such great lords, nasty beast that you are to sit there!"

Next day the brothers were for setting out again, and this time Cinderlad begged them to let him go with them and see who rode; but no, they said he was not fit to do that, for he was much too ugly and dirty. "Well, well, then I will go all alone by myself," said Cinderlad. So the brothers went to the glass hill, and all the princes and knights began to ride again, and this time they had taken care to rough the shoes of their horses; but that did not help them. They rode and they slipped as they had done the day before, and not one of them could even get so far as a yard up the hill. When they had tired out their horses, so that they could do no more, they again had to stop altogether. But just as the king was thinking that it would be well to proclaim that the riding should take place next day for the last time, so that they might have one more chance, he suddenly bethought himself that it would be well to wait a little longer to see if the knight in copper armor would come on this day too. But nothing was to be seen of him.

Just as they were still looking for him, however, came a knight riding on a steed that was much, much finer than that which the knight in copper armor had ridden, and this knight had silver armor and a silver saddle and bridle, and all were so bright that they shone and glistened when he was a long way off. Again the other knights called to him, and said that he might just as well give up the attempt to ride up the glass hill, for it was useless to try; but the knight paid no heed to that, but rode straight away to the glass hill, and went still further up than the knight in copper armor had gone; but when he had ridden two-thirds of the way up he turned his horse round and rode down again. The princess liked this knight still better than she had liked the other, and sat longing that he might be able to get up above, and when she saw him turning back she threw the second apple after him, and it rolled into his shoe, and as soon as he had got down the glass hill he rode away so fast that no one could see what had become of him.

In the evening, when every one was to appear before the king and princess, in order that he who had the golden apple might show it, one knight went in after the other, but none of them had a golden apple to show.

At night the two brothers went home as they had done the night before, and told how things had gone, and how every one had ridden, but no one had been able to get up the hill. "But last of all," they said, "came one in silver armor, and he had a silver bridle on his horse and a silver saddle, and oh, but he could ride! He took his horse two-thirds of the way up the hill, but then he turned back. He was a fine fellow," said the brothers, "and the princess threw the second golden apple to him!"

"Oh, how I should have liked to see him too!" said Cinderlad.

"Oh, indeed! He was a little brighter than the ashes that you sit grubbing among, you dirty black creature!" said the brothers.

On the third day everything went just as on the former days. Cinderlad wanted to go with them to look at the riding, but the two brothers would not have him in their company, and when they got to the glass hill there was no one who could ride even so far as a yard up it, and every one waited for the knight in silver armor, but he was neither to be seen nor heard of. At last, after a long time, came a knight riding upon a horse that was such a fine one its equal had never yet been seen. The knight had golden armor and the horse a golden saddle and bridle, and these were all so bright that they shone and dazzled every one, even while the knight was still at a great distance. The other princes and knights were not able even to call to tell him how useless it was to try to ascend the hill, so amazed were they at the sight of his magnificence. He rode straight away to the glass hill, and galloped up it as if it were no hill at all, so that the princess had not even time to wish that he might get up the whole way. As soon as he had ridden to the top he took the third golden apple from the lap of the princess, and then turned his horse about and rode down again, and vanished from their sight before any one was able to say a word to him.

When the two brothers came home again at night they had much to tell of how the riding had gone off that day, and at last they told about the knight in the golden armor too. " He was a fine fellow, that was! Such another splendid knight is not to be found on earth! " said the brothers.

" Oh, how I should have liked to see him too! " said Cinderlad.

" Well, he shone nearly as brightly as the coal-heaps that thou art always raking among, dirty black creature that thou art! " said the brothers.

Next day all the knights and princes were to appear before the king and the princess — it had been too late for them to do it the night before — in order that he who had the golden apple might produce it. They all went in turn, first princes and then knights, but none of them had a golden apple.

" But somebody must have it," said the king, " for with our own eyes we all saw a man ride up and take it." So he commanded that every one in the kingdom should come to the palace and see if he could show the apple. And one after the other they all came, but no one had the golden apple, and after a long, long time Cinderlad's two brothers came likewise. They were the last of all, so the king inquired of them if there was no one else in the kingdom left to come.

"Oh! yes, we have a brother," said the two, "but he never got the golden apple! He never left the cinder-heap on any of the three days."

"Never mind that," said the king. "As every one else has come to the palace, let him come too."

So Cinderlad was forced to go to the king's palace.

"Hast thou the golden apple?" asked the king.

"Yes, here is the first, and here is the second, and here is the third, too," said Cinderlad, and he took all the three apples out of his pocket, and with that threw off his sooty rags and appeared there before them in his bright golden armor, which gleamed as he stood.

"Thou shalt have my daughter and the half of my kingdom, and thou hast well earned both!" said the king. So there was a wedding, and Cinderlad got the king's daughter, and every one made merry at the wedding, for all of them could make merry, though they could not ride up the glass hill, and if they have not left off their merry-making they must be at it still.

THE YELLOW DWARF

ONCE upon a time there lived a queen who had been the mother of a great many children, and of them all only one daughter was left. But then she was worth at least a thousand.

Her mother, who since the death of the king, her father, had nothing in the world she cared for so much as this little princess, was so terribly afraid of losing her that she quite spoiled her, and never tried to correct any of her faults. The consequence was that this little person, who was as pretty as possible and was one day to wear a crown, grew up so proud and so in love with her own beauty that she despised every one else in the world.

The queen, her mother, by her caresses and flatteries, helped to make her believe that there was nothing too good for her. She was dressed almost always in the prettiest frocks, as a fairy or as a queen going out to hunt, and the ladies of the court followed her dressed as forest fairies.

And to make her more vain than ever the queen caused her portrait to be taken by the cleverest painters and sent it to several neighboring kings with whom she was very friendly.

When they saw this portrait they fell in love with the princess — every one of them, but upon each it had a different effect. One fell ill, one went quite crazy, and a few of the luckiest set off to see her as soon as possible; but these poor princes became her slaves the moment they set eyes on her.

Never has there been a gayer court. Twenty delighted kings did everything they could think of to make themselves agreeable, and after having spent ever so much money in giving a single entertainment thought themselves very lucky if the princess said " That 's pretty."

All this admiration vastly pleased the queen. Not a day passed but she received seven or eight thousand sonnets, and as many elegies, madrigals, and songs, which were sent her by all the poets in the world. All the prose and the poetry that was written just then was about Bellissima — for that was the princess' name — and all the bonfires that they had were made of these verses, which crackled and sparkled better than any other sort of wood.

Bellissima was already fifteen years old and every one of the princes wished to marry her, but not one dared to say so. How could they when they knew that any of them might have cut off his head five or six times a day just to please her, and she would have thought it a mere trifle, so little did she care? You may imagine how hard-hearted her lovers thought her; and the queen, who wished to see her married, did not know how to persuade her to think of it seriously.

" Bellissima," she said, " I do wish you would not be so proud. What makes you despise all these nice kings? I wish you to marry one of them and you do not try to please me."

" I am so happy," Bellissima answered: " do leave me in peace, madam. I don't want to care for any one."

" But you would be very happy with any of these princes," said the queen, " and I shall be very angry if you fall in love with any one who is not worthy of you."

But the princess thought so much of herself that she did not consider any one of her lovers clever or handsome enough for her; and her mother, who was getting really angry at her determination not to be married, began to wish that she had not allowed her to have her own way so much.

At last, not knowing what else to do, she resolved to consult a certain witch who was called the Fairy of the Desert. Now, this was very difficult to do, as she was guarded by some terrible lions, but happily the queen had heard a long time before that whoever wanted to pass these lions safely must throw to them a cake made of millet flour, sugar-candy, and crocodile's eggs. This cake she prepared with her own hands, and putting it in a little basket, she set out to seek the fairy. But as she was not used to walking far, she soon felt very tired and sat down at the foot of a tree to rest, and presently fell fast asleep. When she awoke she was dismayed to find her basket empty. The cake was all gone! and to make matters worse, at that moment she heard the roaring of the great lions, who had found out that she was near and were coming to look for her.

"What shall I do?" she cried; "I shall be eaten up," and being too much frightened to run a single step, she began to cry and leaned against the tree under which she had been asleep.

Just then she heard some one say: "H'm! h'm!"

She looked all round her and then up at the tree, and there she saw a little tiny man who was eating oranges.

"Oh! queen," said he, "I know you very well and I know how much afraid you are of the lions, and you are quite right, too, for they have eaten many other people: and what can you expect, as you have not any cake to give them?"

"I must make up my mind to die," said the poor queen. "Alas! I should not care so much if only my dear daughter were married."

"Oh! you have a daughter," cried the yellow dwarf (who was so called because he was a dwarf and had such a yellow face and lived in the orange-tree). "I'm really glad to hear that, for I've been looking for a wife all over the world. Now if you will promise that she shall marry me, not one of the lions, tigers, or bears shall touch you."

The queen looked at him and was almost as much afraid of his ugly little face as she had been of the lions before, so that she could not speak a word.

"What! you hesitate, madam?" cried the dwarf. "You must be very fond of being eaten up alive."

And as he spoke the queen saw the lions, which were running down a hill toward them.

Each one had two heads, eight feet, and four rows of teeth, and their skins were as hard as turtle-shells and were bright red.

At this dreadful sight the poor queen, who was trembling like a dove when it sees a hawk, cried out as loud as she could: "Oh! dear Mr. Dwarf, Bellissima shall marry you."

"Oh, indeed!" said he disdainfully. "Bellissima is pretty enough, but I don't particularly want to marry her — you can keep her."

"Oh! noble sir," said the queen in great distress, "do not refuse her. She is the most charming princess in the world."

"Oh! well," he replied, "out of charity I will take her; but be sure you don't forget that she is mine."

As he spoke a little door opened in the trunk of the orange-tree, in rushed the queen only just in time, and the door shut with a bang in the faces of the lions.

The queen was so confused that at first she did not notice another little door in the orange-tree, but presently it opened and she found herself in a field of thistles and nettles. It was encircled by a muddy ditch, and a little further on was a tiny thatched cottage, out of which came the yellow dwarf with a very jaunty air. He wore wooden shoes and a little yellow coat, and as he had no hair and very long ears he looked altogether a shocking little object.

"I am delighted," said he to the queen, "that as you are to be my mother-in-law, you should see the little house in which your Bellissima will live with me. With these thistles and nettles she can feed a donkey which she can ride whenever she likes; under this humble roof no weather can hurt her; she will drink the water of this brook and eat frogs — which grow very fat about here; and then she will have me always with her, handsome, agreeable, and gay as you see me now. For if her shadow stays by her more closely than I do I shall be surprised."

The unhappy queen, seeing all at once what a miserable life her daughter would have with this dwarf, could not bear the idea and fell down insensible without saying a word.

When she revived she found to her great surprise that she was lying in her own bed at home, and what was more, that she had on the loveliest lace nightcap that she had ever seen in her life. At first she thought that all her adventures, the terrible lions, and her promise to the yellow dwarf that he should marry Bellissima must have been a dream, but there was the new cap with its beautiful ribbon and lace to remind her that it was all true, which made her so unhappy that she could neither eat, drink, nor sleep for thinking of it.

The princess, who in spite of her willfulness really loved her mother with all her heart, was much grieved when she saw her looking so sad, and often asked her what was the matter, but the queen, who did n't want her to find out the truth, only said that she was ill, or that one of her neighbors was threatening to make war against her. Bellissima knew quite well that something was being hidden from her — and that neither of these was the real reason of the queen's uneasiness. So she made up her mind that she would go and consult the Fairy of the Desert about it, especially as she had often heard how wise she was, and she thought that at the same time she might ask her advice as to whether it would be as well to be married or not.

So with great care she made some of the proper cake to pacify the lions and one night went up to her room very early, pretending that she was going to bed; but instead of that she wrapped herself up in a long white veil and went down a secret staircase and set off all by herself to find the witch.

But when she got as far as the same fatal orange-tree and saw it covered with flowers and fruit, she stopped and began to gather some of the oranges — and then putting down her basket she sat down to eat them. But when it was time to go on again the basket had disappeared, and though she looked everywhere, not a trace of it could she find. The more she hunted for it the more frightened she got, and at last she began to cry. All at once she saw the yellow dwarf.

"What's the matter with you, my pretty one?" said he. "What are you crying about?"

"Alas!" she answered; "no wonder that I am crying, seeing that I have lost the basket of cake that was to help me to get safely to the cave of the Fairy of the Desert."

"And what do you want with her, pretty one?" said the little monster, "for I am a friend of hers, and for the matter of that I am quite as clever as she is."

"The queen, my mother," replied the princess, "has lately fallen into such deep sadness that I fear that she will die; and I am afraid that perhaps I am the cause of it, for she very much wishes me to be married, and I must tell you truly that as yet I have not found any one I consider worthy to be my husband. So for all these reasons I wished to talk to the fairy."

"Do not give yourself any further trouble, princess," answered the dwarf. "I can tell you all you want to know better than she could. The queen, your mother, has promised you in marriage — "

"Has promised me!" interrupted the princess. "Oh! no. I'm sure she has not. She would have told me if she had. I am too much interested in the matter for her to promise anything without my consent — you must be mistaken."

"Beautiful princess," cried the dwarf suddenly, throwing

148

himself on his knees before her, "I flatter myself that you will not be displeased at her choice when I tell you that it is to me she has promised the happiness of marrying you."

"You!" cried Bellissima, starting back. "My mother wishes me to marry you! How can you be so silly as to think of such a thing?"

"Oh! it isn't that I care much to have that honor," cried the dwarf angrily; "but here are the lions coming; they'll eat you up in three mouthfuls and there will be an end of you and your pride."

And, indeed, at that moment the poor princess heard their dreadful howls coming nearer and nearer.

"What shall I do?" she cried. "Must all my happy days come to an end like this?"

The malicious dwarf looked at her and began to laugh spitefully. "At least," said he, "you have the satisfaction of dying unmarried. A lovely princess like you must surely prefer to die rather than be the wife of a poor little dwarf like myself."

"Oh! don't be angry with me," cried the princess, clasping her hands. "I'd rather marry all the dwarfs in the world than die in this horrible way."

"Look at me well, princess, before you give me your word," said he. "I don't want you to promise me in a hurry."

"Oh!" cried she, "the lions are coming. I have looked at you enough. I am so frightened. Save me this minute or I shall die of terror."

Indeed, as she spoke she fell down insensible, and when she recovered she found herself in her own little bed at home; how she got there she could not tell, but she was dressed in the most beautiful lace and ribbons and on her finger was a little ring, made of a single red hair which fitted so tightly that try as she might she could not get it off. When the princess saw all these things and remembered what had happened, she, too, fell into the deepest sadness, which surprised and alarmed the whole court, and the queen more than any one else. A hundred times she asked Bellissima if anything was the matter with her, but she always said that there was nothing.

At last the chief men of the kingdom, anxious to see their princess married, sent to the queen to beg her to choose a husband for her as soon as possible. She replied that nothing would please her better, but that her daughter seemed so unwilling to marry and she recommended them to go and talk to the princess about it themselves; so this they at once did. Now, Bellissima was much less proud since her adventure with the yellow dwarf, and she could not think of a better way of getting rid of the little monster than to marry some powerful king, therefore she replied to their request much more favorably than they had hoped, saying that though she was very happy as she was, still to please them she would consent to marry the King of the Gold Mines. Now, he was a very handsome and powerful prince who had been in love with the princess for years, but had not thought that she would ever care about him at all. You can easily imagine how delighted he was when he heard the news, and how angry it made all the other kings to lose forever the hope of marrying the princess; but after all, Bellissima could not have married twenty kings — indeed, she had found it quite difficult enough to choose one, for her vanity made her believe that there was nobody in the world who was worthy of her.

Preparations were begun at once for the grandest wedding that had ever been held at the palace. The King of the Gold Mines sent such immense sums of money that the whole sea was covered with the ships that brought it. Messengers were sent to all the gayest and most refined courts, particularly to the court of France, to seek out everything rare and precious to adorn the princess, although her beauty was so perfect that nothing she wore could make her look prettier. At least that is what the King of the Gold Mines thought, and he was never happy unless he was with her.

As for the princess, the more she saw of the king the more she liked him; he was so generous, so handsome and clever, that at last she was almost as much in love with him as he was with her. How happy they were as they wandered about in the beautiful gardens together, sometimes listening to sweet music! and the king used to write songs for Bellissima. This is one that she liked very much:

> "In the forest all is gay
> When my princess walks that way.
> All the blossoms then are found
> Downward fluttering to the ground,
> Hoping she may tread on them.
> And bright flowers on slender stem
> Gaze up at her as she passes,
> Brushing lightly through the grasses.
> Oh! my princess, birds above
> Echo back our songs of love,
> As through this enchanted land
> Blithe we wander, hand in hand."

They really were as happy as the day was long. All the king's unsuccessful rivals had gone home in despair. They said good-bye to the princess so sadly that she could not help being sorry for them.

"Ah! madam," the King of the Gold Mines said to her, "how is this? Why do you waste your pity on these princes, who love you so much that all their trouble would be well repaid by a single smile from you?"

"I should be sorry," answered Bellissima, "if you had not noticed how much I pitied these princes who were leaving me forever; but for you, sire, it is very different: you have every

151

reason to be pleased with me, but they are going sorrowfully away, so you must not grudge them my compassion."

The King of the Gold Mines was quite overcome by the princess' good-natured way of taking his interference, and throwing himself at her feet, he kissed her hand a thousand times and begged her to forgive him.

At last the happy day came. Everything was ready for Bellissima's wedding. The trumpets sounded, all the streets of the town were hung with flags and strewn with flowers, and the people ran in crowds to the great square before the palace. The queen was so overjoyed that she had hardly been able to sleep at all, and she got up before it was light to give the necessary orders and to choose the jewels that the princess was to wear. These were nothing less than diamonds, even to her shoes, which were covered with them, and her dress of silver brocade was embroidered with a dozen of the sun's rays. You may imagine how much these had cost, but then nothing could have been more brilliant except the beauty of the princess! Upon her head she wore a splendid crown, her lovely hair waved nearly to her feet, and her stately figure could easily be distinguished among all the ladies who attended her.

The King of the Gold Mines was not less noble and splendid. It was easy to see by his face how happy he was, and every one who went near him returned loaded with presents, for all round the great banqueting hall had been arranged a thousand barrels full of gold and numberless bags made of velvet embroidered with pearls and filled with money, each one containing at least a hundred thousand gold-pieces, which were given away to every one who liked to hold out his hand, which numbers of people hastened to do, you may be sure; indeed, some found this by far the most amusing part of the wedding festivities.

The queen and the princess were just ready to set out with the king when they saw advancing towards them from the end of the long gallery two great basilisks dragging after them a very badly made box; behind them came a tall old woman, whose ugliness was even more surprising than her extreme old age. She wore a ruff of black taffeta, a red velvet hood, and a farthingale all in rags, and she leaned heavily upon a crutch. This strange old woman without saying a single word hobbled three times round the gallery followed by the basilisks, then stopping in the middle and brandishing her crutch threateningly she cried:

"Ho, ho, queen! Ho, ho, princess! Do you think you are going to break with impunity the promise that you made to my friend the yellow dwarf? I am the Fairy of the Desert; without the yellow dwarf and his orange-tree my great lions would soon have eaten you up, I can tell you, and in Fairyland we do not suffer ourselves to be insulted like this. Make up your minds at once what you will do, for I vow that you shall marry the yellow dwarf. If you don't, may I burn my crutch!"

"Ah! princess," said the queen, weeping, "what is this that I hear? What have you promised?"

"Ah! my mother," replied Bellissima sadly, "what did you promise yourself?"

The King of the Gold Mines, indignant at being kept from his happiness by this wicked old woman, went up to her, and threatening her with his sword said:

"Get away out of my country at once and forever, miserable creature, lest I take your life and so rid myself of your malice."

He had hardly spoken these words when the lid of the box fell back on the floor with a terrible noise and to their horror out sprang the yellow dwarf, mounted upon a great Spanish cat. "Rash youth!" he cried, rushing between the Fairy of the Desert and the king. "Dare to lay a finger upon this illustrious fairy! Your quarrel is with me only. I am your enemy and your rival. That faithless princess who would have married you is promised to me. See if she has not upon her finger a ring made of one of my hairs. Just try to take it off and you will soon find out that I am more powerful than you are!"

"Wretched little monster!" said the king; "do you dare to call yourself the princess' lover and to lay claim to such a treasure? Do you know that you are a dwarf — that you are so ugly that one cannot bear to look at you — and that I should have killed you myself long before this if you had been worthy of such a glorious death?"

The yellow dwarf, deeply enraged at these words, set spurs to his cat, which yelled horribly and leaped hither and thither — terrifying everybody except the brave king, who pursued the dwarf closely, till he, drawing a great knife with which he was armed, challenged the king to meet him in single combat, and rushed down into the courtyard of the palace with a terrible clatter. The king, quite provoked, followed him hastily, but they had hardly taken their places facing one another, and the whole court had only just had time to rush out upon the balconies to watch what was going on, when suddenly the sun became as red as blood, and it was so dark that they could scarcely see at all. The thunder crashed and the lightning seemed as if it must burn up everything; the two basilisks appeared, one on each side of the bad dwarf like giants mountains high, and fire flew from their mouths and ears until they looked like flaming furnaces. None of these things could terrify the noble young king, and the boldness of his looks and actions reassured those who were looking on, and perhaps even embarrassed the yellow dwarf himself; but even his courage gave way when he saw what was happening to his beloved princess. For the Fairy of the Desert, looking more terrible than before, mounted upon a winged griffin and with long snakes coiled round her neck, had given her such a blow with the lance she carried that Bellissima fell into the queen's arms bleeding and senseless. Her fond mother, feeling as much hurt by the blow as the princess herself, uttered such piercing cries and lamentations that the king, hearing them, entirely lost his courage and presence of mind. Giving up the combat, he flew toward the princess to rescue or to die with her, but the yellow dwarf was too quick for him. Leaping with his Spanish cat upon the balcony, he snatched Bellissima from the queen's arms, and before any of the ladies of the court could stop him he had sprung upon the roof of the palace and disappeared with his prize.

The king, motionless with horror, looked on despairingly at this dreadful occurrence, which he was quite powerless to prevent, and to make matters worse his sight failed him, everything became dark, and he felt himself carried along through the air by a strong hand.

This new misfortune was the work of the wicked Fairy of the Desert, who had come with the yellow dwarf to help him carry off the princess, and had fallen in love with the handsome young King of the Gold Mines directly she saw him. She thought that if she carried him off to some frightful chasm and chained him to a rock, then the fear of death would make him forget Bellissima and become her slave. So as soon as they reached the place she gave him back his sight, but without releasing him from his chains, and by her magic power she appeared before him as a young and beautiful fairy and pretended to have come there quite by chance.

"What do I see?" she cried. "Is it you, dear prince? What misfortune has brought you to this dismal place?"

The king, who was quite deceived by her altered appearance, replied:

"Alas! beautiful fairy, the fairy who brought me here first took away my sight, but by her voice I recognized her as the Fairy of the Desert, though what she should have carried me off for I cannot tell you."

"Ah!" cried the pretended fairy, "if you have fallen into her hands, you won't get away until you have married her. She has carried off more than one prince like this, and she will certainly have anything she takes a fancy to." While she was thus pretending to be sorry for the king he suddenly noticed her feet, which were like those of a griffin, and knew in a moment that this must be the Fairy of the Desert, for her feet were the one thing she could not change, however pretty she might make her face.

Without seeming to have noticed anything, he said, in a confidential way:

" Not that I have any dislike to the Fairy of the Desert, but I really cannot endure the way in which she protects the yellow dwarf and keeps me chained here like a criminal. It is true that I love a charming princess, but if the fairy should set me free my gratitude would oblige me to love her only."

" Do you really mean what you say, prince? " said the fairy, quite deceived.

" Surely," replied the prince; " how could I deceive you? You see it is so much more flattering to my vanity to be loved by a fairy than by a simple princess. But even if I am dying of love for her, I shall pretend to hate her until I am set free."

The Fairy of the Desert, quite taken in by these words, resolved at once to transport the prince to a pleasanter place. So making him mount her chariot, to which she had harnessed swans instead of the bats which generally drew it, away she flew with him. But imagine the distress of the prince when, from the giddy height at which they were rushing through the air, he saw his beloved princess in a castle built of polished steel, the walls of which reflected the sun's rays so hotly that no one could approach it without being burned to a cinder! Bellissima was sitting in a little thicket by a brook, leaning her head upon her hand and weeping bitterly, but just as they passed she looked up and saw the king and the Fairy of the Desert. Now the fairy was so clever that she could not only seem beautiful to the king, but even the poor princess thought her the most lovely being she had ever seen.

"What!" she cried; "was I not unhappy enough in this lonely castle to which that frightful yellow dwarf brought me? Must I also be made to know that the King of the Gold Mines ceased to love me as soon as he lost sight of me? But who can my rival be whose fatal beauty is greater than mine?"

While she was saying this the king, who really loved her as much as ever, was feeling terribly sad at being so rapidly torn away from his beloved princess, but he knew too well how powerful the fairy was to have any hope of escaping from her except by great patience and cunning.

The Fairy of the Desert had also seen Bellissima, and she tried to read in the king's eyes the effect that this unexpected sight had had upon him.

"No one can tell what you wish to know better than I can," said he. "This chance meeting with an unhappy princess for whom I once had a passing fancy before I was lucky enough to meet you has affected me a little, I admit, but you are so much more to me than she is that I would rather die than leave you."

"Ah! prince," she said, "can I believe that you really love me so much?"

"Time will show, madam," replied the king; "but if you wish to convince me that you have some regard for me, do not I beg of you, refuse to aid Bellissima."

"Do you know what you are asking?" said the Fairy of the Desert, frowning and looking at him suspiciously. "Do you want me to employ my art against the yellow dwarf, who is my best friend, and take away from him a proud princess whom I can but look upon as my rival?"

The king sighed, but made no answer — indeed, what was there to be said to such a clear-sighted person? At last they reached a vast meadow, gay with all sorts of flowers; a deep river surrounded it and many little brooks murmured softly under the shady trees, where it was always cool and fresh. A little way off stood a splendid palace, the walls of which were of transparent emeralds. As soon as the swans which drew the fairy's chariot had alighted under a porch, which was paved with diamonds and had arches of rubies, they were greeted on all sides by thousands of beautiful beings, who came to meet them joyfully singing these words:

"When Love within a heart would reign,
  Useless to strive against him 't is.
The proud but feel a sharper pain,
  And make a greater triumph his."

The Fairy of the Desert was delighted to hear them sing of her triumphs. She led the king into the most splendid room that can be imagined and left him alone for a little while, just that he might not feel that he was a prisoner; but he felt sure that she had not really gone quite away, but was watching him from some hiding-place. So walking up to a great mirror he said to it: "Trusty counselor, let me see what I can do to make myself agreeable to the charming Fairy of the Desert; for I can think of nothing but how to please her."

And he at once set to work to curl his hair, and seeing upon a table a grander coat than his own he put it on carefully. The fairy came back so delighted that she could not conceal her joy.

"I am quite aware of the trouble you have taken to please me," said she, "and I must tell you that you have succeeded perfectly already. You see it is not difficult to do if you really care for me."

The king, who had his own reasons for wishing to keep the old fairy in a good humor, did not spare pretty speeches, and after a time he was allowed to walk by himself upon the seashore. The Fairy of the Desert had by her enchantments raised such a terrible storm that the boldest pilot would not venture out in it, so she was not afraid of her prisoner's being able to escape; and he found it some relief to think sadly over his terrible situation without being interrupted by his cruel captor.

Presently, after walking wildly up and down, he wrote these verses upon the sand with his stick:

> " At last may I upon this shore
>   Lighten my sorrow with soft tears.
> Alas! alas! I see no more
>   My love, who yet my sadness cheers.
>
> " And thou, O raging, stormy sea,
>   Stirred by wild winds, from depth to height,
> Thou hold'st my loved one far from me,
>   And I am captive to thy might.
>
> " My heart is still more wild than thine,
>   For fate is cruel unto me.
> Why must I thus in exile pine?
>   Why is my princess snatched from me?
>
> " O lovely nymphs, from ocean caves,
>   Who know how sweet true love may be,
> Come up and calm the furious waves
>   And set a desperate lover free! "

While he was still writing he heard a voice which attracted his attention in spite of himself. Seeing that the waves were rolling in higher than ever he looked all round him, and presently saw a lovely lady floating gently toward him upon the crest of a huge billow, her long hair spread all about her; in one hand she held a mirror and in the other a comb, and instead of feet she had a beautiful tail like a fish, with which she swam.

The king was struck dumb with astonishment at this unexpected sight, but as soon as she came within speaking distance she said to him: " I know how sad you are at losing your princess and being kept a prisoner by the Fairy of the Desert; if you like I will help you to escape from this fatal place, where you may otherwise have to drag on a weary existence for thirty years or more."

The King of the Gold Mines hardly knew what answer to make to this proposal. Not because he did not wish very much to escape, but he was afraid that this might be only another device by which the Fairy of the Desert was trying to deceive him. As he hesitated the mermaid, who guessed his thoughts, said to him:

" You may trust me; I am not trying to entrap you. I am so angry with the yellow dwarf and the Fairy of the Desert that I am not likely to wish to help them, especially since I constantly see your poor princess, whose beauty and goodness make me pity her so much: and I tell you that if you will have confidence in me I will help you to escape."

" I trust you absolutely," cried the king, " and I will do whatever you tell me; but if you have seen my princess I beg of you to tell me how she is and what is happening to her."

" We must not waste time in talking," said she. " Come with me and I will carry you to the castle of steel, and we will leave upon this shore a figure so like you that even the fairy herself will be deceived by it."

So saying she quickly collected a bundle of sea-weed, and blowing it three times she said:

" My friendly sea-weeds, I order you to stay here stretched upon the sand until the Fairy of the Desert comes to take you away." And at once the sea-weeds became like the king, who stood looking at them in great astonishment, for they were even dressed in a coat like his, but they lay there pale and still as the king himself might have lain if one of the great waves had overtaken him and thrown him senseless upon the shore. And then the mermaid caught up the king and away they swam joy-fully together.

"Now," said she, "I have time to tell you about the princess. In spite of the blow which the Fairy of the Desert gave her, the yellow dwarf compelled her to mount behind him upon his terrible Spanish cat; but she soon fainted away with pain and terror and did not recover till they were within the walls of his frightful castle of steel. Here she was received by the prettiest girls it was possible to find, who had been carried there by the yellow dwarf, who hastened to wait upon her and showed her every possible attention. She was laid upon a couch covered with cloth-of-gold, embroidered with pearls as big as nuts."

"Ah!" interrupted the King of the Gold Mines, "if Bellissima forgets me and consents to marry him, I shall break my heart."

"You need not be afraid of that," answered the mermaid; "the princess thinks of no one but you, and the frightful dwarf cannot persuade her to look at him."

"Pray go on with your story," said the king.

"What more is there to tell you?" replied the mermaid. "Bellissima was sitting in the wood when you passed and saw you with the Fairy of the Desert, who was so cleverly disguised that the princess took her to be prettier than herself; you may imagine her despair, for she thought that you had fallen in love with her."

"She believes that I love her!" cried the king. "What a fatal mistake! What is to be done to undeceive her?"

"You know best," answered the mermaid, smiling kindly at him. "When people are as much in love with one another as you two are they don't need advice from any one else."

As she spoke they reached the castle of steel, the side next the sea being the only one which the yellow dwarf had left un-protected by the dreadful burning walls.

"I know quite well," said the mermaid, "that the princess is sitting by the brook-side just where you saw her as you passed, but as you will have many enemies to fight with before you can reach her, take this sword; armed with it you may dare any danger and overcome the greatest difficulties, only beware of one thing — that is never to let it fall from your hand. Farewell; now I will wait by that rock, and if you need my help in carrying off your beloved princess I will not fail you, for the queen her mother is my best friend, and it was for her sake that I went to rescue you."

So saying she gave to the king a sword made from a single diamond, which was more brilliant than the sun. He could not find words to express his gratitude, but he begged her to believe that he fully appreciated the importance of her gift, and would never forget her help and kindness.

We must now go back to the Fairy of the Desert. When she found that the king did not return she hastened out to look for him, and reached the shore with a hundred of the ladies of her train, loaded with splendid presents for him. Some carried baskets full of diamonds, others golden cups of wonderful workmanship, and amber, coral, and pearls, others again balanced upon their heads bales of the richest and most beautiful stuffs, while the rest brought fruit and flowers and even birds. But what was the horror of the fairy, who followed this gay troop, when she saw stretched upon the sands the image of the king which the mermaid had made with the sea-weeds. Struck with astonishment and sorrow, she uttered a terrible cry and threw herself down beside the pretended king, weeping and howling and calling upon her eleven sisters, who were also fairies and who came to her assistance. But they were all taken in by the image of the king, for clever as they were the mermaid was still cleverer, and all they could do was to help the Fairy of the Desert to make a wonderful monument over what they thought was the grave of the King of the Gold Mines. But while they were collecting jasper and porphyry, agate and marble, gold and bronze, statues and devices, to immortalize the king's memory, he was thanking the good mermaid and begging her still to help him, which she graciously promised to do as she disappeared; and then he set out for the castle of steel. He walked fast, looking anxiously round him and longing once more to see his darling Bellissima, but he had not gone far before he was surrounded by four terrible sphinxes, who would very soon have torn him to pieces with their sharp talons if it had not been for the mermaid's diamond sword. For no sooner had he flashed it before their eyes than down they fell at his feet quite helpless, and he killed them with one blow. But he had hardly turned to continue his search when he met six dragons covered with scales that were harder than iron. Frightful as this encounter was, the king's courage was unshaken, and by the aid of his wonderful sword he cut them in pieces one after the other. Now he hoped his difficulties were over, but at the next turning he was met by one which he did not know how to overcome. Twenty-four pretty and graceful nymphs advanced toward him, holding garlands of flowers with which they barred the way.

"Where are you going, prince?" they said; "it is our duty to guard this place, and if we let you pass great misfortune will happen to you and to us. We beg you not to insist upon going on. Do you want to kill twenty-four girls who have never displeased you in any way?"

The king did not know what to do or to say. It went against all his ideas as a knight to do anything a lady begged him not to do; but as he hesitated a voice in his ear said:

"Strike! strike! and do not spare, or your princess is lost forever!"

So without replying to the nymphs he rushed forward instantly, breaking their garlands and scattering them in all directions; and then went on without further hindrance to the little wood where he had seen Bellissima. She was seated by the brook looking pale and weary when he reached her, and he would have thrown himself down at her feet, but she drew herself away from him with as much indignation as if he had been the yellow dwarf.

" Ah! princess," he cried, " do not be angry with me. Let me explain everything. I am not faithless or to blame for what has happened. I am a miserable wretch who has displeased you without being able to help himself."

" Ah!" cried Bellissima, " did I not see you flying through the air with the loveliest being imaginable? Was that against your will? "

" Indeed it was, princess," he answered; " the wicked Fairy of the Desert, not content with chaining me to a rock, carried me off in her chariot to the other end of the earth, where I should even now be a captive but for the unexpected help of a friendly mermaid, who brought me here to rescue you, my princess, from the unworthy hands that hold you. Do not refuse the aid of your most faithful lover." So saying he threw himself at her feet and held her by her robe. But, alas! in so doing he let fall the magic sword, and the yellow dwarf, who was crouching behind a lettuce, no sooner saw it than he sprang out and seized it, well knowing its wonderful power.

The princess gave a cry of terror on seeing the dwarf, but this only irritated the little monster; muttering a few magical words he summoned two giants, who bound the king with great chains of iron.

" Now," said the dwarf, " I am master of my rival's fate, but I will give him his life and permission to depart unharmed if you, princess, will consent to marry me."

" Let me die a thousand times rather," cried the unhappy king.

"Alas!" cried the princess, "must you die? Could anything be more terrible?"

"That you should marry that little wretch would be far more terrible," answered the king.

"At least," continued she, "let us die together."

"Let me have the satisfaction of dying for you, my princess," said he.

"Oh, no, no!" she cried, turning to the dwarf; "rather than that I will do as you wish."

"Cruel princess!" said the king, "would you make my life horrible to me by marrying another before my eyes?"

"Not so," replied the yellow dwarf; "you are a rival of whom I am too much afraid: you shall not see our marriage." So saying, in spite of Bellissima's tears and cries, he stabbed the king to the heart with the diamond sword.

The poor princess, seeing her lover lying dead at her feet, could no longer live without him; she sank down by him and died of a broken heart.

So ended these unfortunate lovers, whom not even the mermaid could help, because all the magic power had been lost with the diamond sword.

As to the wicked dwarf, he preferred to see the princess dead rather than married to the King of the Gold Mines; and the Fairy of the Desert, when she heard of the king's adventure, pulled down the grand monument which she had built, and was so angry at the trick that had been played her that she hated him as much as she had loved him before.

The kind mermaid, grieved at the sad fate of the lovers, caused them to be changed into two tall palm trees, which stand always side by side, whispering together of their faithful love and caressing one another with their interlacing branches.

TOM THUMB

IN the days of King Arthur, Merlin, the most learned magician of his time in old England, was on a journey; and being very weary stopped one day at the cottage of an honest ploughman to ask for refreshment. The ploughman's wife, with great civility, immediately brought him some milk in a wooden bowl, and some brown bread on a wooden platter.

Merlin could not help observing that, although everything within the cottage was particularly neat and clean and in good order, the ploughman and his wife had the most sorrowful air imaginable. So he asked them the cause of this, and learned that they were very miserable because they had no children. The poor woman declared, with tears in her eyes, that she would be the happiest creature in the world if she had a son, although he were no bigger than his father's thumb. Merlin was much amused with the thought of a boy no bigger than a man's thumb, and as soon as he returned home he sent for the queen of the fairies (with whom he was very intimate) and related to her the desire of the ploughman and his wife to have a son the size of his father's thumb.

The queen of the fairies was also amused at the idea, and declared that their wish should speedily be granted. And so the ploughman's wife had a son who in a few minutes grew as tall as his father's thumb.

The queen of the fairies came in at the window as the mother

---

[1] "Tom Thumb" is an English version of "Little Thumb" in Perrault's collection. This character is the germ of the most ancient folk tales of the Far East, of Africa, and of every country of Europe.

was sitting up in bed admiring the child. The queen kissed the infant, and giving it the name of Tom Thumb, immediately summoned several fairies from Fairy Land to clothe her new little favorite.

> An oak-leaf hat he had for his crown,
> His shirt it was by spiders spun;
> With doublet wove of thistle's down,
> His trousers up with points were done.
> His stockings, of apple rind, they tie
> With eye-lash plucked from his mother's eye.
> His shoes were made of a mouse's skin,
> Tanned with the downy hair within.

Tom never was any bigger than his father's thumb, which was not a large thumb either. But, as he grew older, he became very cunning and sly, for which his mother did not sufficiently correct him; so that when he was able to play with the boys for cherry stones, and had lost all his own, he used to creep into the boys' bags, fill his pockets, and come out again to play. But one day as he was getting out of a bag of cherry stones, the boy to whom it belonged chanced to see him.

"Ah, ha, my little Tom Thumb!" said the boy, "have I caught you at your bad tricks at last? Now I will reward you for thieving."

Then drawing the string of the bag tight round his neck, and shaking the bag heartily, the cherry stones bruised Tom's legs, thighs, and body sadly, which made him beg to be let out, and promise never to be guilty of such things any more.

Shortly afterwards, Tom's mother was making a batter pudding, and that he might see how she mixed it, he climbed upon the edge of the bowl. But his foot slipped, he fell over head and ears into the batter, and his mother, not observing him, stirred him into the pudding, and popped him into the pot to boil.

The hot water made Tom kick and struggle; and his mother, seeing the pudding jump up and down in such a furious manner, thought it was bewitched; and a tinker coming by just at the time, she quickly gave him the pudding, and he put it into his bag and walked on.

As soon as Tom could get the batter out of his mouth, he began to cry aloud, which so frightened the poor tinker that he flung the pudding over the hedge and ran away from it as fast as he could run. The pudding being broken to pieces by the fall, Tom was released, and walked home to his mother, who gave him a kiss and put him to bed.

Tom Thumb's mother once took him with her when she went to milk the cow; and it being a very windy day, she tied him with a needleful of thread to a thistle, that he might not be blown away. The cow, liking his oak-leaf hat, took him and the thistle up at one mouthful. While the cow chewed the thistle, Tom, terrified at her great teeth, which seemed ready to crush him to pieces, roared, " Mother, mother! " as loud as he could bawl.

" Where are you, Tommy, my dear Tommy? " said the mother.

" Here, mother, here in the red cow's mouth."

The mother began to cry and wring her hands; and the cow, surprised at such odd noises in her throat, opened her mouth and let him drop out. His mother then clapped him into her apron and ran home with him as fast as she could.

A little later Tom's father made him a whip of barley straw to drive the cattle with, and being one day in the field he slipped into a deep furrow. A raven flying over, picked him up with a grain of corn, and flew with him to the top of a giant's castle by the seaside, where he left him; and old Grumbo the giant coming soon after to walk upon his terrace, swallowed Tom like a pill, clothes and all. Tom presently made the giant very uncomfortable, and he threw him up into the sea. A large fish then swallowed him. This fish was soon after caught, and bought for the table of King Arthur. When it was cut open, everybody was delighted with little Tom Thumb.

The king made him his dwarf, and he became the favorite of the whole court. By his merry pranks he often amused the queen and the Knights of the Round Table. The king, when he rode on horseback, frequently took Tom in his hand; and if a shower of rain came on, he used to creep into his Majesty's waistcoat pocket and sleep till the rain was over. The king one day questioned Tom concerning his parents, and when Tom informed his Majesty they were very poor people, the king led him into his treasury and told him he should pay his friends a visit, and take with him as much money as he could carry. Tom procured a little purse, which was made of a water-bubble, and putting a threepenny piece into it, with much labor and difficulty got it upon his back, and after traveling two days and nights arrived at his father's house.

His mother met him at the door, and he was tired almost to death, having in forty-eight hours traveled about half a mile with a huge silver three-penny piece upon his back. His parents were glad to see him, especially when he had brought such an amazing sum of money with him. They placed him in a walnut shell by the fireside, and feasted him for three days upon a hazel nut, which made him sick, for a whole nut usually served him a month.

Tom got well again though, but could not travel because it rained. Therefore his mother took him in her hand, and with one puff blew him into King Arthur's court, where he entertained the king, queen, and nobility at tilts and tournaments. At this he exerted himself so much that he brought on a fit of sickness, and his life was despaired of.

Hearing of this, the queen of the fairies came in a chariot drawn by flying mice, placed Tom by her side, and drove through the air without stopping till they arrived at her palace; when, after restoring him to health, and permitting him to enjoy all the gay diversions of Fairy Land, the queen summoned a great wind, and, placing Tom before it, blew him straight to the court of King Arthur.

But just as Tom should have alighted in the courtyard of the palace, the cook happened to pass along with the king's great bowl of firmity (King Arthur loved firmity), and poor Tom Thumb fell plump into the middle of it, and splashed the hot firmity into the cook's eyes. Down went the bowl.

" Oh, dear! oh, dear! " cried Tom.

" Murder! murder! " bellowed the cook. And away ran the king's nice firmity into the gutter.

The cook was a red-faced, cross fellow, and swore to the king that Tom had done it out of mere mischief; so he was taken up, tried, and sentenced to be beheaded. Tom, hearing this dreadful sentence and seeing a miller stand by with his mouth wide open, took a good spring and jumped down the miller's throat, unperceived by all, even by the miller himself.

Tom being lost, the court broke up, and away went the miller to his mill. But Tom did not leave him long at rest; he began to roll and tumble about, so that the miller felt himself bewitched, and sent for a doctor. When the doctor came, Tom began to dance and sing; the doctor was as much frightened as the miller, and sent in great haste for five more doctors and twenty learned men.

While all these were considering what they should do, the miller happened to yawn, and Tom, taking the opportunity, made another jump, and alighted on his feet, in the middle of the table. The miller, provoked to be thus tormented by such a little creature, fell into a great passion, caught hold of Tom, and threw him out of the window into the river. A large salmon swimming by, snapped him up in a minute. The salmon was soon caught and sold in the market to the steward of a lord. The lord, thinking it an uncommon fine fish, made a present of it to the king, who ordered it to be dressed immediately. When the cook cut open the salmon, he found poor Tom, and ran with him directly to the king; but the king being busy with state affairs, desired that he might be brought another day.

The cook resolving to keep him safely this time, as he had so lately given him the slip, clapped him into a mouse-trap, and left him to amuse himself for a whole week by peeping through the wires. At last the king sent for him, and, forgiving him for causing the firmity to be thrown down, ordered him new clothes and knighted him.

> Of butterflies' wings his shirt was made,
>   His boots of chickens' hide;
> And by a nimble fairy blade,
> Well learnèd in the tailoring trade,
>   His clothing was supplied.
>   A needle dangled by his side;
>   A dapper mouse he used to ride,
>   Thus strutted Tom in stately pride!

Thus dressed and mounted, he rode a hunting with the king and nobility, all of whom laughed heartily at Tom and his fine prancing steed.

As they rode by a farm-house one day, a cat jumped from behind the door, seized the mouse and little Tom, and began to devour the mouse. However, Tom boldly drew his sword and attacked the cat, who then let him fall.

The king and his nobles, seeing Tom falling, went to his assistance, and one of the lords caught him in his hat; but poor Tom was sadly scratched, and his clothes were torn by the claws of the cat. In this condition he was carried home, when a bed of down was made for him in a little ivory cabinet.

The queen of the fairies came and took him again to Fairy

Land, where she kept him for some years; and then, dressing him in bright green, sent him flying once more through the air to earth, in the days of King Thunstone. The people flocked far and near to look at him; and the king before whom he was carried asked him who he was, whence he came, and where he lived. Tom answered: —

> " My name is Tom Thumb,
> From the Fairies I come;
> When King Arthur shone,
> This court was my home.
> In me he delighted,
> By him I was knighted,
> Did you never hear of
> Sir Thomas Thumb? "

The king was so charmed with this address that he ordered a little chair to be made, in order that Tom might sit on his table; and also a palace of gold a span high, with a door an inch wide, for little Tom to live in. He also gave him a coach drawn by six small mice. This made the queen angry, because she had not a new coach too. Therefore, resolving to ruin Tom, she complained to the king that he had been saucy to her. The king sent for him in a rage. Tom, to escape his fury, crept into an empty snail-shell, and there lay until he was almost starved; when peeping out of the shell, he saw a fine large butterfly settled on the ground. He now ventured out, and getting astride, the butterfly took wing, and mounted into the air with little Tom on his back. Away he flew from field to field and from tree to tree, and at last returned to the king's court. The king, queen, and nobles all strove to catch him but could not. At length poor Tom slipped from his seat, and fell into a watering pot, in which he was almost drowned.

The queen vowed his head should be cut off; but while they were getting ready to do it, he was secured once more in a mouse-trap; when the cat seeing something stir, and supposing it to be a mouse, patted the trap about till she broke it, and set Tom at liberty.

Soon afterwards a spider, taking him for a fly, made at him. Tom drew his sword and fought valiantly, but the spider's poisonous breath at last overcame him.

> He fell dead on the ground where late he had stood,
> And the spider sucked up the last drop of his blood.

King Thunstone and his whole court went into mourning for little Tom Thumb. They buried him under a rosebush, and raised a nice white marble monument over his grave, with the following epitaph: —

> " Here lies Tom Thumb, King Arthur's knight,
> Who died by spider's cruel bite.
> He was well known in Arthur's court,
> Where he afforded gallant sport;
> He rode at tilt and tournament,
> And on a mouse a-hunting went;
> Alive he filled the court with mirth,
> His death to sorrow soon gave birth.
> Wipe, wipe your eyes, and shake your head
> And cry, ' Alas! Tom Thumb is dead.' "

THE STORY OF MR. VINEGAR

M R. and Mrs. Vinegar lived in a vinegar bottle. One day, when Mr. Vinegar was away from home, Mrs. Vinegar, who was a very good housewife, was busily sweeping her house, when an unlucky thump of the broom brought the whole house clitter-clatter, clitter-clatter about her ears. Bursting into tears she ran forth to meet her husband, and, on seeing him she exclaimed, "Oh, Mr. Vinegar, we are ruined! I have knocked the house down, and it is all in pieces!" Mr. Vinegar then said, "My dear, let us see what can be done. Here is the door; I will take it on my back, and we will go forth and seek our fortune."

They walked all that day, and at night entered a forest. They were both very tired, and Mr. Vinegar said, "My love, I will climb up into a tree, drag the door up, and you shall follow." He did so, and they both lay down upon the door and fell asleep. In the middle of the night Mr. Vinegar was awakened by the sound of voices underneath, and to his dismay perceived that a party of thieves were dividing their booty. "Here, Jack," said one, "here's five pounds for you; here, Bill, here's ten pounds for you; here, Bob, here's three pounds for you."

Mr. Vinegar was so frightened that his trembling shook down the door on their heads. The thieves ran away, but Mr. Vinegar did not quit his retreat until broad daylight.

He then scrambled out of the tree, and went to lift up the

174

door. What did he see but a number of golden guineas! "Come down, Mrs. Vinegar," he cried, "come down, our fortune's made, our fortune's made!" Mrs. Vinegar got down as fast as she could, and saw the money with equal delight. "Now, my dear," said she, "I'll tell you what to do. There is a fair in the neighborhood; you take these forty guineas and buy a cow. I can make butter and cheese, which you shall sell, and we shall be able to live comfortably." Mr. Vinegar joyfully assents, takes the money and goes off to the fair. When he arrived, he walked up and down, and at length saw a beautiful red cow. It was an excellent milker, and Mr. Vinegar thought, "Oh! if I only had that cow, I should be the happiest man alive." So he offers the forty guineas for the cow, and the owner declaring that, as he was a friend, he would oblige him, and the bargain was made. Proud of his purchase, he drove the cow backwards and forwards to show it. Presently he saw a man playing the bagpipes, tweedledum, tweedledee; the children followed him about, and he was pocketing money on all sides. "Well," thought Mr. Vinegar, "if I had but that beautiful instrument I should be the happiest man alive — my fortune would be made."

So he went up to the man, and said, "Friend, what a beautiful instrument that is, and what a lot of money you must make." "Why, yes," said the man, "I make a great deal of money, to be sure, and it is a wonderful instrument." "Oh!" cried Mr. Vinegar, "how I should like to possess it." "Well," said the man, "as you are a friend, you shall have it for that red cow." "Done," said the delighted Mr. Vinegar; so he exchanged the beautiful red cow for the bagpipes. He walked up and down with his purchase, but he could n't play a tune, and instead of pocketing pence, the boys followed him hooting and laughing.

His fingers grew very cold, and very much ashamed, he was leaving the town, when he met a man with a fine thick pair of

175

gloves. "Oh, my fingers are so very cold," said Mr. Vinegar to himself; "if I only had those beautiful gloves I should be the happiest man alive." He went up to the man, and said to him, "Friend, you have a capital pair of gloves there." "Yes, truly!" cried the man, "and my hands are as warm as toast." "Well," said Mr. Vinegar, "I should like to have them." "What will you give?" said the man; "as you are a friend, you may have them for those bagpipes." "Done," cried Mr. Vinegar. He put on the gloves, and felt very happy as he walked homeward.

At last he grew very tired, when he saw a man coming toward him with a good stout stick in his hand. "Oh," said Mr. Vinegar, "if I had but that stick; I should then be the happiest man alive." He spoke to the man: "Friend, what a fine stick you have there." "Yes," said the man, "I have used it for many a long mile, and a good friend it has been; but if you have a fancy for it, I don't mind letting you have it for that pair of gloves." Mr. Vinegar's hands now being warm, and his legs tired, he gladly made the exchange.

As he drew near to the wood where he had left his wife, he heard a parrot on a tree calling out to him: "Mr. Vinegar, you foolish man, you simpleton! You laid out all your money at the fair in buying a cow; not content with that, you changed it for bagpipes, on which you could not play, and which were not worth one tenth of the money. You no sooner had the bagpipes than you changed them for the gloves, which were not worth one quarter of the money, and when you had the gloves, you changed them for a miserable stick, which you might have cut in any hedge." The bird burst into laughter, and Mr. Vinegar, being very angry, threw the stick at its head. The stick lodged in the tree, and he returned to his wife without money, cow, bagpipes, gloves, or stick.

THE SUN AND THE WIND

ONE day the sun and the wind had a quarrel. The wind said, "I am stronger than you." "No," said the sun, "I am stronger than you."

While they were disputing they saw a traveler coming along the road. He wore a heavy coat.

"See that man!" cried the wind. "Let us see which of us can take off his coat. The one who can do that is the stronger."

"Agreed," said the sun. "You may begin."

The wind blew and blew and blew. But the traveler only drew his coat closer about him.

The wind now blew more fiercely than before. The trees rocked, and the dust flew, but the traveler only buttoned up his coat.

"What a gale this is!" cried he, and turned up his coat collar to his ears.

"I give it up," said the wind.

Then the sun had his turn. He shone and shone and shone.

"How the weather has changed," said the traveler, and he unbuttoned his coat.

Still the sun shone, and presently the traveler wiped the moisture from his face.

"This thick coat is too much for me; I will have to take it off and carry it on my arm," said he, and he took it off.

"You have won," said the wind. "I see now that gentleness succeeds where rudeness fails."

THE LION AND THE MOUSE

ONE day a great lion lay asleep in the sunshine. A little mouse ran across his paw and wakened him. The great lion was just going to eat him up when the little mouse cried, " O please, let me go, sir, some day I may help you."

The lion laughed at the thought that the little mouse could be of any use to him. But he was a good-natured lion, and he set the mouse free.

Not long after, the lion was caught in a net. He tugged and pulled with all his might, but the ropes were too strong. Then he roared loudly. The little mouse heard him, and ran to the spot.

" Be still, dear Lion, and I will set you free. I will gnaw the ropes."

With his sharp little teeth, the mouse cut the ropes, and the lion came out of the net.

" You laughed at me once," said the mouse. " You thought I was too little to do you a good turn. But see, you owe your life to a poor little mouse."

THE DOG AND HIS IMAGE

A DOG once stole a piece of meat and ran away. Down the road he went, and across the brook on a plank. Midway across he stopped and looked into the water. He thought he saw another dog with a piece of meat in his mouth.

This meat looked larger to him than his own.

"I'll have it!" growled he, and sprang into the water. But he lost the first piece of meat, and did not get the other, for what he saw was his own reflection.

Do not be greedy, or you may lose all you have.

THE TORTOISE AND THE HARE

A HARE once made fun of a tortoise. "What a slow way you have!" he said. "How you creep along!"

"Do I?" said the tortoise. "Try a race with me and I 'll beat you."

"What a boaster you are," said the hare. "But come! I will race with you. Whom shall we ask to mark off the bounds and see that the race is fair?"

"Let us ask the fox," said the tortoise. The fox was very wise and fair. He showed them where they were to start, and how far they were to run.

The tortoise lost no time. He started out at once, and jogged straight on.

The hare leaped along swiftly for a few minutes till he had left the tortoise far behind. He knew he could reach the mark very quickly, so he lay down by the road under a shady tree and took a nap.

By and by he awoke, and remembered the race. He sprang up and ran as fast as he could. But when he reached the mark the tortoise was there!

"Slow and steady wins the race," said the fox.

THE FOX AND THE GRAPES

ONE warm day a thirsty fox found some bunches of grapes growing high up on a vine. " I must have those grapes," he thought.

Again and again he sprang into the air but he could not reach them. At last he went away, saying, " The grapes are very sour! Even the birds would not peck at them."

That is what people sometimes do when they cannot get what they want: they make believe that what they want is good for nothing.

THE STRAW, THE COAL, AND THE BEAN

IN a village dwelt a poor old woman, who had gathered together a dish of beans and wanted to cook them. So she made a fire on her hearth, and that it might burn the quicker, she lighted it with a handful of straw. When she was emptying the beans into the pan, one dropped without her observing it, and lay on the ground beside a straw, and soon afterward a burning coal from the fire leaped down to the two.

Then the straw began and said, "Dear friends, from whence do you come here?"

The coal replied, "I fortunately sprang out of the fire, and if I had not escaped by main force, my death would have been certain — I should have been burned to ashes."

The bean said, "I too have escaped with a whole skin, but if the old woman had got me into the pan I should have been made into broth without any mercy, like my comrades."

"And would a better fate have fallen to my lot?" said the straw. "The old woman has destroyed all my brethren in fire and smoke; she seized sixty of them at once, and took their lives. I luckily slipped through her fingers."

"But what are we to do now?" said the coal.

"I think," answered the bean, "that as we have so fortunately escaped death, we should keep together like good companions, and lest a new mischance should overtake us here, we should go away together, and repair to a foreign country."

The proposition pleased the two others, and they set out

182

on their way in company. Soon, however, they came to a little brook, and as there was no bridge or foot-plank they did not know how they were to get over it.

The straw hit on a good idea, and said, " I will lay myself straight across, and then you can walk over me as on a bridge."

The straw thereupon stretched itself from one bank to the other, and the coal, who was very impetuous, tripped quite boldly on to the newly built bridge. But when she had reached the middle, and heard the water rushing beneath her, she was afraid, and stood still and ventured no further. The straw, however, began to burn, broke in two pieces, and fell into the stream. The coal slipped after her, hissed when she got into the water, and breathed her last.

The bean, who had prudently stayed behind on the shore, could not help laughing at the event, and laughed so heartily that she burst. It would have been all over with her, likewise, had not a tailor, who was traveling in search of work, sat down by the brook to rest. As he had a compassionate heart he pulled out his needle and thread, and sewed her together. The bean thanked him most prettily, but as the tailor used black thread, all beans since then have had a black seam.

THE GOLDEN GOOSE

THERE was once a man who had three sons. The youngest of them was called Dullhead, and was sneered and jeered at and snubbed on every possible opportunity.

One day it happened that the eldest son wished to go into the forest to cut wood, and before he started his mother gave him a fine rich cake and a bottle of wine, so that he might be sure not to suffer from hunger or thirst.

When he reached the forest he met a little old gray man who wished him "Good-morning," and said: "Do give me a piece of that cake you have in your pocket, and let me have a draught of your wine — I am so hungry and thirsty."

But this clever son replied: "If I give you my cake and wine I shall have none left for myself: you must go your own way;" and he left the little man standing there and went further into the forest. There he began to cut down a tree, but before long he made a false stroke with his ax and cut his own arm so badly that he was obliged to go home and have it bound up.

Then the second son went to the forest and his mother gave him a good cake and a bottle of wine as she had to his elder brother. He too met the little old gray man, who begged him for a morsel of cake and a draught of wine.

But the second son spoke most sensibly too, and said: "Whatever I give you I deprive myself of. Just go your own way, will you?" Not long after his punishment overtook him, for no sooner had he struck a couple of blows on a tree with his ax, than he cut his leg so badly that he had to be carried home.

184

So then Dullhead said: "Father, let me go out and cut wood."

But his father answered: "Both your brothers have injured themselves. You had better leave it alone; you know nothing about it."

But Dullhead begged so hard to be allowed to go that at last his father said: "Very well, then — go. Perhaps when you have hurt yourself, you may learn to know better." His mother only gave him a very plain cake made with water and baked in cinders, and a bottle of sour beer.

When he got to the forest, he too met the little old gray man, who greeted him, and said: "Give me a piece of your cake and a draught from your bottle; I am so hungry and thirsty."

And Dullhead replied: "I've only got a cinder cake and some sour beer, but if you care to have that, let us sit down and eat."

So they sat down, and when Dullhead brought out his cake he found it had turned into a fine rich cake, and the sour beer into excellent wine. Then they ate and drank, and when they had finished the little man said: "Now I will bring you luck, because you have a kind heart and are willing to share what you have with others. There stands an old tree; cut it down, and among its roots you'll find something." With that the little man took leave.

Then Dullhead fell to at once to hew down the tree, and when it fell he found among its roots a goose, whose feathers were all of pure gold. He lifted it out, carried it off, and took it with him to an inn where he meant to spend the night.

Now the landlord of the inn had three daughters, and when they saw the goose they were filled with curiosity as to what this wonderful bird could be, and each longed to have one of its beautiful feathers.

The eldest thought to herself: "No doubt I shall soon find

a good opportunity to pluck out one of its feathers," and the first time Dullhead happened to leave the room she caught hold of the goose by its wing. But, lo and behold! her fingers seemed to stick fast to the goose, and she could not take her hand away.

Soon after the second daughter came in, and thought to pluck a golden feather for herself, too; but hardly had she touched her sister than she stuck fast as well. At last the third sister came with the same intention, but the other two cried: "Keep off! for Heaven's sake, keep off!"

The younger sister could not imagine why she was to keep off, and thought to herself: "If they are both there, why should not I be there, too?"

So she sprang to them; but no sooner had she touched one of them than she stuck fast to her. So they all three had to spend the night with the goose.

Next morning Dullhead tucked the goose under his arm and went off, without in the least troubling himself about the three girls who were hanging on to it. They just had to run after him right or left as best they could. In the middle of the field they met a parson, and when he saw this procession he cried:

"For shame, you bold girls! What do you mean by running after a young fellow through the fields like that? Do you call that proper behaviour?" And with that he caught the youngest girl by the hand to try and draw her away. But directly he touched her he hung on himself, and had to run along with the rest of them.

Not long after the clerk came that way, and was much surprised to see the parson following the footsteps of three girls. "Why, where is your reverence going so fast?" cried he; "don't forget there is to be a christening to-day," and he ran after him, caught him by the sleeve, and hung on to it himself.

As the five of them trotted along in this fashion, one after the other, two peasants were coming from their work with their hoes.

On seeing them the parson called out and begged them to come and rescue him and the clerk. But no sooner did they touch the clerk than they stuck on, too, and so there were seven of them running after Dullhead and the goose.

After a time they all came to a town where a king reigned whose daughter was so serious and solemn that no one could ever manage to make her laugh. So the king had decreed that whoever should succeed in making her laugh should marry her.

When Dullhead heard this he marched before the princess with his goose and its appendages, and as soon as she saw these seven people continually running after each other she burst out laughing, and could not stop herself. Then Dullhead claimed her as his bride, but the king, who did not much fancy him as a son-in-law, made all sorts of objections, and told him he must first find a man who could drink up a whole cellarful of wine.

Dullhead bethought him of the little gray man, who could, he felt sure, help him; so he went off to the forest, and on the very spot where he had cut down the tree he saw a man sitting with a most dismal expression of face.

Dullhead asked him what he was taking so much to heart, and the man answered: " I don't know how I am ever to quench the terrible thirst I am suffering from. Cold water does n't suit me at all. To be sure, I 've emptied a whole barrel of wine, but what is one drop on a hot stove? "

" I think I can help you," said Dullhead. " Come with me, and you shall drink to your heart's content." So he took him to the king's cellar, and the man sat down before the huge casks and drank and drank till he drank up the whole contents of the cellar before the day closed.

Then Dullhead asked once more for his bride, but the king felt vexed at the idea of a stupid fellow whom people called " Dullhead " carrying off his daughter, and he began to make fresh conditions. He required Dullhead to find a man who could eat a mountain of bread. Dullhead did not wait to consider long, but went straight off to the forest, and there on the same spot sat a man who was drawing in a strap as tight as he could around his body, and making a most woeful face. Said he: "I've eaten up a whole ovenful of loaves, but what's the good of that to a man who is as hungry as I am? I declare my stomach feels quite empty, and I must draw my belt tight if I'm not to die of starvation."

Dullhead was delighted, and said: "Get up and come with me, and you shall have plenty to eat," and he brought him to the king's court.

Now the king had given orders to have all the flour in his kingdom brought together, and to have a huge mountain baked of it. But the man from the wood just took up his stand before the mountain and began to eat, and in one day it had all vanished.

For the third time Dullhead asked for his bride, but again the king tried to make some evasion, and demanded a ship "which could sail on land and water. When you come sailing in such a ship," said he, "you shall have my daughter without any further delay."

Again Dullhead started off to the forest, and there he found the little old gray man with whom he had shared his cake, and who said: "I have eaten and I have drunk for you, and now I will give you the ship. I have done all this for you because you were kind and merciful to me."

Then he gave Dullhead a ship which could sail on land or water, and when the king saw it he felt he could no longer refuse him his daughter.

So they celebrated the wedding with great rejoicings; and after the king's death Dullhead succeeded to the kingdom, and lived happily with his wife for many years after.

THE FOX AND THE LITTLE RED HEN

THERE was once a little red hen that lived in a house by herself in the wood. And over the hill, in a hole in the rocks, lived a sly, crafty old fox.

Now this crafty old fellow of a fox lay awake nights, and prowled slyly about days, trying to think how he should get the little red hen. He wanted to carry her home to boil for his supper.

But the wise little hen never left her house without locking the door and putting the key in her pocket; so the old fox watched and prowled and lay awake nights till he grew pale and thin, but he found no way to get the wise little red hen.

At last one morning he took a big bag over his shoulder, and said to his mother:

"Mother, have the pot boiling when I come home, for I'll bring the little red hen for our supper."

Away he went over the hill and through the wood to where the red hen lived in her snug little house.

Just at that moment out came the little red hen to pick up sticks for her fire, and in slipped the fox and hid behind the door.

In came the hen in a minute and locked the door, and put the key in her pocket. When she saw the fox she dropped her sticks and flew with a great flutter up to the beam across the house under the roof.

"Ah," said the sly fox, "I'll soon bring you down." And

he began to whirl around and around and around, faster and faster and faster, after his big, bushy tail.

The little red hen looked at him till she got so dizzy that she fell off the beam to the floor. The fox caught her and put her into his bag and started straight for home.

Up the wood and down the wood he went with the little red hen shut tight in the bag. She thought it was all over with her.

After a while the fox lay down to rest. Then she came to her wits, and put her hand into her pocket and took out a bright little pair of scissors. With them she snipped a hole in the bag. She leaped out and picked up a big stone and dropped it into the bag and ran home as fast as her legs could carry her.

The fox waked up and started again with his bag over his shoulders. "How heavy the little red hen is," he said, "that I am to have for my supper."

His mother was standing at the door of his den waiting for him. "Mother," he said, "have you the pot boiling?"

"Yes, to be sure!" said she, "and have you the little red hen?"

"Yes, here in my bag. Lift the lid, and let me put her in," said the fox.

The fox untied the bag and held it over the boiling water and shook it. The heavy stone fell into the water with a splash which went up over the fox and his mother and scalded them. And the little red hen lived safe in her house in the wood.

THE LITTLE RED HEN AND THE GRAIN OF WHEAT

A LITTLE red hen once found a grain of wheat. "Who will plant this wheat?" she said.

"I won't," says the dog.

"I won't," says the cat.

"I won't," says the pig.

"I won't," says the turkey.

"Then I will," says the little red hen. "Cluck! cluck!"

So she planted the grain of wheat. Very soon the wheat began to grow and the green leaves came out of the ground. The sun shone and the rain fell and the wheat kept on growing until it was tall, strong, and ripe.

"Who will reap this wheat?" says the little red hen.

"I won't," says the dog.

"I won't," says the cat.

"I won't," says the pig.

"I won't," says the turkey.

"I will, then," says the little red hen. "Cluck! cluck!"

So she reaped the wheat.

"Who will thresh this wheat?" says the little red hen.

"I won't," says the dog.

"I won't," says the cat.

"I won't," says the pig.

"I won't," says the turkey.

"I will, then," says the little red hen. "Cluck! cluck!"

So she threshed the wheat.

"Who will take this wheat to mill to have it ground?" says the little red hen.

"I won't," says the dog.

"I won't," says the cat.

"I won't," says the pig.

"I won't," says the turkey.

"I will, then," says the little red hen. "Cluck! cluck!"

So she took the wheat to mill, and by and by she came back with the flour.

"Who will bake this flour?" says the little red hen.

"I won't," says the dog.

"I won't," says the cat.

"I won't," says the pig.

"I won't," says the turkey.

"I will, then," says the little red hen. "Cluck! cluck!"

So she baked the flour and made a loaf of bread.

"Who will eat this bread?" says the little red hen.

"I will," says the dog.

"I will," says the cat.

"I will," says the pig.

"I will," says the turkey.

"*I* will," says the little red hen. "Cluck! cluck!"

And she ate up the loaf of bread.

THE GINGERBREAD MAN

ONCE upon a time there were a little old woman and a little old man, and they lived all alone in a little old house. They had n't any little girls or any little boys at all. So one day, the little old woman made a boy out of gingerbread; she made him a chocolate jacket, and put cinnamon seeds in it for buttons; his eyes were made of fine, fat currants; his mouth was made of rose-colored sugar; and he had a gay little cap of orange sugar-candy. When the little old woman had rolled him out, and dressed him up, and pinched his ginger-bread shoes into shape, she put him in a pan; then she put the pan in the oven and shut the door; and she thought, "Now I shall have a little boy of my own."

When it was time for the Gingerbread Boy to be done she opened the oven door and pulled out the pan. Out jumped the little Gingerbread Boy on to the floor, and away he ran, out of the door and down the street. The little old woman and the little old man ran after him as fast as they could, but he just laughed, and shouted:

> "Run! run! as fast as you can!
> You can't catch me, I 'm the Gingerbread Man!"

And they could n't catch him.

The little Gingerbread Boy ran on and on, until he came to a cow by the roadside. "Stop, little Gingerbread Boy," said the cow; "I want to eat you." The little Gingerbread Boy laughed, and said, —

> "I have run away from a little old woman,
> And a little old man,
> And I can run away from you, I can!"

And, as the cow chased him, he looked over his shoulder and cried, —

> "Run! run! as fast as you can!
> You can't catch me, I'm the Gingerbread Man!"

And the cow could n't catch him.

The little Gingerbread Boy ran on, and on, and on, till he came to a horse in the pasture. "Please stop, little Gingerbread Boy," said the horse, "you look very good to eat." But the little Gingerbread Boy laughed out loud. "O ho! Oho!" he said.

> "I have run away from a little old woman,
> A little old man,
> A cow,
> And I can run away from you, I can!"

And, as the horse chased him, he looked over his shoulder and cried, —

> "Run! run! as fast as you can!
> You can't catch me, I'm the Gingerbread Man!"

And the horse could n't catch him.

By and by the little Gingerbread Boy came to a barn full of threshers. When the threshers smelled the Gingerbread Boy, they tried to pick him up, and said, "Don't run so fast, little Gingerbread Boy; you look very good to eat." But the little Gingerbread Boy ran harder than ever, and as he ran he cried out, —

"I have run away from a little old woman,
A little old man,
A cow,
A horse,
And I can run away from you, I can!"

And when he found that he was ahead of the threshers, he turned and shouted back to them, —

"Run! run! as fast as you can!
You can't catch me, I 'm the Gingerbread Man!"

And the threshers could n't catch him.

Then the little Gingerbread Boy ran faster than ever. He ran and ran until he came to a field full of mowers. When the mowers saw how fine he looked, they ran after him, calling out, "Wait a bit! wait a bit, little Gingerbread Boy, we wish to eat you!" But the little Gingerbread Boy laughed harder than ever, and ran like the wind. "O ho! O ho!" he said.

"I have run away from a little old woman,
A little old man,
A cow,
A horse,
A barn full of threshers,
And I can run away from you, I can!"

And when he found he was ahead of the mowers, he turned and shouted back to them, —

"Run! run! as fast as you can!
You can't catch me, I 'm the Gingerbread Man!"

And the mowers could n't catch him.

By this time the little Gingerbread Boy was so proud that he did n't think anybody could catch him. Pretty soon he saw a fox coming across a field. The fox looked at him and began

to run. But the little Gingerbread Boy shouted across to him,
" You can't catch me!" The fox began to run faster, and the
little Gingerbread Boy ran faster, and as he ran he said, —

> " I have run away from a little old woman,
>   A little old man
>   A cow,
>   A horse,
>   A barn full of threshers,
>   A field full of mowers,
>   And I can run away from you, I can!
>   Run! run! as fast as you can!
>   You can't catch me, I'm the Gingerbread Man!"

" Why," said the fox, " I would not catch you if I could.
I would not think of disturbing you."

Just then, the little Gingerbread Boy came to a river. He
could not swim across, and he wanted to keep running away
from the cow and the horse and the people.

" Jump on my tail and I will take you across," said the fox.

So the Gingerbread Boy jumped on the fox's tail, and the
fox swam into the river. A little distance from the shore he
said, " Little Gingerbread Boy, I think you had better get on
my back, or you may fall off."

So the little Gingerbread Boy jumped on his back.

After swimming a little farther, the fox said, " I am afraid
you will get wet there. You had better jump on my shoulder."

So the little Gingerbread Boy jumped on his shoulder.

When they were near the other side of the river, the fox said,
" Little Gingerbread Boy, my back is tired, will you jump on
my nose?"

So the little Gingerbread Boy jumped on his nose.

As soon as the fox reached the shore he threw back his head,
and into his mouth fell the little Gingerbread Boy.

THE WOLF AND THE SEVEN YOUNG GOSLINGS

THERE was once an old goose who had seven young goslings, and loved them as only a mother could love her children. One day she was going into the wood to seek for food, and before setting off she called all seven to her and said, " Dear children, I am obliged to go into the wood, so be on your guard against the wolf; for if he gets in here he will eat you up, feathers, skin, and all. The villain often disguises himself, but you can easily recognize him by his rough voice and black paws."

The children answered, "Dear mother, we will take great care; you may go without any anxiety." So the old lady was comforted, and set off cheerfully for the wood.

Before long some one knocked at the door, and cried, " Open, open, my dear children; your mother is here, and has brought something for each of you."

But the goslings soon perceived, by the rough voice, that it was the wolf. "We will not open," said they; " you are not our mother, for she has a sweet and lovely voice; but your voice is rough — you are the wolf."

Thereupon the wolf set off to a merchant and bought a large lump of chalk; he ate it, and it made his voice sweet. Back he came, knocked at the door, and cried, " Open, open, my dear children; your mother is here, and has brought something for each of you."

But the wolf had laid his black paw on the window-sill, and

when the children saw it they cried, " We will not open; our mother has not black feet like you — you are the wolf."

So the wolf ran off to the baker, and said, " I have hurt my foot, put some dough on it." And when the baker had plastered it with dough the wolf went to the miller and cried, " Strew some meal on my paws." But the miller thought to himself, " The wolf wants to deceive someone," and he hesitated to do it, till the wolf said, " If you don't do it at once I will eat you up." So the miller was afraid and made his paws white. Such is the way of the world!

Now came the rogue back for the third time, knocked, and said, " Open the door, dear children; your mother has come home, and has brought something for each of you out of the wood."

The little goslings cried, " Show us your paws first, that we may see whether you are indeed our mother." So he laid his paws on the window-sill, and when the goslings saw that they were white they believed it was all right and opened the door; and who should come in but the wolf!

They screamed out and tried to hide themselves: one jumped under the table, another into the bed, the third into the oven, the fourth ran into the kitchen, the fifth hopped into a chest, the sixth under the wash-tub, and the seventh got into the clock-case. But the wolf seized them, and stood on no ceremony with them; one after another he gobbled them all up, except the youngest, who being in the clock-case he couldn't find. When the wolf had eaten his fill he strolled forth, laid himself down in the green meadow under a tree, and went fast asleep.

Not long after, back came the old goose home from the wood; but what, alas! did she see? The house-door stood wide open; table, chairs, benches, were all overthrown; the wash-tub lay in the ashes; blankets and pillows were torn off the bed. She looked for her children, but nowhere could she find them;

she called them each by name, but nobody answered. At last, when she came to the youngest, a little squeaking voice answered, "Dear mother, I am in the clock-case." She pulled him out, and he told her how the wolf had come and had eaten up all the others. You may think how she wept for her dear children.

At last, in her grief, she went out, and the youngest gosling ran beside her. And when she came to the meadow there lay the wolf under the tree, snoring till the boughs shook. She walked round and examined him on all sides, till she perceived that something was moving and kicking about inside him.

"Can it be," thought she, "that my poor children whom he has swallowed for his supper are yet alive?" So she sent the little gosling back to the house for scissors, needle, and thread, and began to slit up the monster's stomach. Scarcely had she given one snip when out came the head of a gosling, and when she had cut a little further the six jumped out, one after another, not having taken the least hurt, because the greedy monster had swallowed them down whole. That was a joy! They embraced their mother tenderly, and skipped about as lively as a tailor at his wedding.

But the old goose said, "Now go and find me six large stones, which we will put inside the greedy beast while he is still asleep." So the goslings got the stones in all haste, and they put them inside the wolf; and the old goose sewed him up again in a great hurry, while he never once moved nor took any notice.

Now, when the wolf at last woke up and got upon his legs he found he was very thirsty, and wished to go to the spring to drink. But as soon as he began to move the stones began to shake and rattle inside him, till he cried:

"What's this rumbling and tumbling,
    What's this rattling like bones?
I thought I had eaten six little geese,
    But they've turned out only stones."

And when he came to the spring and bent down his head to drink the heavy stones overbalanced him, and in he went head over heels. Now, when the seven goslings saw this they came running up, crying loudly, " The wolf is dead! the wolf is dead! " and danced for joy all round the spring, and their mother with them.

MR. MIACCA

TOMMY GRIMES was sometimes a good boy, and sometimes a bad boy; and when he was a bad boy, he was a very bad boy. Now his mother used to say to him: "Tommy, Tommy, be a good boy, and don't go out of the street, or else Mr. Miacca will take you." But still when he was a bad boy he would go out of the street; and one day, sure enough, he had scarcely got round the corner, when Mr. Miacca did catch him and popped him into a bag upside down, and took him off to his house.

When Mr. Miacca got Tommy inside, he pulled him out of the bag and sat him down, and felt his arms and legs. "You 're rather tough," says he; "but you 're all I 've got for supper, and you 'll not taste bad boiled. But body o' me, I 've forgot the herbs, and it 's bitter you 'll taste without herbs. Sally! Here, I say, Sally!" and he called Mrs. Miacca.

So Mrs. Miacca came out of another room and said: "What d 'ye want, my dear?"

"Oh, here 's a little boy for supper," said Mr. Miacca, "and I 've forgot the herbs. Mind him, will ye, while I go for them."

"All right, my love," says Mrs. Miacca, and off he goes.

Then Tommy Grimes said to Mrs. Miacca: "Does Mr. Miacca always have little boys for supper?"

"Mostly, my dear," said Mrs. Miacca, "if little boys are bad enough, and get in his way."

"And don't you have anything else but boy-meat? No pudding?" asked Tommy.

"Ah, I love pudding," says Mrs. Miacca. "But it's not often I get it."

"Why, my mother is making a pudding this very day," said Tommy Grimes, "and I am sure she'd give you some, if I ask her. Shall I run and get some?"

"Now, that's a thoughtful boy," said Mrs. Miacca, "only don't be long and be sure to be back for supper."

So off Tommy pelted, and right glad he was to get off so cheap; and for many a long day he was as good as good could be, and never went round the corner of the street. But he could n't always be good; and one day he went round the corner, and as luck would have it, he had scarcely got round it when Mr. Miacca grabbed him, popped him in his bag, and took him home.

When he got him there, Mr. Miacca dropped him out; and when he saw him, he said: "Ah, you're the youngster that served us such a shabby trick, leaving us without any supper. Well, you sha'n't do it again. I'll watch over you myself. Here, get under the sofa, and I'll sit on it and watch the pot boil for you."

So poor Tommy Grimes had to creep under the sofa, and Mr. Miacca sat on it and waited for the pot to boil. And they waited and they waited, but still the pot did n't boil, till at last Mr. Miacca got tired of waiting, and he said: "Here, you under there, I'm not going to wait any longer; put out your leg, and I'll stop your giving us the slip."

So Tommy put out a leg and Mr. Miacca got a chopper, and chopped it off, and pops it into the pot.

Suddenly he calls out: "Sally, my dear, Sally!" and nobody answered. So he went into the next room to look out for Mrs. Miacca, and while he was there, Tommy crept out from under the sofa and ran out of the door. For it was a leg of the sofa that he had put out.

So Tommy Grimes ran home, and he never went round the corner again till he was old enough to go alone.

THE CAT AND THE MOUSE

THE cat and the mouse
Play'd in the malt-house:

The cat bit the mouse's tail off. " Pray, puss, give me my tail." " No," says the cat, " I 'll not give you your tail, till you go to the cow, and fetch me some milk."

First she leapt, and then she ran,
Till she came to the cow, and thus began:

" Pray, Cow, give me milk, that I may give cat milk, that cat may give me my own tail again." " No," said the cow, " I will give you no milk, till you go to the farmer, and get me some hay."

First she leapt, and then she ran,
Till she came to the farmer, and thus began:

" Pray, Farmer, give me hay, that I may give cow hay, that cow may give me milk, that I may give cat milk, that cat may give me my own tail again." " No," says the farmer, " I 'll give you no hay till you go to the butcher and fetch me some meat."

First she leapt, and then she ran,
Till she came to the butcher, and thus began:

" Pray, Butcher, give me meat, that I may give farmer meat, that farmer may give me hay, that I may give cow hay, that cow may give me milk, that I may give cat milk, that cat may give

203

me my own tail again." "No," says the butcher, "I 'll give you no meat, till you go to the baker and fetch me some bread."

> First she leapt, and then she ran,
> Till she came to the baker, and thus began:

"Pray, Baker, give me bread, that I may give butcher bread, that butcher may give me meat, that I may give farmer meat, that farmer may give me hay, that I may give cow hay, that cow may give me milk, that I may give cat milk, that cat may give me my own tail again."

> "Yes," says the baker, "I 'll give you some bread,
> But if you eat my meal, I 'll cut off your head."

Then the baker gave mouse bread, and mouse gave butcher bread, and butcher gave mouse meat, and mouse gave farmer meat, and farmer gave mouse hay, and mouse gave cow hay, and cow gave mouse milk, and mouse gave cat milk, and cat gave mouse her own tail again.

THE FOOLHARDY FROGS AND
THE STORK

THERE was once a pond full of young frogs. These frogs peeped up out of the water, and made a great noise, each trying to cry louder than the rest. Why they did this, I don't know; but then, many children make a noise, too, and don't know why they do it. Only one old frog sat quite silent, moving his head and eyes anxiously, first on one side and then on the other. Suddenly he called out, —

"Silence! Duck your heads; the stork's coming!"

Then in a moment there was a dead silence, and all the round heads and goggle-eyes disappeared under the water. For, although they had not seen the stork until now, the old frog had often told them about him — how he was a terrible fellow, with long legs, long neck, and long beak; and how he could make a hideous clappering with the said beak, which he used, moreover, to drag out of the water all the frogs he could snap up, and whom he subsequently devoured. But the stork who came that day, and of whose arrival the old frog had warned his comrades, had already eaten as much as he wanted in some other pond; consequently, he walked gravely to and fro by the side of the water, without looking round to seek for a frog; and then, establishing himself by the shore, he drew up one leg, and bent down his head and beak, as it is the custom of storks to do when about to go to sleep. And, standing thus, he looked exactly like a bag of feathers on a long stick.

For a time there was perfect silence in the pond; but then the

205

young frog-people began to find the time hang heavy on their paws, so they opened their eyes, which they had at first closed in great terror, and began to look round them. And one of them whispered to another, —

" Just look and see if the stork is still there."

" Yes," said the other, " there he stands."

" That's not the stork," cried two or three together; " for they say the stork has a long neck and a long beak."

But the old frog said, in a warning voice, —

> " Don't wake the stork, for frogs he doth kill:
> The danger that sleeps is a danger still."

Now, most of the frogs listened to these words of warning. But one of them, named Cax, a forward fellow, who liked to hear himself croak, exclaimed, —

" Nonsense! the old chap only wants to make us afraid, because he does not like to hear the sound of our voices. That thing by the water's edge looks much more like a scarecrow than a bird."

" It may frighten sparrows, but no valiant frog will be afraid of it," croaked another frog, whose name was Kix, and who liked to say and do whatever Cax said and did.

" Whoever has courage, follow me! " cried Cax. " We'll have a closer look at the thing yonder, and, as sure as my name's Cax, I'll jump upon it! " The old frog raised his voice in these warning words, —

> " Foolhardy frogs, foolhardy pack,
> Listen to me! quack, quack! quack, quack!
> Beware, beware! for danger is near,
> And those must feel who will not hear! "

But those who would not hear were, in this case, Kix and Cax. Cax hopped away in advance, and Kix followed after him, till they came to the place where the stork stood. The affair now began to seem a little formidable to them, as generally happens to boasters when danger is near.

" After all," they thought, " it looks very much like the stork."

But they felt ashamed to turn back, so Cax said, " You jump first, Kix; you 're the younger of us two."

" No," replied Kix; " you should jump first, for you 're the elder of us two. I 'm in no hurry."

" No more am I," said Cax.

And so, for a time, they both sat quite still.

The stork, meanwhile, was fast asleep, dreaming of the nest he had built the year before far away in Africa, and of the young he had brought up there, and of the wife who had helped him to feed and educate them. When Kix and Cax saw that he did not move at all, they began to take courage. Cax stuck up his head out of the water, and quacked at the stork in a low voice. Kix followed his comrade's example. The stork never moved. Now they began to quack in a louder tone, and at last to dabble about in the water, and to splash the stork with their legs. When the other frogs, who had been watching these proceedings at a distance, saw that the sport seemed a safe one, they came hopping up to take part in it; only the wary old frog remained behind.

At last the increasing noise woke up the stork, but as he was somewhat drowsy with sleep and with the meal he had lately made, he let the frogs cry out to their hearts' content for a time, and splash about just as they liked, for he thought, " Wait a little — I 'll have you presently!" At last Cax said to the rest, —

" Look at me now! I 'll jump upon the thing, as I told you I would."

And Kix added, " And so will I, as I told you I would."

But when they both jumped up at the stork, he suddenly

thrust out his bill, with a snap to the left and a snap to the right, and in a twinkling Kix and Cax were eaten up and swallowed down. Then the stork turned round three times in the pond, clapped his beak, as a man might clap his hands, and said, —

> " Klipp, clap! klipp, clap!
> Fish and frog, snail and crab!
> I hope you all will act like these,
> That I may eat you at my ease."

Then the other frogs scampered away as fast as ever they could, and there was a great silence in the pond for a long time. The stork went to sleep again, seeing that nothing more seemed inclined to jump into his mouth; but the old frog repeated his warning to his young friends, and they all listened, with very grave faces indeed, while he sang, —

> " Fool-hardy frogs, foolhardy pack,
> Listen to me! quack, quack! quack, quack!
> Beware, beware! for danger is near,
> And those must feel who will not hear!"

And then, wishing to improve the terrible disaster which had just taken place, he added a new verse, which was considered by all the other frogs to be a masterpiece. It ran thus, —

> " My dear young friends, my dear young friends,
> You 've seen, quack, quack! how boasting ends;
> If one of you discretion lacks,
> Let him think of the fate of Kix and Cax."

And the young frogs listened to these words of wisdom and were so thoroughly determined to profit by the sage advice they had received, that not one head poked up over the water during the whole evening, and early next morning the stork went away in disgust, wondering what had become of all the frogs in the pond. But the old frog, to the last day of his life, looked upon himself as the preserver of all the frogs in the pond, and was very proud when he thought what a beautiful talent it was to be able to make such verses as those he had recited to his young friends.

TIRED OF BEING A LITTLE GIRL

"OH, dear me," sighed little Eva one fine morning, "I am tired of being a little girl. I wish I could be something else."

"Well," said a voice near her, "what would you like to be?"

Eva looked about in surprise. She saw no one, but the voice repeated the words, "What would you like to be?"

Just to see what would happen, Eva spoke up quite loud and said, "I should like to be a rosebud."

The words were hardly out of her mouth before she felt her skirts twisting close around her body in a very queer way. She had on a little pink cambric frock, but when she touched it she found it was not cambric any longer, it was made of rose-leaves. She looked down at her feet. They felt very queer; they seemed to be turning green, and up and down her legs were funny little sharp things.

The next moment Eva knew she was a rosebud. She was growing on a bush in the garden. The wind swayed her gently back and forth. It was charming. Although she was a rosebud she knew everything that went on around her. Suddenly she saw a lovely fairy bending over her.

"Ah," said the fairy, "this rose-petal is filled with dew. First I will drink the dew, then I will eat the tender end of the bud for breakfast."

"Don't, don't," cried Eva, "if you do you will eat my head."

The fairy began to laugh.

"Please make me something else, quick," cried Eva, "make me into a bird."

Before Eva knew how it happened she was hopping round among the daisies, a real live bird.

"This is great fun," she cried, "but I begin to feel hungry."

"Do you?" cried a voice beside her, "then I'll feed you."

To her horror in front of her stood a frightful little elf, holding in his hand an ugly worm, which he wanted to force into her mouth. Eva tried to scream; she looked round, hoping to see a friendly face, but the only faces she saw were those of some dreadful green apples, which seemed to be jeering at her from a tree.

"I won't eat that worm," she screamed; "I'm not a real bird! I'm a — I'm a —" Just then the sky grew dark, the wind blew fiercely; Eva put her hands to her head, frightened, yet glad, glad to find that she had hands and head, that she was not a bird.

"Why, it's raining hard," she said; "where have I been? I must have fallen asleep under the apple tree." And then Eva ran into the house as fast as she could go, to tell her strange dream to her mother.

"And, oh, mamma," she cried, "I've decided that I would rather be a little girl than anything."

THE PANCAKE

ONCE upon a time there was a goody who had seven hungry bairns, and she was frying a pancake for them. It was a sweet-milk pancake, and there it lay in the pan bubbling and frizzling, so thick and good it was a sight for sore eyes to look at. And the bairns stood round about, and the goodman sat by and looked on.

"Oh, give me a bit of pancake, mother, dear; I am so hungry," said one bairn.

"Oh, darling mother," said the second.

"Oh, darling, good mother," said the third.

"Oh, darling, good, nice mother," said the fourth.

"Oh, darling, pretty, good, nice mother," said the fifth.

"Oh, darling, pretty, good, nice, clever mother," said the sixth.

"Oh, darling, pretty, good, nice, clever, sweet mother," said the seventh.

So they begged for the pancake all round, the one more prettily than the other; for they were so hungry and so good.

"Yes, yes, bairns, only wait a bit till it turns itself," — she ought to have said, "till I can get it turned," — "and then you shall all have some; a lovely, sweet-milk pancake; only look how fat and happy it lies there."

When the pancake heard that, it got afraid, and in a trice it turned itself all of itself, and tried to jump out of the pan; but it fell back into it again t' other side up, and so when it had been fried a little on the other side, too, till it got firmer in its flesh, it sprang out on the floor, and rolled off like a wheel through the door and down the hill.

"Halloa! Stop, Pancake!" and away went the goody after it, with the frying-pan in one hand and the ladle in the other, as fast as she could, and her bairns behind her, while the goodman limped after them last of all.

"Hi! Won't you stop? Seize it! Stop, Pancake," they all screamed out, one after the other, and tried to catch it on the run and hold it; but the pancake rolled on and on, and in the twinkling of an eye it was so far ahead that they could n't see it, for the pancake was faster than any of them.

So when it had rolled awhile it met a man.

"Good-day, Pancake," said the man.

"The same to you, Manny Panny," said the pancake.

"Dear Pancake," said the man, "don't roll so fast; stop a little and let me eat you."

"When I have given the slip to Goody Poody, and the goodman, and seven squalling children, I may well slip through your fingers, Manny Panny," said the pancake, and rolled on and on till it met a hen.

"Good-day, Pancake," said the hen.

"The same to you, Henny Penny," said the pancake.

"Pancake, dear, don't roll so fast; bide a bit and let me eat you up," said the hen.

"When I have given the slip to Goody Poody, and the goodman, and seven squalling children, and to Manny Panny, I may well slip through your claws, Henny Penny," said the pancake, and so it rolled on like a wheel down the road.

Just then it met a cock. "Good-day, Pancake," said the cock.

"The same to you, Cocky Locky," said the pancake.

"Pancake, dear, don't roll so fast, but bide a bit and let me eat you up."

"When I have given the slip to Goody Poody, and the goodman, and seven squalling children, and to Manny Panny, and Henny Penny, I may well slip through your claws, Cocky Locky," said the pancake, and off it set rolling away as fast as it could; and when it had rolled a long way it met a duck.

"Good-day, Pancake," said the duck.

"The same to you, Ducky Lucky."

"Pancake, dear, don't roll away so fast; bide a bit and let me eat you up."

"When I have given the slip to Goody Poody, and the goodman, and seven squalling children, and to Manny Panny, and Henny Penny, and Cocky Locky, I may well slip through your fingers, Ducky Lucky," said the pancake, and with that it took to rolling faster than ever; and when it had rolled a long, long while, it met a goose.

"Good-day, Pancake," said the goose.

"The same to you, Goosey Poosey."

"Pancake, dear, don't roll so fast; bide a bit and let me eat you up."

"When I have given the slip to Goody Poody, and the goodman, and seven squalling children, and to Manny Panny, and Henny Penny, and Cocky Locky, and Ducky Lucky, I can well slip through your feet, Goosey Poosey," said the pancake, and off it rolled.

So when it had rolled a long, long way farther, it met a gander.

"Good-day, Pancake," said the gander.

"The same to you, Gander Pander," said the pancake.

"Pancake, dear, don't roll so fast; bide a bit and let me eat you up."

"When I have given the slip to Goody Poody, and the goodman, and seven squalling children, and to Manny Panny, and Henny Penny, and Cocky Locky, and Ducky Lucky, and

Goosey Poosey, I may well slip through your feet, Gander Pander," said the pancake, which rolled off as fast as ever.

So, when it had rolled a long, long time, it met a pig.

" Good-day, Pancake," said the pig.

" The same to you, Piggy Wiggy," said the pancake, which, without another word began to roll swiftly away.

" Oh!" cried the pig, " you need n't be in such a hurry; we two can go together and see one another over the wood, where it is not too safe."

The pancake thought it might be well to do that, so they went together. But after they had gone awhile they came to a brook. Piggy was so fat that he could easily swim across, but the poor pancake could n't get over.

" Sit on my snout," said the pig, " and I 'll carry you over."

So the pancake sat on his snout.

" Ouf, ouf," said the pig, and swallowed the pancake at one gulp; and then, as the poor pancake could go no farther, why — this story can go no farther either.

THE FOX AND THE RABBIT

ONCE upon a time a fox and a rabbit were neighbors, and one fine spring morning the fox asked the rabbit if he would go hunting with him. The rabbit said, " I do not think I can go with you to-day, as I shall be very busy."

But when the fox had gone, the rabbit, who really had nothing to do, sat in the sun and enjoyed the beautiful morning air. After a while he spied the fox returning from his hunt, and he thought out a scheme whereby he might secure possession of the fox's game bag.

He went a little way into the forest, and lay down as if he were dead. When the fox came up to him, he touched him with his paw, and said to himself, " Here is a nice fat rabbit for which I will presently return, and add to my larder."

When the rabbit saw the fox go on, he got up, took a short cut ahead of him, and lay down as before. Seeing, as he supposed, another rabbit fast asleep, the fox said to himself, " Fat rabbits seem to be very plentiful this season; I will take this one home with me." Then he thought he would go back and get the other one; so he put his game-bag down on the grass by the stump of a tree, and started back.

When the rabbit saw that he was alone, he took the bag and hid it in a thick clump of bushes. Then he ran behind a tree, and waited to see what would happen.

The fox returned with a disgusted look on his face. He, a fox, had been fooled, and when he saw that his game-bag had been taken, he became very angry indeed. A cunning trick had been played upon him, and he looked about to see if he could find the culprit.

The rabbit was very proud of the fact that he had outwitted his neighbor, and, seeing the look of anger and disgust on the fox's face, laughed so loudly that he betrayed his hiding-place. Fortunately for him, his burrow was close by, and he reached it only just in time to escape the fox, who would have made short work of him if he had caught him.

While the fox was watching for the rabbit to come out, a boy passing by saw the game-bag in the clump of bushes, and, picking it up, threw it over his shoulder, and walked off with it. And so neither the fox nor the rabbit had the game.

HENNY PENNY

ONE day Henny Penny was picking up corn in the corn-yard when — whack! — something hit her upon the head. "Goodness gracious me!" said Henny Penny; "the sky's a-going to fall; I must go and tell the King."

So she went along and she went along and she went along till she met Cocky Locky. "Where are you going, Henny Penny?" says Cocky Locky. "Oh! I'm going to tell the King the sky's a-falling," says Henny Penny. "May I come with you?" says Cocky Locky. "Certainly," says Henny Penny. So Henny Penny and Cocky Locky went to tell the King the sky was falling.

They went along, and they went along, and they went along, till they met Ducky Daddles. "Where are you going to, Henny Penny and Cocky Locky?" says Ducky Daddles. "Oh! we're going to tell the King the sky's a-falling," said Henny Penny and Cocky Locky. "May I come with you?" says Ducky Daddles. "Certainly," said Henny Penny and Cocky Locky. So Henny Penny, Cocky Locky, and Ducky Daddles went to tell the King the sky was a-falling.

So they went along, and they went along, and they went along, till they met Goosey Poosey. "Where are you going to, Henny Penny, Cocky Locky, and Ducky Daddles?" said Goosey Poosey. "Oh! we're going to tell the King the sky's a-falling,"

[1] Another popular variant of "The Story of Henny Penny" is "The Story of Chicken Licken."

said Henny Penny and Cocky Locky and Ducky Daddles. "May I come with you?" said Goosey Poosey. "Certainly," said Henny Penny, Cocky Locky, and Ducky Daddles. So Henny Penny, Cocky Locky, and Ducky Daddles, and Goosey Poosey went to tell the King the sky was a-falling.

So they went along, and they went along, and they went along, till they met Turkey Lurkey. "Where are you going, Henny Penny, Cocky Locky, Ducky Daddles, and Goosey Poosey?" says Turkey Lurkey. "Oh! we're going to tell the King the sky's a-falling," said Henny Penny, Cocky Locky, Ducky Daddles, and Goosey Poosey. "May I come with you, Henny Penny, Cocky Locky, Ducky Daddles, and Goosey Poosey?" said Turkey Lurkey. "Oh, certainly, Turkey Lurkey," said Henny Penny, Cocky Locky, Ducky Daddles, and Goosey Poosey. So Henny Penny, Cocky Locky, Ducky Daddles, Goosey Poosey, and Turkey Lurkey all went to tell the King the sky was a-falling.

So they went along, and they went along, and they went along, till they met Foxy Woxy, and Foxy Woxy said to Henny Penny, Cocky Locky, Ducky Daddles, Goosey Poosey, and Turkey Lurkey, "Where are you going, Henny Penny, Cocky Locky, Ducky Daddles, Goosey Poosey, and Turkey Lurkey?" And Henny Penny, Cocky Locky, Ducky Daddles, Goosey Poosey, and Turkey Lurkey said to Foxy Woxy, "We're going to tell the King the sky's a-falling." "Oh! but this is not the way to the King, Henny Penny, Cocky Locky, Ducky Daddles, Goosey Poosey, and Turkey Lurkey," said Foxy Woxy; "I know the proper way; shall I show it to you?" "Oh, certainly, Foxy Woxy," said Henny Penny, Cocky Locky, Ducky Daddles, Goosey Poosey, and Turkey Lurkey. So Henny Penny, Cocky Locky, Ducky Daddles, Goosey Poosey, Turkey Lurkey, and Foxy Woxy all went to tell the King the sky was a-falling. So they went along, and they went along, and they went along, till they came to a narrow and dark hole. Now this was the door of Foxy Woxy's cave. But Foxy Woxy said to Henny Penny, Cocky Locky, Ducky Daddles, Goosey Poosey, and Turkey Lurkey, "This is the short way to the King's palace: you'll soon get there if you follow me. I will go first and you come after, Henny Penny, Cocky Locky, Ducky Daddles, Goosey Poosey, and Turkey Lurkey." "Why, of course, certainly, without doubt, why not?" said Henny Penny, Cocky Locky, Ducky Daddles, Goosey Poosey, and Turkey Lurkey.

So Foxy Woxy went into his cave, and he did n't go very far, but turned round to wait for Henny Penny, Cocky Locky, Ducky Daddles, Goosey Poosey, and Turkey Lurkey. So at last, first Turkey Lurkey went through the dark hole into the cave. He had n't got far when " Hrumph," Foxy Woxy snapped off Turkey Lurkey's head and threw his body over his left shoulder. Then Goosey Poosey went in, and " Hrumph," off went her head and Goosey Poosey was thrown beside Turkey Lurkey. Then Ducky Daddles waddled down, and " Hrumph," snapped Foxy Woxy, and Ducky Daddles' head was off and Ducky Daddles was thrown alongside Turkey Lurkey and Goosey Poosey. Then Cocky Locky strutted down into the cave, and he had n't gone far when " Snap! Hrumph!" went Foxy Woxy, and Cocky Locky was thrown alongside of Turkey Lurkey, Goosey Poosey and Ducky Daddles.

But Foxy Woxy had made two bites at Cocky Locky, and when the first snap only hurt Cocky Locky, but did n't kill him, he called out to Henny Penny. But she turned tail and off she ran home, so she never told the King the sky was a-falling.

THE OLD WOMAN AND HER PIG

AN old woman was sweeping her house and found a little crooked sixpence. "What," said she, "shall I do with this little sixpence? I will go to the market and buy a little pig." As she was coming home, she came to a stile; the piggy would not go over the stile.

She went a little farther, and she met a dog. So she said to the dog, "Dog! bite pig; piggy won't go over the stile, and I sha'n't get home to-night." But the dog would not. She went a little farther, and she met a stick. So she said, "Stick! stick! beat dog; dog won't bite pig, piggy won't go over the stile, and I sha'n't get home to-night." But the stick would not. She went a little farther, and she met a fire. So she said, "Fire! fire! burn stick; stick won't beat dog, dog won't bite pig, pig won't go over the stile, and I sha'n't get home to-night." But the fire would not. She went a little farther, and she met some water. So she said, "Water! water! quench fire; fire won't burn stick, stick won't beat dog, dog won't bite pig, pig won't go over the stile, and I sha'n't get home to-night." But the water would not. She went a little farther, and she met an ox. So she said, "Ox! ox! drink water; water won't quench fire, fire won't burn stick, stick won't beat dog, dog won't bite pig, pig won't go over the stile, and I sha'n't get home to-night." But the ox would not. She went a little farther, and she met a butcher. So she said, "Butcher! butcher! kill ox; ox won't drink water, water won't quench fire, fire won't burn stick, stick won't beat dog, dog won't bite pig, pig won't go over the stile, and I sha'n't get home to-night." But the butcher would not. She went a little farther, and she met a rope. So she said, " Rope! rope! hang butcher; butcher won't kill ox, ox won't drink water, water won't quench fire, fire won't burn stick, stick won't beat dog, dog won't bite pig, pig won't go over the stile, and I sha'n't get home to-night." But the rope would not. She went a little farther, and she met a rat. So she said, " Rat! rat! gnaw rope; rope won't hang butcher, butcher won't kill ox, ox won't drink water, water won't quench fire, fire won't burn stick, stick won't beat dog, dog won't bite pig, pig won't go over the stile, and I sha'n't get home to-night." But the rat would not. She went a little farther, and she met a cat. So she said, " Cat! cat! kill rat; rat won't gnaw rope, rope won't hang butcher, butcher won't kill ox, ox won't drink water, water won't quench fire, fire won't burn stick, stick won't beat dog, dog won't bite pig, pig won't go over the stile, and I sha'n't get home to-night." But the cat said to her, " If you will go to yonder cow and fetch me a saucer of milk, I will kill the rat." So away went the old woman to the cow. But the cow said to her, " If you will go to yonder haystack, and bring me a handful of hay, I 'll give you the milk." So away went the old woman to the haystack, and she brought the hay to the cow. As soon as the cow had eaten the hay she gave the old woman the milk, and away she went with it in a saucer to the cat. As soon as the cat had lapped up the milk, the cat began to kill the rat, the rat began to gnaw the rope, the rope began to hang the butcher, the butcher began to kill the ox, the ox began to drink the water, the water began to quench the fire, the fire began to burn the stick, the stick began to beat the dog, the dog began to bite the pig, the little pig in a fright jumped over the stile, and so the old woman got home that night.

TEENY-TINY

ONCE upon a time there was a teeny-tiny woman lived in a teeny-tiny house in a teeny-tiny village. Now, one day this teeny-tiny woman put on her teeny-tiny bonnet, and went out of her teeny-tiny house to take a teeny-tiny walk. And when this teeny-tiny woman had gone a teeny-tiny way, she came to a teeny-tiny gate; so the teeny-tiny woman opened the teeny-tiny gate, and went into a teeny-tiny churchyard. And when this teeny-tiny woman had got into the teeny-tiny churchyard, she saw a teeny-tiny bone on a teeny-tiny grave, and the teeny-tiny woman said to her teeny-tiny self, " This teeny-tiny bone will make me some teeny-tiny soup for my teeny-tiny supper." So the teeny-tiny woman put the teeny-tiny bone into her teeny-tiny pocket, and went to her teeny-tiny house.

Now, when the teeny-tiny woman got home to her teeny-tiny house she was a teeny-tiny tired; so she went up her teeny-tiny stairs to her teeny-tiny bed, and put the teeny-tiny bone into a teeny-tiny cupboard. And when this teeny-tiny woman had been to sleep for a teeny-tiny time, she was awakened by a teeny-tiny voice from the teeny-tiny cupboard, which said, " Give me my bone!" And this teeny-tiny woman was a teeny-tiny frightened, so she hid her teeny-tiny head under the teeny-tiny clothes, and went to sleep again. And when she had been to sleep again a teen-tiny time, the teeny-tiny voice again cried out from the teeny-tiny cupboard, a teeny-tiny louder, " *Give me my bone!* " This made the teeny-tiny woman a teeny-tiny more frightened, so she hid her teeny-tiny head a teeny-tiny farther under the teeny-tiny clothes. And when the teeny-tiny woman had been to sleep again a teeny-tiny time, the teeny-tiny voice from the teeny-tiny cupboard said again, a teeny-tiny louder, " GIVE ME MY BONE!" And this teeny-tiny woman was a teeny-tiny bit more frightened, but she put her teeny-tiny head out of the teeny-tiny clothes, and said in her loudest teeny-tiny voice, —

"TAKE IT!!"

SO-SO

"BE sure, my child," said the widow to her little daughter, "that you always do just as you are told."

"Very well, mother."

" Or at any rate do what will do just as well," said the small house-dog, as he lay blinking at the fire.

" You darling," cried little Joan, and she sat down on the hearth and hugged him. But he got up and shook himself, and moved three turns nearer the stove, to be out of the way; for though her arms were soft, she had kept her doll in them, and that was made of wood, which hurts.

" What a dear, kind house-dog you are!" said little Joan, and she meant what she said, for it does feel nice to have the sharp edges of one's duty a little softened off for one.

He was no particular kind of dog, but he was very smooth to stroke, and had a nice way of blinking with his eyes, which it was soothing to see. There had been a difficulty about his name. The name of the house-dog before him was Faithful, and well it became him, as his tombstone testified. The one before that was called Wolf. He was very wild and came to a bad end for worrying sheep. The little house-dog never chased anything, to the widow's knowledge. There was no reason whatever for giving him a bad name, and she thought of several good ones, such as Faithful, and Trusty, and Keeper, which are fine old-fashioned titles, but none of these seemed quite perfectly to suit him. So he was called So-so; and a very nice soft name it is.

The widow was only a poor woman, though she contrived by

her industry to keep a decent home together, and to get now one and now another little comfort for herself and her child. One day she was going out on business, and she called her little daughter and said to her, " I am going out for two hours. You are too young to protect yourself and the house, and So-so is not as strong as Faithful was. But when I go, shut the house door and bolt the big wooden bar, and be sure you do not open it for any reason until I return. If strangers come So-so may bark, which he can do as well as a bigger dog. Then they will go away. With this summer's savings I have bought a quilted petticoat for you and a duffle coat for myself against the winter, and if I get the work I am going after to-day, I shall buy enough wool to knit warm stockings for us both, so be patient till I return, and then we will have the plum-cake that is in the cupboard for tea."

" Thank you, Mother."

" Good-bye, my child. Be sure you do just as I have told you," said the woman.

" Very well, Mother."

Little Joan laid down her doll, and shut the house door, and fastened the big bolt. It was very heavy, and the kitchen looked gloomy when she had done it.

" I wish Mother had taken us all three with her, and had locked the house and put the key in her big pocket, as she has done before," said little Joan, as she got into the rocking-chair, to put her doll to sleep.

" Yes, it would have done just as well," So-so replied, as he stretched himself on the hearth.

By and by Joan grew tired of hush-a-bying the doll, who looked none the sleepier for it, and she took the three-legged stool and sat down in front of the clock to watch the hands. After awhile she drew a deep sigh.

" There are sixty seconds in every single minute, So-so," said she.

"So I have heard," said So-so. He was snuffling in the back place, which was not usually allowed.

"And sixty whole minutes in every hour, So-so."

"You don't say so," growled So-so. He had not found a bit, and the cake was on the top shelf. There was not so much as a spilt crumb, though he snuffed in every corner of the kitchen, till he stood snuffing under the house door.

"The air smells fresh," said he.

"It's a beautiful day, I know," said little Joan. "I wish Mother had allowed us to sit on the doorstep. We could have taken care of the house —"

"Just as well," said So-so.

Little Joan came to smell the air at the key-hole, and, as So-so had said, it smelt very fresh. Besides, one could see from the window how fine the evening was.

"It's not exactly what mother told us to do," said Joan, "but I do believe —"

"It would do just as well," said So-so.

By and by little Joan unfastened the bar, and opened the door, and she and the doll and So-so went out and sat on the doorstep.

Not a stranger was to be seen. The sun shone delightfully. An evening sun, and not too hot. All day it had been ripening the corn in the field close by, and this glowed and waved in the breeze.

"It does just as well, and better," said little Joan, "for if any one comes we can see him coming up the field-path."

"Just so," said So-so, blinking in the sunshine.

Suddenly Joan jumped up.

"Oh!" cried she, "there's a bird, a big bird. Dear So-so, can you see him? I can't, because of the sun. What a queer noise he makes — Crake! Crake! Oh, I can see him now! He is not flying, he is running, and he has gone into the corn. I do wish I were in the corn. I would catch him and put him in a cage."

"I'll catch him," said So-so, and he put up his tail, and started off.

"No, no!" cried Joan. "You are not to go. You must stay and take care of the house, and bark if any one comes."

"You could scream, and that would do just as well," replied So-so, with his tail still up.

"No, it wouldn't," cried little Joan.

"Yes, it would," reiterated So-so.

Whilst they were bickering, an old woman came up to the door; she had a brown face, and black hair, and a very old red cloak.

"Good-evening, my little dear," said she. "Are you all at home this fine evening?"

"Only three of us," said Joan; "I, and my doll, and So-so. Mother has gone to the town on business, and we are taking care of the house, but So-so wants to go after the bird we saw run into the corn."

"Was it a pretty bird, my little dear?" asked the old woman.

"It was a very curious one," said Joan, "and I should like to go after it myself, but we can't leave the house."

"Dear, dear! Is there no neighbor would sit on the doorstep for you, and keep house till you slip down to the field after the curious bird?" said the old woman.

"I'm afraid not," said little Joan. "Old Martha, our neighbor, is now bed-ridden. Of course, if she had been able to mind the house instead of us, it would have done just as well."

"I have some distance to go this evening," said the old woman, "but I do not object to a few minutes' rest, and sooner than that you should lose the bird, I will sit on the doorstep to oblige you, while you run down to the cornfield."

"But can you bark if any one comes?" asked little Joan. "For if you can't So-so must stay with you."

"I can call you and the dog if I see any one coming, and that will do just as well," said the old woman.

"So it will," replied little Joan, and off she ran to the cornfield, where, for that matter, So-so had run before her, and was bounding and barking and springing among the corn stalks.

They did not catch the bird, though they stayed longer than they had intended, and though So-so seemed to know more about hunting than was supposed.

"I dare say Mother has come home," said little Joan, as they went back up the field-path. "I hope she won't think we ought to have stayed in the house."

"It was taken care of," said So-so, "and that must do just as well."

When they reached the house, she had not come home.

But the old woman had gone, and she had taken the quilted petticoat and the duffle cloak, and the plum-cake from the top shelf away with her; and no more was ever heard of any of the lot.

"For the future, my child," said the widow, "I hope you will always do just as you are told, whatever So-so may say."

"I will, Mother," said little Joan (and she did). But the house-dog sat and blinked. He dared not speak, he was in disgrace.

I do not feel quite sure about So-so. Wild dogs often amend their ways, and the Faithful sometimes fall; but when anyone begins by being only So-so, he is very apt to be So-so to the end. So-sos so seldom change.

But this one was *very* soft and nice, and he got no cake that tea-time. On the whole, we will hope that he lived to be a good dog ever after.

WHY?

"NOW, you must not go in there," said an old dog to a puppy, who stood on the steps of a large house. "You must stay out now."

"Why?" asked the puppy. For it was a habit (and a bad habit) of his to say "Why?" when he was told to do, or not to do, a thing.

"Why," said the old dog. "I cannot say why. I do not know why. But I do know that if you go in when it is a wet day like this, the maid will drive you out."

"But why?" went on the puppy. "It is not fair. There is no sense in it. I have been in the house for days, and no one turned me out, so why should they now?"

"Those were fine days," said the old dog.

"Well, on the wet days I want to be in doors most," said the puppy. "And I don't see why I should stay out. So in I go."

And he did so.

But he soon found that though no one stopped to tell him "why" he must not come in, it was quite true that he might not.

The first to see him was the cook, who had a broom in her hand.

"That dirty puppy!" she cried. "Look at his feet!"

"What is wrong with my feet?" barked the puppy.

She did not wait to tell him. She hit him with the broom, and he fled with a howl up the stairs.

WHY?

"Oh, that puppy!" cried the maid, as she saw the marks of his feet. "He ought not to come in the house at all, if he will not keep out on wet days."

"But why?" yelped the puppy, as the maid threw a broom at his head.

Still no one told him why. But a man just then came upstairs.

"Why, what a mess!" he said. "Oh, I see. It is that puppy. I thought he knew he must not come in."

"So I did, but I did not know why," growled the puppy, as with sore back and lame feet he crept under a chair.

"Come out, come out," cried the man. "I will not have you in the house at all. Out with you!" And he seized him, and chained him up in the kennel.

"You might have played on the grass if you had stayed there," he said. "But as you will come in the house when you ought not you must be kept where you cannot do so."

And so the young puppy had to stay in the dull kennel. And when at last he was let out, he did not ask "Why?" if he was told to do, or not to do, a thing, but did as he ought at once, like a wise dog.

THE FIR TREE

FAR away in the forest stood a pretty little fir tree. The warm sun shone upon it, the fresh breeze blew about it, but the fir tree was not happy. All about it were many tall companions, pines and firs, and the little fir tree wanted to be tall like them. So it did not heed the warm sunlight, or the soft air which fluttered its leaves, or even the little pleasant children who passed by, prattling merrily. Sometimes the children would bring a basketful of raspberries or strawberries, and seat themselves near the fir tree, saying of the tree, " What a pretty little one this is! " which made it feel more unhappy than ever.

And yet, all this time, the tree grew a whole joint or ring taller every year, for by the number of rings on the trunk of a fir tree we can tell its age.

Still, as it grew, it complained, " Oh, if I were only as tall as the other trees! then I should spread out my branches on every side, and my crown would overlook the wide world. The birds would build their nests in my branches, and when the wind blew, I should bow with stately dignity like the others."

So discontented was the tree that it took no pleasure in the sunshine, or in the birds, or in the rosy clouds that floated over it morning and evening.

Sometimes in winter, when the snow lay white and sparkling on the grounds, a hare would come leaping along and jump right over the little tree's head; then how mortified it felt!

Two winters passed, and when the third came, the tree had grown so tall that the hare was obliged to run round it.

"Ah, to grow and grow! to become tall and old! That is the only thing in the world worth caring for," the fir tree sighed.

In the autumn the woodcutters always came and cut down several of the tallest trees, and the young fir, which had now grown to a very good height, shuddered as the noble trees fell to the ground with a crash. After the branches were lopped off, the trunks looked so slender and bare that they could scarcely be recognized. Then the trees were placed one upon another, on wagons, and dragged by horses out of the forest. "Where were they going? What was going to become of them?" The young fir tree wondered a great deal about it.

So in the spring when the swallows and the storks came, it asked them: "Do you know where those trees were taken? Did you meet them?"

The swallows knew nothing about them, but the stork, after a little reflection, nodded his head and said: "Yes, I think I know. As I flew from Egypt I met several new ships, and they had fine masts that smelt like fir. These must have been the trees, and I assure you they were most stately and grand; they towered majestically."

"Oh, how I wish I were tall enough to go on the sea!" said the fir tree. "Tell me what is the sea, and what does it look like?"

"It would take too much time to explain,—a great deal too much," said the stork, flying quickly away.

"Rejoice in thy youth," said the sunbeam, "rejoice in the fresh growing time, and in the young life that is within thee!"

And the wind kissed the tree, and the dew wept tears over it; but the fir tree did not understand.

Christmas time drew near, and many young trees were cut down, some that were even smaller and younger than the fir tree, which had no peace or rest from its longing to leave the forest. These young trees which were chosen for their beauty, kept their branches, but were also laid on wagons and drawn by horses out of the forest.

"Where are they going?" asked the fir tree. "They are not taller than I am; indeed, one was not so tall. And why do they keep all their branches? Where are they going?"

"We know! we know!" sang the sparrows. "We have looked in at the windows of the houses in town and we know what is done with them. Oh, you cannot think what honor and glory they receive! They are dressed up in the most splendid manner. We have looked in and seen them standing in the middle of a warm room, adorned with all sorts of beautiful things, — gilded apples, sweetmeats, playthings, and hundreds of candles."

"And then," asked the fir tree, trembling in all its branches, "and then what happens?"

"We did not see any more," said the sparrows; "but indeed it was simply wonderful!"

"I wonder whether anything so brilliant will ever happen with me," thought the fir tree. "That would be even better than sailing over the sea. Oh, when will Christmas be here! I am now as tall and well grown as those who were taken away last year. O that I were now laid on the wagon or standing in the warm room with all that brightness and splendor about me! Something better and more beautiful is sure to follow, or the trees would not be so decked out. Yes, something better, something still more splendid must follow — but what can it be? I am weary with longing. I scarcely know myself what is the matter with me."

"Rejoice in our love," said the air and the sunlight; "rejoice in thine own bright life in the fresh air."

But the tree would not rejoice though it grew taller every

day, and, winter and summer, its evergreen foliage might be in the forest, and passers-by would say, " What a beautiful tree! "

A short time before the next Christmas this discontented fir tree was the first to fall. As the ax cut sharply into its trunk, deep in through the pit, the tree fell to the ground with a groan, conscious only of pain and faintness, and forgetting all its dreams of happiness in the sorrow of leaving its home in the forest. It knew it would never again see its dear old companions the trees, nor the little bushes, nor the flowers that had grown by its side — perhaps not even the birds.

Nor was the journey at all pleasant. The tree first recovered itself while it was being unloaded, with several other trees, in the courtyard of a house; and it heard a man say, " We want only one and this is the prettiest. This one is beautiful."

Then came two servants in grand livery, and carried the fir tree into a large and beautiful room. Pictures hung on the walls, and near the large stove stood great china jars with lions on the lids. There were rocking-chairs, silken sofas, large tables, with picture books and toys that had cost a hundred times a hundred dollars — at least so the children said.

Then the fir tree was placed in a large tub full of sand, but no one could see it was a tub, for it was hung with green cloth, and it stood on a very handsome carpet. Oh, how the tree trembled! What was going to happen to it now? Some young ladies came, and the servants helped them to adorn the tree.

On some branches they hung little bags cut out of colored paper, and each bag was full of sweetmeats; from other branches there hung gilded apples and walnuts, as if they had grown there; and above and all around were hundreds of red, blue, and white candles, which were fastened upon the branches. Dolls, exactly like real men and women, were placed under the green leaves, — the fir tree had never seen any before, — and at the very top was fastened a glittering star, made of gold tinsel. Oh, it was very beautiful!

"This evening," they all exclaimed; "this evening, how bright it will be!"

"Oh, that evening were come," thought the tree, "and the candles were lighted! Then I should know what else is going to happen. Will the trees come from the forest to see me? Will the sparrows peep in the windows, I wonder? Shall I grow faster here, and keep on all these ornaments during summer and winter?"

But guessing was of very little use. Its back ached with trying; and this pain is as bad for a slender tree as headache is for us.

At last the candles were lighted, and then what a shining blaze of splendor the tree presented! It trembled so with joy in all its branches that one of the candles fell on a green twig and set fire to it. "Help! Help!" exclaimed the young ladies, and they quickly extinguished the fire.

After this the tree did not dare even to tremble (though the fire frightened it), it was so anxious not to hurt any of the beautiful ornaments which so dazzled and bewildered it by their brilliance.

And now the folding doors were thrown open, and a troop of children rushed in as if they intended to upset the tree. They were followed more slowly by the older people. For a moment the little ones stood silent with delight, and then they shouted for joy till the room rang; and they danced merrily round the tree, and snatched off one present after another.

"What are they doing?" thought the tree. "What will happen next?"

The candles burned down to the branches and were put out one by one. Then the children were given permission to plunder the tree. Oh, how they rushed upon it. Its branches creaked with the strain, and if it had not been fastened by the gold star to the ceiling, it must have been thrown down.

Then the children danced about their pretty toys, and no one paid any attention to the tree except the old nurse, who came and peeped among the branches to see if any apple or fig had been forgotten.

"A story! a story!" cried the children, and dragged a little stout man toward the tree.

"Now we are in the greenwood," said the man, as he sat down beneath it, "and the tree will have the pleasure of hearing, too. But I am going to tell only one story. What shall it be? Henny Penny? or Humpty Dumpty, who fell downstairs, but soon got up again, and at last married a princess?"

"Henny Penny!" cried some. "Humpty Dumpty!" cried others; and there was a great uproar. But the fir tree kept silent and thought. "What am I supposed to do now? Have I nothing to do with all this?" But it had already been in the entertainment, and had played out its part.

Then the old man told the story of Humpty Dumpty,—how he fell downstairs, but soon got up again, and married a princess. And the children clapped their hands and cried, "Another! another!" for they wanted to hear the story of Henny Penny, too; but this time they had only Humpty Dumpty. The fir tree stood quiet and thoughtful. The birds in the forest had never told anything like that,—how Humpty Dumpty fell downstairs, and yet married a princess.

"Ah, yes, that is the way it happens in the world, I suppose," thought the fir tree. And it believed the story because such a nice man told it.

"Well," it thought, "who knows? Perhaps I shall fall downstairs, too, and marry a princess," and it looked forward eagerly to the next evening, expecting to be again decked out with candles and toys, tinsel and fruit. "To-morrow I will not tremble," thought the tree; "I will enjoy to the full all my splendor, and I shall hear the story of Humpty Dumpty again, and perhaps Henny Penny, too." And the tree stood silent and lost in thought all night.

In the morning the servants came in. "Now," thought the tree, "all the decking me out will begin again." But they dragged it out of the room and upstairs to the garret, and threw it on the floor in a dark corner where no daylight shone, and there they left it. "What does this mean?" thought the tree. "What am I to do here? What is there for me to hear in a place like this?" and it leaned against the wall and thought and thought.

And it had time enough to think, for days and nights passed and no one came near it; and when at last some one did come, it was only to put some great boxes in the corner. So the tree was completely hidden from sight; it seemed as if it had been quite forgotten.

"It is winter now out of doors," thought the tree. "The ground is hard and covered with snow, so that the people cannot plant me yet. That is doubtless why I am left here under cover till the spring comes. How thoughtful and kind everybody is to me! Still, I wish it were not so dark here, and so terribly lonely, with not even a hare to look at. How pleasant it was out in the forest, while the snow lay on the ground, when the hare would run by — yes, and jump over me, too; but I did not like it at all then. Oh, it is terribly lonely here!"

"Squeak! Squeak!" said a little mouse, stealing out of his hole and creeping cautiously toward the tree; then came another, and they both sniffed at the fir tree and crept in and out between the branches.

"Oh, it is very cold!" said the little mouse. "If it were not, we should be very comfortable here, should n't we, old fir tree?"

THE FIR TREE

"I am not old at all," said the fir tree. "There are many who are much older than I am."

"Where do you come from?" asked the mice, who were full of curiosity; "and what do you know? What is the most beautiful place on earth that you know about? Do tell us all about it! Have you been in the storeroom, where cheeses lie on the shelves, and hams hang from the ceiling? One can run about the tallow candles there. Ah! that is a place were one goes in thin and comes out fat."

"I know nothing about that," said the fir tree; "but I know of the wood, where the sun shines and the birds sing."

And then the tree told the mice all about its youth. The mice had never heard anything like that before, and they listened with all their ears, and said: "How much you have seen! How happy you must have been!"

"Happy!" exclaimed the fir tree; and then, as it thought over what it had been telling them, it added, "Ah, yes, those were happy days."

But when it went on and told them about Christmas eve and how it had been adorned with sweetmeats and candles, the mice repeated once more, "How happy, how very fortunate you have been, you old fir tree!"

"I am not old at all," replied the tree. "I only came from the forest this winter. I am now checked in my growth."

"What splendid stories you do tell!" said the little mice. And the next night they came with four others, to have them hear what the tree had to tell. The more it talked the more it remembered, and then it thought to itself: "Yes, those were happy days, but they may come again. Humpty Dumpty fell downstairs and yet married a princess. Perhaps I, too, may marry a princess." And the tree thought of a pretty little birch tree that grew in the forest; she was a princess, a real princess, to the fir tree.

"Who is Humpty Dumpty?" asked the little mice. And then the tree told the whole story; it could remember every single word. And the little mice were so delighted with it that they were ready to jump with joy up to the very top of the tree. The next night a great many more mice made their appearance, and on Sunday two rats came; but they did not care about the story at all, and that troubled the mice, for it made them also think less of it.

"Is that the only story you know?" asked the rats.

"The only one," answered the tree. "I heard it on the happiest evening of my life; but I did not know I was so happy at the time."

"We think it is a very poor story," said the rats. "Don't you know any stories about bacon or tallow candles in the storeroom?"

"No," replied the tree.

"Then we are much obliged to you," said the rats, and they went their way.

The little mice also kept away after this, and the tree sighed and said: "Really it was very pleasant when the lively little mice sat round me and listened while I told them stories. Now that is all past, too. However, I shall consider myself happy when some one comes to take me out of this place."

But would this ever happen? Yes; one morning people came to clear up the garret; the boxes were moved aside and the tree was pulled out of the corner and thrown roughly on the floor; then the servants dragged it out to the stairs, where the daylight shone.

"Now life is beginning again," thought the tree, rejoicing in the sunshine and fresh air.

It was carried downstairs and put out in the yard so quickly that it forgot to look at itself, and gazed about it, for there was so much to be seen.

THE FIR TREE

The yard opened into a garden where everything was bloom-
ing. Fresh and sweet roses hung over a little trellis; the linden
trees were in blossom; and swallows flew here and there, calling,
" Twit, twit, twit, my mate is coming "; but it was not the fir
tree they meant.

" Now I shall live," thought the tree joyfully, stretching out
its branches; but, alas! they were all withered and yellow, and
it was lying in a corner among weeds and nettles.

The star of gold paper still stuck in the top of the tree and
glittered in the sunshine. In the yard two of the merry children
who had danced round the tree at Christmas were playing. One
of them saw the gilded star, and ran up and tore it off.

" See what is sticking to the ugly old fir tree," he cried, and
stamped on the boughs till they crackled under his boots.

And the tree saw all the fresh, bright flowers in the garden
and looked at itself, and wished it had been left lying in the
dark corner of the garret. It thought of its fresh youth in
the forest, of the merry Christmas eve, and of the little mice
that had listened so happily to the tale of Humpty Dumpty.

" Past! past!" said the poor tree. " O had I only enjoyed myself when I could! But now it is too late, — it is all
past."

Then a lad came and chopped the tree into small pieces, till
a large pile lay heaped on the ground. The pieces were placed
in a fire, where they blazed up brightly, and the tree sighed so
deeply that each sigh was like a pistol shot, and the children who
were at play came and sat in front of the fire and looked at it,
and cried, " Puff! puff!" But at each explosion, which was a
deep sigh, the tree thought of a summer day in the woods,
or of a winter night there, when the stars were bright; or of
Christmas eve, or of Humpty Dumpty, the only story it
had ever heard or knew how to tell, — and then the tree was
burned.

The children played in the garden, and the youngest had on his breast the golden star which the tree had worn on its happiest evening. Now that was past, the tree's life was past, and this story is past, too, as all stories must come to an end.

THE MAGIC SWAN

ONCE upon a time there were three brothers, and the youngest of them was named Peter. The two bigger boys treated him very badly. Almost every day they beat him until he cried aloud.

One day as he was crying an old woman passed by. She felt sorry for the poor boy, and said that she would help him to become rich and happy.

Peter thanked her, and then the old woman said: " To-morrow morning, when the sun rises, go to the cross-roads, and there you will find a large swan tied to a tree. Untie it and bring it away with you. The first man that you meet will wish to have a feather from the swan's tail. You must let him try to take one. As soon as he touches the swan it will scream. Then you must say, ' Swan, hold fast,' and the man will be stuck fast until you touch him with this little stick I will give you. All the people who try to set the man free will be held fast in the same way.

" When a number of people have been held fast you must go to the king's palace. There you will find a poor, sad princess, who has never been known to laugh. If you can make her laugh the king will give you a rich reward, and you will be happy ever after."

Peter thanked the old lady, and at sunrise he went to the cross-roads, where he found the swan. At once he untied it, and, putting it under his arm, walked away.

Soon he met a man who said: "I want a feather from that swan."

"Take it," cried Peter.

When the man took hold of the swan's tail the bird screamed, and Peter said, "Swan, hold fast!" At once the man found himself stuck to the swan so tightly that he could not get free. He pulled his hardest, but all in vain.

A girl who was washing clothes in the brook thought she would come to the help of the man; but as soon as she touched him Peter cried, "Swan, hold fast!" Then the girl was caught, too.

On they went, and soon they met a chimney-sweep. "Come and help me to get free," cried the girl. The sweep took hold of the girl, and at once the swan screamed. "Swan, hold fast!" said Peter, and the sooty man found that he was stuck fast, too.

Soon they came to a village where a fair was going on. A clown saw the three people following Peter and the swan, and began to make fun of them. "Don't laugh at us," said the sweep, "but help us to get free."

The clown did so; but no sooner had he touched the sweep than the swan screamed, and Peter said, "Swan, hold fast!" Then the clown found that he could not get free and that he was forced to go with the others.

Just then a policeman came up. "What is the matter here?" he asked, and then he took hold of the clown's arm, meaning to take him off to prison. Once more the swan screamed, and once more Peter said, "Swan, hold fast!" Then the policeman found himself stuck fast to the clown.

The policeman's wife, who was looking out of the window, saw her husband being dragged along. At once she rushed out and took hold of his hand, and tried to pull him away; but the swan screamed, and Peter cried, "Swan, hold fast!" So the policeman's wife had to follow Peter, too.

On they went until they came to the king's palace. Looking out of the window was a beautiful princess, with the saddest face you could ever see. When she saw Peter and the people behind him she began to laugh. At once the servants told the king, and he was very glad to hear the joyful news.

When he saw the man, the girl, the chimney-sweep, the clown, the policeman, and the policeman's wife all struggling to get free, he laughed, too, and could hardly stop.

"Set these people free," said he, "and I will give you a great reward for making the princess laugh."

Then Peter touched them with his little stick, and away they ran as fast as they could. At this the princess and the king laughed louder than ever.

Then the king gave Peter much gold and silver, and made him a great man in the land. In time the princess became his wife, and when her father died Peter became king.

He did not forget the old lady who had told him what to do that he might become rich and great. He gave her a house and servants to wait upon her, and she and the princess and Peter lived happily ever after.

THE RAGAMUFFINS

THE cock said to the little hen: " The nuts are getting ripe, wifie, so let us make a little picnic to the hill where they grow, and have a nice feast before the squirrels have eaten them all."

The little hen was delighted. " We will have fine fun together," she said, and away they went, arm in arm, to the place where the nuts grew. The day was fine, and they enjoyed themselves so much that they stayed there until night began to fall, and then they were so tired that they felt they really could not walk home. So the cock began to build a carriage of nutshells.

When it was finished, the little hen seated herself in it and told the cock to harness himself to the carriage and take her home.

" Indeed, no! " answered the cock, " I am as tired as you, and I have no mind to draw you, madam. Your coachman I will be and sit upon a box, but more I will not do."

So they squabbled with each other, until a duck came waddling by.

" Hello! you thieves! " cried she, " what are you doing on my nut-hill? Wait a minute, and I 'll teach you to keep away in the future! "

She flew at the cock with wings outspread, but the plucky little fellow met her with equal fury, and after a time the duck found she was getting the worst of it, and had to beg for mercy.

246

So, as a punishment, she was made to harness herself to the carriage. The cock seated himself upon the box, cracked the whip, and away they went like the wind.

Before they had gone far, they met a couple of foot passengers — a pin and a needle. They called to the cock to stop, and asked if he and his wife would give them a lift as they were too tired to go another step, and the roads were too muddy to make a comfortable resting-place. They said that they had stayed at the Tailor's Inn for refreshment, and had not noticed how quickly the time was passing, and how late it was.

When the cock saw what thin little folks they were, he bade them get inside the carriage, but made them promise on no account to crush his wife or tread on her toes.

Late that night they came to an inn, at which they alighted, for they felt sure they would get no farther before morning. The duck was an unsteady steed, and besides shaking the carriage violently from side to side, complained terribly of pains in her feet, for she was not a good walker.

But the host did not like the appearance of the travelers, and made all sorts of excuses to get rid of them.

However, the cock spoke so persuasively, — promising him the egg which his wife had laid coming along, as well as that of the duck, which, he said, laid one every day, — that at last he consented to let the company of ragamuffins stay one night.

So they set to work to enjoy themselves, ordered the best of food and drink and passed the night in comfortable beds.

As soon as the morning began to dawn, the cock awakened the hen, pecked a hole in the egg, and together they ate it up, and threw the shell upon the hearth.

Then they went to the needle, which was still asleep, picked it up by the eye and stuck it in the host's chair; the pin they stuck in the poor man's towel, and after that they flew away, over hedge, ditch, and field as fast as ever they could.

The duck, who had slept in the courtyard all night, heard the cock and the hen fluttering overhead and waddled away well pleased to the stream, splashed in, and swam away far more quickly than ever she had drawn the carriage.

Two hours later, the host got up, washed himself and took the towel to dry himself with, when the pin scratched him in the face and made a red scar from ear to ear.

He went down to the kitchen, and stooped over the hearth to light his pipe. At once the egg-shells flew up into his face.

" Everything seems to fly at my head this morning," he said, quite crossly, and sat down in the old grandfather chair.

With a cry of pain he sprang up as though he had been shot.

He was now thoroughly angry, but happening to remember the guests who had arrived the night before, he went to see how they had slept. But they had disappeared!

So the host made a vow that never again would he harbor a troop of ragamuffins, who ate folk out of house and home, paid nothing and played one such shabby tricks into the bargain.

THE FOX AS HERDSMAN

ONCE upon a time there was a woman who went out to hire a herdsman, and she met a bear.

"Where are you going, Goody?" said Bruin.

"Oh, I'm going out to hire a herdsman," answered the woman.

"Why not have me for a herdsman?" said Bruin.

"Well, why not?" said the woman. "If you only knew how to call the flock! Just let me hear how you would do it."

"O-ow! o-ow!" growled the bear.

"No, no! I won't have you," said the woman, as soon as she heard him say that; and off she went on her way.

So when she had gone a bit farther, she met a wolf.

"Where are you going, Goody?" asked the wolf.

"Oh," said she, "I'm going out to hire a herdsman."

"Why not have me for a herdsman?" asked the wolf.

"Well, why not? If you could only call the flock! Just let me hear how you would do it," said she.

"Uh! uh!" said the wolf.

"No, no!" said the woman; "that would never do."

After she had gone a while longer, she met a fox.

"Where are you going, Goody?" asked the fox.

"Oh, I'm just going out to hire a herdsman," said the woman.

"Why not have me for your herdsman?" asked the fox.

"Well, why not?" said she. "If you could only call the flock! How would you do it?"

"Dil-dal-holm," called out the fox in a clear voice.

" Yes, you 'll do," said the woman; and so she set the fox to herd her flock.

The first day the fox ate up all the woman's goats; the second day he made an end of all her sheep; and the third day he ate up all her cows. When he came home on the evening of the third day, the woman asked him where her flocks were.

" Oh," said the fox, " their skulls are in the stream, and their bodies in the woods."

Now the woman was churning when the fox said this, but she thought she might as well go out and look after her flock; and while she was away the fox crept into the churn and ate up the cream. When the woman came back and saw what he had done, she was so angry that she snatched up what cream there was left and threw it at the fox as he ran off, and some of it stuck to his tail. So that is the reason why the fox has a white tip to his brush.

THREE BILLY GOATS GRUFF

ONCE upon a time there were three billy goats, who went up the hillside to make themselves fat, and the name of all three was " Gruff."

On the way up was a bridge over a brook; and under the bridge lived a great, ugly Troll, with eyes as big as saucers, and a nose as long as your arm.

First of all came the youngest Billy Goat Gruff to cross the bridge.

Trip trap! trip trap! went the bridge. " Who 's that tripping over my bridge? " roared the Troll.

" Oh, it is only I, the Tiniest Billy Goat Gruff; and I 'm going up the hillside to make myself fat," said the billy goat, with such a small voice.

" Now I 'm coming to gobble you up," said the Troll.

" Oh, no, pray don't take me! I 'm too little," said the billy goat. " Wait a bit till the next Billy Goat Gruff comes; he 's much bigger."

" Well, be off with you! " said the Troll.

A little while after came the Second Billy Goat Gruff to cross the bridge.

Trip trap! trip trap! trip trap! went the bridge.

" Who 's that tripping over my bridge? " roared the Troll.

" Oh, it 's only the Second Billy Goat Gruff; and I 'm going up the hillside to make myself fat," said the billy goat, who had n't such a small voice.

"Now I'm coming to gobble you up," said the Troll.

"Oh, no, don't take me! Wait a little till the Big Billy Goat Gruff comes; he's much bigger."

"Very well, be off with you!" said the Troll.

But just then came the Big Billy Goat Gruff.

Trip trap! trip trap! trip trap! went the bridge, for the billy goat was so heavy that the bridge creaked under him.

"Who's that tramping over my bridge?" roared the Troll.

"It's I, the Big Billy Goat Gruff," said the billy goat, who had an ugly, hoarse voice of his own.

"Now I'm coming to gobble you up," roared the Troll.

> "Well, come along! I've got two spears,
> And I'll poke your eyeballs out at your ears;
> I've got besides two curling-stones,
> And I'll crush you to bits, body and bones."

That was what the big billy goat said; and so he flew at the Troll, and poked his eyes out with his horns, and crushed him to bits, body and bones, and tossed him out into the stream, and after that he went up to the hillside. There the billy goats got so fat they were scarce able to walk home again; and if the fat hasn't fallen off them, why, they're still fat; and so —

> "Snip, snap, snout,
> This tale's told out."

HOW JACK WENT TO SEEK HIS FORTUNE

ONCE on a time there was a boy named Jack, and one morning he started to go and seek his fortune.

He had n't gone very far before he met a cat.

" Where are you going, Jack? " said the cat.

" I am going to seek my fortune."

" May I go with you? "

" Yes," said Jack, " the more the merrier."

So on they went, jiggelty-jolt, jiggelty-jolt.

They went a little further and they met a dog.

" Where are you going, Jack? " said the dog.

" I am going to seek my fortune."

" May I go with you? "

" Yes," said Jack, " the more the merrier."

So on they went, jiggelty-jolt, jiggelty-jolt.

They went on a little further and they met a bull.

" Where are you going, Jack? " said the bull.

" I am going to seek my fortune."

" May I go with you? "

" Yes," said Jack, " the more the merrier."

So on they went, jiggelty-jolt, jiggelty-jolt.

They went a little further and they met a goat.

" Where are you going, Jack? " said the goat.

" I am going to seek my fortune."

" May I go with you? "

253

"Yes," said Jack, "the more the merrier."

So on they went, jiggelty-jolt, jiggelty-jolt.

They went a little further and they met a rooster.

"Where are you going, Jack?" said the rooster.

"I am going to seek my fortune."

"May I go with you?"

"Yes," said Jack, "the more the merrier."

So on they went, jiggelty-jolt, jiggelty-jolt.

Well, they went on till it was about dark, and they began to think of some place where they could spend the night. About this time they came in sight of a house, and Jack told them to keep still while he went up and looked in through the window. And there were some robbers counting over their money. Then Jack went back and told them to wait till he gave the word, and then to make all the noise they could. So when they were all ready Jack gave the word, and the cat mewed, and the dog barked, and the goat bleated, and the bull bellowed, and the rooster crowed, and altogether they made such a dreadful noise that it frightened the robbers away.

And then they went in and took possession of the house. Jack was afraid the robbers would come back in the night, and so when it came time to go to bed he put the cat in the rocking-chair, and he put the dog under the table, and he put the goat upstairs, and he put the bull in the cellar, and the rooster flew up to the roof, and Jack went to bed.

By and by the robbers saw that the house was all in darkness, and they sent one man back to look after their money. Before long he came back in a great fright and told them his story.

"I went back to the house," said he, "and went in and tried to sit down in the rocking-chair, and there was an old woman knitting, and she stuck her knitting-needles into me." That was the cat, you know.

"I went to the table to look after the money and there was a shoemaker under the table, and he stuck his awl into me." That was the dog, you know.

"I started to go upstairs, and there was a man up there threshing, and he knocked me down with his flail. That was the goat, you know.

"I started to go down cellar, and there was a man down there chopping wood, and he knocked me up with his ax." That was the bull, you know.

"But I should n't have minded all that if it had n't been for that little fellow on top of the house, who kept a-hollering, 'Chuck him up to me-e! Chuck him up to me-e!'" Of course that was the cock-a-doodle-do.

PUSS IN BOOTS; OR, THE MASTER CAT

THERE was a miller who left no more estate to the three sons he had than his mill, his ass, and his cat. The partition was soon made. Neither scrivener nor attorney was sent for. They would soon have eaten up all the poor patrimony. The eldest had the mill, the second the ass, and the youngest nothing but the cat. The poor young fellow was quite comfortless at having so poor a lot.

"My brothers," said he, "may get their living handsomely enough by joining their stocks together; but for my part, when I have eaten up my cat and made me a muff of his skin I must die of hunger."

The cat, who heard all this, but made as if he did not, said to him with a grave and serious air:

"Do not thus afflict yourself, my good master. You have nothing else to do but to give me a bag and get a pair of boots made for me that I may scamper through the dirt and the brambles, and you shall see that you have not so bad a portion of me as you imagine."

The cat's master did not build very much upon what he said. He had often seen him play a great many cunning tricks to catch rats and mice, as when he used to hang by the heels, or hide himself in the meal, and make as if he were dead; so that he did not altogether despair of his affording him some help in his miserable condition. When the cat had what he asked for he booted himself very gallantly, and putting his bag about his neck, he held the strings of it in his two fore paws and went into a warren where was great abundance of rabbits. He put bran and sow-thistle into his bag, and stretching out at length, as if he had been dead, he waited for some young rabbits, not yet acquainted with the deceits of the world, to come and rummage his bag for what he had put into it.

Scarce was he lain down but he had what he wanted. A rash and foolish young rabbit jumped into his bag, and Monsieur Puss, immediately drawing close the strings, took and killed him without pity. Proud of his prey, he went with it to the palace and asked to speak with his majesty. He was shown upstairs into the king's apartment, and making a low reverence said to him:

" I have brought you, sir, a rabbit of the warren, which my noble lord the Marquis of Carabas " (for that was the title which puss was pleased to give his master) " has commanded me to present to your Majesty from him."

" Tell thy master," said the king, " that I thank him and that he does me a great deal of pleasure."

Another time he went and hid himself among some standing corn, holding still his bag open, and when a brace of partridges ran into it he drew the strings and so caught them both. He went and made a present of these to the king, as he had done before of the rabbit which he took in the warren. The king, in like manner, received the partridges with great pleasure and ordered him some money for drink.

The cat continued for two or three months thus to carry his Majesty, from time to time, game of his master's taking. One day in particular, when he knew for certain that he was to take the air along the river-side with his daughter, the most beautiful princess in the world, he said to his master:

" If you will follow my advice your fortune is made. You

have nothing else to do but go and wash yourself in the river, in that part I shall show you, and leave the rest to me."

The Marquis of Carabas did what the cat advised him to, without knowing why or wherefore. While he was washing the king passed by, and the cat began to cry out: "Help! help! My Lord Marquis of Carabas is going to be drowned."

At this noise the king put his head out of the coach-window, and finding it was the cat who had so often brought him such good game, he commanded his guards to run immediately to the assistance of his lordship the Marquis of Carabas. While they were drawing the poor marquis out of the river, the cat came up to the coach and told the king that while his master was washing there came by some rogues, who went off with his clothes, though he had cried out "Thieves! thieves!" several times as loud as he could.

This cunning cat had hidden them under a great stone. The king immediately commanded the officers of his wardrobe to run and fetch one of his best suits for the Marquis of Carabas.

The king caressed him after a very extraordinary manner, and as the fine clothes he had given him extremely set off his good mien (for he was well made and very handsome in his person), the king's daughter took a secret inclination to him, and the Marquis of Carabas had no sooner cast two or three respectful and somewhat tender glances but she fell in love with him to distraction. The king would needs have him come into the coach and take part of the airing. The cat, quite overjoyed to see his project begin to succeed, marched on before, and meeting with some countrymen who were mowing a meadow, he said to them:

"Good people, you who are mowing, if you do not tell the king that the meadow you mow belongs to my Lord Marquis of Carabas, you shall be chopped as small as herbs for the pot."

The king did not fail asking of the mowers to whom the meadow they were mowing belonged.

"To my Lord Marquis of Carabas," answered they altogether, for the cat's threats had made them terribly afraid.

"You see, sir," said the marquis, "this is a meadow which never fails to yield a plentiful harvest every year."

The master cat, who went still on before, met with some reapers and said to them:

"Good people, you who are reaping, if you do not tell the king that all this corn belongs to the Marquis of Carabas, you shall be chopped as small as herbs for the pot."

The king, who passed by a moment after, would needs know to whom all that corn, which he then saw, did belong.

"To my Lord Marquis of Carabas," replied the reapers, and the king was very well pleased with it, as well as the marquis, whom he congratulated thereupon. The master cat, who went always before, said the same words to all he met, and the king was astonished at the vast estates of my Lord Marquis of Carabas.

Monsieur Puss came at last to a stately castle, the master of which was an ogre, the richest had ever been known; for all the lands which the king had then gone over belonged to this castle. The cat, who had taken care to inform himself who this ogre was and what he could do, asked to speak with him, saying he could not pass so near his castle without having the honor of paying his respects to him.

The ogre received him as civilly as an ogre could do and made him sit down.

"I have been assured," said the cat, "that you have the gift of being able to change yourself into all sorts of creatures you have a mind to. You can, for example, transform yourself into a lion, or an elephant, and the like."

"That is true," answered the ogre very briskly; "and to convince you, you shall see me now become a lion."

Puss was so sadly terrified at the sight of a lion so near him that he immediately got into the gutter, not without abundance of trouble and danger, because of his boots, which were of no use at all to him in walking upon the tiles. A little while after, when puss saw that the ogre had resumed his natural form, he came down and owned he had been very much frightened.

"I have been moreover informed," said the cat, "but I know not how to believe it, that you have also the power to take on you the shape of the smallest animals; for example, to change yourself into a rat or a mouse; but I must own to you I take this to be impossible."

"Impossible!" cried the ogre. "You shall see that presently."

And at the same time he changed himself into a mouse and began to run about the floor. Puss no sooner perceived this but he fell upon him and ate him up.

Meanwhile the king, who saw, as he passed, this fine castle of the ogre's, had a mind to go into it. Puss, who heard the noise of his Majesty's coach running over the drawbridge, ran out and said to the king:

"Your Majesty is welcome to this castle of my Lord Marquis of Carabas."

"What! my lord marquis," cried the king, "and does this castle also belong to you? There can be nothing finer than this court and all the stately buildings which surround it. Let us go into it, if you please."

The marquis gave his hand to the princess and followed the king, who went first. They passed into a spacious hall, where they found a magnificent collation, which the ogre had prepared for his friends who were that very day to visit him, but dared not enter, knowing the king was there. His Majesty was perfectly charmed with the good qualities of my Lord Marquis of Carabas, as was his daughter, who had fallen violently in love with him, and seeing the vast estate he possessed, said to him, after having drunk five or six glasses:

" It will be owing to yourself only, my lord marquis, if you are not my son-in-law."

The marquis, making several low bows, accepted the honor which his Majesty conferred upon him, and forthwith, that very same day, married the princess.

Puss became a great lord and never ran after mice any more but only for his diversion.

BLUE BEARD

THERE was a man who had fine houses, both in town and country, a deal of silver and gold plate, embroidered furniture, and coaches gilded all over with gold. But this man was so unlucky as to have a blue beard, which made him so frightfully ugly that all the women and girls ran away from him.

One of his neighbors, a lady of quality, had two daughters who were perfect beauties. He desired of her one of them in marriage, leaving to her choice which of the two she would bestow on him. They would neither of them have him, and sent him backward and forward from one another, not being able to bear the thoughts of marrying a man who had a blue beard, and what besides gave them disgust and aversion was his having already been married to several wives, and nobody ever knew what became of them.

Blue Beard, to engage their affection, took them, with the lady their mother and three or four ladies of their acquaintance, with other young people of the neighborhood, to one of his country seats, where they stayed a whole week.

There was nothing then to be seen but parties of pleasure, hunting, fishing, dancing, mirth, and feasting. Nobody went to bed, but all passed the night in rallying and joking with each other. In short, everything succeeded so well that the youngest daughter began to think the master of the house not to have a beard so very blue, and that he was a mighty civil gentleman.

BLUE BEARD

As soon as they returned home the marriage was concluded. About a month afterward, Blue Beard told his wife that he was obliged to take a country journey for six weeks at least, about affairs of very great consequence, desiring her to divert herself in his absence, to send for her friends and acquaintances, to carry them into the country if she pleased, and to make good cheer wherever she was.

"Here," said he, "are the keys of the two great wardrobes, wherein I have my best furniture; these are of my silver and gold plate, which is not every day in use; these open my strong-boxes, which hold my money, both gold and silver; these my caskets of jewels; and this is the master-key to all my apartments. But for this little one here, it is the key of the closet at the end of the great gallery on the ground-floor. Open them all; go into all and every one of them, except that little closet, which I forbid you, and forbid it in such a manner that, if you happen to open it, there's nothing but what you may expect from my just anger and resentment."

She promised to observe, very exactly, whatever he had ordered; when he, after having embraced her, got into his coach and proceeded on his journey.

Her neighbors and good friends did not stay to be sent for by the new-married lady, so great was their impatience to see all the rich furniture of her house, not daring to come while her husband was there, because of his blue beard, which frightened them. They ran through all the rooms, closets, and wardrobes, which were all so fine and rich that they seemed to surpass one another.

After that they went up into the two great rooms, where were the best and richest furniture; they could not sufficiently admire the number and beauty of the tapestry, beds, couches, cabinets, stands, tables, and looking-glasses, in which you might see yourself from head to foot; some of them were framed with glass, others with silver, plain and gilded, the finest and most magnificent ever were seen.

They ceased not to extol and envy the happiness of their friend, who in the mean time in no way diverted herself in looking upon all these rich things, because of the impatience she had to go and open the closet on the ground-floor. She was so much pressed by her curiosity that, without considering that it was very uncivil to leave her company, she went down a little back staircase, and with such excessive haste that she had twice or thrice like to have broken her neck.

Being come to the closet door, she made a stop for some time, thinking upon her husband's orders and considering what unhappiness might attend her if she was disobedient; but the temptation was so strong she could not overcome it. She then took the little key and opened it, trembling, but could not at first see anything plainly, because the windows were shut. After some moments she began to perceive that the floor was all covered over with clotted blood, on which lay the bodies of several dead women, ranged against the walls. (These were all the wives whom Blue Beard had married and murdered, one after another.) She thought she should have died for fear, and the key, which she pulled out of the lock, fell out of her hand.

After having somewhat recovered her surprise, she took up the key, locked the door, and went upstairs into her chamber to recover herself; but she could not, so much was she frightened. Having observed that the key of the closet was stained with blood, she tried two or three times to wipe it off, but the blood would not come out; in vain did she wash it, and even rub it with soap and sand: the blood still remained, for the key was magical and she could never make it quite clean; when the blood was gone off from one side it came again as bright as ever on the other.

Blue Beard returned from his journey the same evening, and

said he had received letters upon the road informing him that the affair he went about was ended to his advantage. His wife did all she could to convince him she was extremely glad of his speedy return.

Next morning he asked her for the keys, which she gave him, but with such a trembling hand that he easily guessed what had happened.

" What! " said he, " is not the key of my closet among the rest? "

" I must certainly," said she, " have left it above upon the table."

" Fail not," said Blue Beard, " to bring it to me presently."

After several goings backward and forward she was forced to bring the key. Blue Beard, having very attentively considered it, said to his wife:

" How comes this blood upon the key? "

" I do not know," cried the poor woman, paler than death.

" You do not know! " replied Blue Beard. " I very well know. You were resolved to go into the closet, were you not? Mighty well, madam; you shall go in and take your place among the ladies you saw there."

Upon this she threw herself at her husband's feet and begged his pardon with all the signs of a true repentance, vowing that she would never more be disobedient. She would have melted a rock, so beautiful and sorrowful was she; but Blue Beard had a heart harder than any rock!

" You must die, madam," said he, " and that presently."

" Since I must die," answered she, looking upon him with her eyes all bathed in tears, " give me some little time to say my prayers."

" I give you," replied Blue Beard, " half a quarter of an hour, but not one moment more."

When she was alone she called out to her sister and said to her:

"Sister Anne," for that was her name, "go up, I beg you, upon the top of the tower, and look if my brothers are not coming; they promised me that they would come to-day, and if you see them, give them a sign to make haste."

Her sister Anne went up upon the top of the tower, and the poor afflicted wife cried out from time to time:

"Anne, sister Anne, do you see any one coming?"

And sister Anne said:

"I see nothing but the sun, which makes a dust, and the grass, which looks green."

In the mean while Blue Beard, holding a great saber in his hand, cried out as loud as he could bawl to his wife:

"Come down instantly, or I shall come up to you."

"One moment longer, if you please," said his wife; and then she cried out very softly: "Anne, sister Anne, dost thou see anybody coming?"

And sister Anne answered:

"I see nothing but the sun, which makes a dust, and the grass, which is green."

"Come down quickly," cried Blue Beard, "or I will come up to you."

"I am coming," answered his wife; and then she cried: "Anne, sister Anne, dost thou not see any one coming?"

"I see," replied sister Anne, "a great dust, which comes on this side here."

"Are they my brothers?"

"Alas! no, my dear sister, I see a flock of sheep."

"Will you not come down?" cried Blue Beard.

"One moment longer," said his wife, and then she cried out: "Anne, sister Anne, dost thou see nobody coming?"

"I see," said she, "two horsemen, but they are yet a great way off."

"God be praised," replied the poor wife joyfully: "they are

my brothers; I will make them a sign, as well as I can, for them to make haste."

Then Blue Beard bawled out so loud that he made the whole house tremble. The distressed wife came down and threw herself at his feet, all in tears, with her hair about her shoulders.

"This signifies nothing," says Blue Beard; "you must die"; then, taking hold of her hair with one hand and lifting up the sword with the other, he was going to take off her head. The poor lady, turning about to him and looking at him with dying eyes, desired him to afford her one little moment to collect herself.

"No, no," said he, "recommend thyself to God," and was just ready to strike.

At this very instant there was such a loud knocking at the gate that Blue Beard made a sudden stop. The gate was opened, and presently entered two horsemen, who, drawing their swords, ran directly to Blue Beard. He knew them to be his wife's brothers, one a dragoon, the other a musketeer, so that he ran away immediately to save himself; but the two brothers pursued so close that they overtook him before he could get to the steps of the porch, when they ran their swords through his body and left him dead. The poor wife was almost as dead as her husband, and had not strength enough to rise and welcome her brothers.

Blue Beard had no heirs, and so his wife became mistress of all his estate. She made use of one part of it to marry her sister Anne to a young gentleman who had loved her a long while; another part to buy captains' commissions for her brothers; and the rest to marry herself to a very worthy gentleman, who made her forget the ill time she had passed with Blue Beard.

THE BRAVE LITTLE TAILOR

ONE summer's day a little tailor sat on his table by the window in the best of spirits and sewed for dear life. As he was sitting thus a peasant-woman came down the street, calling out: "Good jam to sell! good jam to sell!" This sounded sweetly in the tailor's ears. He put his frail little head out of the window and shouted: "Up here, my good woman, and you'll find a willing customer." The woman climbed up the three flights of stairs with her heavy basket to the tailor's room, and he made her spread out all the pots in a row before him. He examined them all, lifted them up and smelled them, and said at last: "This jam seems good. Weigh me four ounces of it, my good woman; and even if it's a quarter of a pound I won't stick at it." The woman, who had hoped to find a good market, gave him what he wanted, but went away grumbling wrathfully. "Now Heaven shall bless this jam for my use," cried the little tailor, "and it shall sustain and strengthen me." He fetched some bread out of a cupboard, cut a round off the loaf, and spread the jam on it. "That won't taste amiss," he said; "but I'll finish that waistcoat first before I take a bite." He placed the bread beside him, went on sewing, and out of the lightness of his heart kept on making his stitches bigger and bigger. In the mean time the smell of the sweet jam rose to the ceiling, where heaps of flies were sitting, and attracted them to such an extent that they swarmed on to it in masses. "Ha! who invited you?" said the tailor, and chased the unwelcome guests away. But the flies, who did n't understand English, refused to let themselves be warned off, and returned again in even greater numbers. At last the little tailor, losing all patience, reached out of his chimney-corner for a duster, and exclaiming, " Wait, and I 'll give it to you," he beat them mercilessly with it. When he left off he counted the slain, and no fewer than seven lay dead before him with outstretched legs. " What a desperate fellow I am! " said he, and was filled with admiration at his own courage. " The whole town must know about this "; and in great haste the little tailor cut out a girdle, hemmed it, and embroidered on it in big letters, " Seven at a blow." " What did I say, the town? No, the whole world shall hear of it," he said; and his heart beat for joy as a lamb wags his tail.

The tailor strapped the girdle round his waist and set out into the wide world, for he considered his workroom too small a field for his prowess. Before he set forth he looked round about him, to see if there was anything in the house he could take with him on his journey; but he found nothing except an old cheese, which he took possession of. In front of the house he observed a bird that had been caught in some bushes, and this he put into his wallet beside the cheese. Then he went on his way merrily, and being light and agile he never felt tired. His ways led up a hill, on the top of which sat a powerful giant who was calmly surveying the landscape. The little tailor went up to him, and greeting him cheerfully said: " Good-day, friend. There you sit at your ease viewing the whole wide world. I 'm just on my way there. What do you say to accompanying me? " The giant looked contemptuously at the tailor and said: " What a poor wretched little creature you are! " " That 's a good joke," answered the little tailor, and unbuttoning his coat he showed the giant the girdle. " There now, you can read what sort of a fellow I am."

The giant read, " Seven at a blow," and thinking they were

human beings the tailor had slain, he conceived a certain respect for the little man. But first he thought he 'd test him, so taking up a stone in his hand he squeezed it till some drops of water ran out. "Now you do the same," said the giant, "if you really wish to be thought strong." "Is that all?" said the little tailor. "That 's child's play to me." So he dived into his wallet, brought out the cheese, and pressed it till the whey ran out. "My squeeze was in sooth better than yours," said he. The giant did n't know what to say, for he could n't have believed it of the little fellow. To prove him again, the giant lifted a stone and threw it so high that the eye could hardly follow it. "Now, my little pygmy, let me see you do that." "Well thrown," said the tailor; "but, after all, your stone fell to the ground. I 'll throw one that won't come down at all." He dived into his wallet again, and grasping the bird in his hand, he threw it up into the air. The bird, enchanted to be free, soared up into the sky and flew away never to return. "Well, what do you think of that little piece of business, friend?" asked the tailor. "You can certainly throw," said the giant; "but now let 's see if you can carry a proper weight."

With these words he led the tailor to a huge oak tree which had been felled to the ground and said: "If you are strong enough, help me to carry the tree out of the wood." "Most certainly," said the little tailor. "Just you take the trunk on your shoulder. I 'll bear the top and branches, which is certainly the heaviest part." The giant laid the trunk on his shoulder, but the tailor sat at his ease among the branches; and the giant, who could n't see what was going on behind him, had to carry the whole tree and the little tailor into the bargain. There he sat behind in the best of spirits, lustily whistling a tune, as if carrying the tree were mere sport. The giant, after dragging the heavy weight for some time, could get on no further and shouted out: "Hi! I must let the tree fall." The tailor sprang nimbly down, seized the tree with both hands as if he had carried it the whole way, and said to the giant: " Fancy a big lout like you not being able to carry a tree! "

They continued to go on their way together, and as they passed by a cherry tree the giant grasped the top of it, where the ripest fruit hung, gave the branches into the tailor's hand, and bade him eat. But the little tailor was far too weak to hold the tree down, and when the giant let go the tree swung back into the air, bearing the little tailor with it. When he had fallen to the ground again without hurting himself, the giant said: " What! do you mean to tell me you have n't the strength to hold down a feeble twig? " " It was n't strength that was wanting," replied the tailor. " Do you think that would have been anything for a man who has killed seven at a blow? I jumped over the tree because the huntsmen are shooting among the branches near us. Do you do the like if you dare." The giant made an attempt, but could n't get over the tree, and stuck fast in the branches, so that here too the little tailor had the better of him.

" Well, you 're a fine fellow, after all," said the giant. " Come and spend the night with us in our cave." The little tailor willingly consented to do this, and following his friend they went on till they reached a cave where several other giants were sitting round a fire, each holding a roast sheep in his hand, of which he was eating. The little tailor looked about him and thought, " Yes, there 's certainly more room to turn round in here than in my workshop." The giant showed him a bed and bade him lie down and have a good sleep. But the bed was too big for the little tailor, so he did n't get into it, but crept away into the corner. At midnight, when the giant thought the little tailor was fast asleep, he rose up, and taking his big iron walking-stick, he broke the bed in two with a blow, and thought he had made an end of the little grasshopper. At early dawn the giants went off to the wood and quite forgot about the little tailor, till all of a sudden they met him trudging along in the most cheerful manner. The giants were terrified at the apparition, and, fearful lest he should slay them, they all took to their heels as fast as they could.

The little tailor continued to follow his nose, and after he had wandered about for a long time he came to the courtyard of a royal palace, and feeling tired he lay down on the grass and fell asleep. While he lay there the people came, and looking him all over read on his girdle: " Seven at a blow." " Oh! " they said, " what can this great hero of a hundred fights want in our peaceful land? He must indeed be a mighty man of valor." They went and told the king about him, and said what a weighty and useful man he 'd be in time of war, and that it would be well to secure him at any price. This counsel pleased the king, and he sent one of his courtiers down to the little tailor, to offer him, when he awoke, a commission in their army. The messenger remained standing by the sleeper and waited till he stretched his limbs and opened his eyes, when he tendered his proposal. " That 's the very thing I came here for," he answered. " I am quite ready to enter the king's service." So he was received with all honor and given a special house of his own to live in.

But the other officers resented the success of the little tailor and wished him a thousand miles away. " What 's to come of it all? " they asked each other. " If we quarrel with him he 'll let out at us, and at every blow seven will fall. There 'll soon be an end of us." So they resolved to go in a body to the king and all to send in their papers. " We are not made," they said, " to hold out against a man who kills seven at a blow." The king was grieved at the thought of losing all his faithful servants for the sake of one man, and he wished heartily that he had never set eyes on him or that he could get rid of him. But he did n't dare to send him away, for he feared he might kill him along with his people and place himself on the throne. He pondered long and deeply over the matter and finally came to a conclusion. He sent to the tailor and told him that, seeing what a great and warlike hero he was, he was about to make him an offer. In a certain wood of his kingdom there dwelt two giants who did much harm by the way they robbed, murdered, burned, and plundered everything about them. No one could approach them without endangering his life. But if he could overcome and kill these two giants he should have his only daughter for a wife and half his kingdom into the bargain. He might have a hundred horsemen, too, to back him up. " That 's the very thing for a man like me," thought the little tailor. " One does n't get the offer of a beautiful princess and half a kingdom every day." " Done with you," he answered. " I 'll soon put an end to the giants. But I have n't the smallest need of your hundred horsemen. A fellow who can slay seven men at a blow need not be afraid of two."

The little tailor set out and the hundred horsemen followed him. When he came to the outskirts of the wood he said to his followers: " You wait here. I 'll manage the giants by myself." He went on into the wood, casting his sharp little eyes right and left about him. After a while he spied the two giants lying asleep under a tree and snoring till the very boughs bent with the breeze. The little tailor lost no time in filling his wallet with stones, and then climbed up the tree under which they lay. When he got to about the middle of it he slipped along a branch till he sat just above the sleepers, when he threw down one stone after the other on the nearest giant. The giant felt nothing for a long time, but at last he woke up, and pinching his companion said: " What did you strike me for? " " I did n't strike you," said the other. " You must be dreaming." They both lay down to sleep again, and the tailor threw down a stone on the second giant, who sprang up and cried: " What 's that for? Why did you throw something at me? " " I did n't throw anything," growled the first one. They wrangled on for a time, till, as both were tired, they made up the matter and fell asleep again. The little tailor began his game once more, and flung the largest stone he could find in his wallet with all his force and hit the first giant on the chest. "This is too much of a good thing!" he yelled, and springing up like a madman, he knocked his companion against the tree till he trembled. He gave, however, as good as he got, and they became so enraged that they tore up trees and beat each other with them till they both fell dead at once on the ground. Then the little tailor jumped down. "It's a mercy," he said, "that they did n't root up the tree on which I was perched, or I should have had to jump like a squirrel on to another, which, nimble though I am, would have been no easy job." He drew his sword and gave each of the giants a very fine thrust or two on the breast, and then went to the horsemen and said: "The deed is done. I 've put an end to the two of them; but I assure you it has been no easy matter, for they even tore up trees in their struggle to defend themselves; but all that 's of no use against one who slays seven men at a blow." "Were n't you wounded?" asked the horsemen. "No fear," answered the tailor. "They have n't touched a hair of my head." But the horsemen would n't believe him till they rode into the wood and found the giants weltering in their blood and the trees lying around torn up by the roots.

The little tailor now demanded the promised reward from the king, but he repented his promise and pondered once more how he could rid himself of the hero. "Before you obtain the hand of my daughter and half my kingdom," he said to him, "you must do another deed of valor. A unicorn is running about loose in the wood and doing much mischief. You must first catch it." "I 'm even less afraid of one unicorn than of two giants. Seven at a blow — that 's my motto." He took a piece of cord and an ax with him, went out to the wood, and again told the men who had been sent with him to remain outside. He had n't to search long, for the unicorn soon passed by, and on perceiving the tailor dashed straight at him as though it were going to spike him on the spot. "Gently, gently," said he; "not so fast, my friend"; and standing still he waited till the beast was quite near, when he sprang lightly behind a tree. The unicorn ran with all its force against the tree, and rammed its horn so firmly into the trunk that it had no strength left to pull it out again, and was thus successfully captured. "Now I've caught my bird," said the tailor, and he came out from behind the tree, placed the cord round its neck first, then struck the horn out of the tree with his ax, and, when everything was in order, led the beast before the king.

Still the king did n't want to give him the promised reward, and made a third demand. The tailor was to catch a wild boar for him that did a great deal of harm in the wood, and he might have the huntsmen to help him. "Willingly," said the tailor. "That's mere child's play." But he did n't take the huntsmen into the wood with him, and they were well enough pleased to remain behind, for the wild boar had often received them in a manner which did not make them desire its further acquaintance. As soon as the boar perceived the tailor it ran at him with foaming mouth and gleaming teeth and tried to knock him down; but our alert little friend ran into a chapel that stood near and got out of the window again with a jump. The boar pursued him into the church, but the tailor skipped round to the door and closed it securely. So the raging beast was caught, for it was far too heavy and unwieldly to spring out of the window. The little tailor summoned the huntsmen together, that they might see the prisoner with their own eyes. Then the hero betook himself to the king, who was obliged now, whether he liked it or not, to keep his promise and hand him over his daughter and half his kingdom. Had he known that no hero-warrior, but only a little tailor, stood before him, it would have gone even more to his heart. So the wedding was celebrated with much splendor and little joy, and the tailor became a king.

After a time the queen heard her husband saying one night in his sleep: "My lad, make that waistcoat and patch those trousers, or I'll box your ears." Thus she learned in what rank the young gentleman had been born, and next day she poured forth her woes to her father and begged him to help her to get rid of a husband who was nothing more nor less than a tailor. The king comforted her and said: "Leave your bedroom door open to-night. My servants shall stand outside, and when your husband is fast asleep they shall enter, bind him fast, and carry him on to a ship, which shall sail away out into the wide ocean." The queen was well satisfied with the idea, but the armor-bearer, who had overheard everything, being much attached to his young master, went straight to him and revealed the whole plot. "I'll soon put a stop to the business," said the tailor. That night he and his wife went to bed at the usual time, and when she thought he had fallen asleep she got up, opened the door, and then lay down again. The little tailor, who had only pretended to be asleep, began to call out in a clear voice: "My lad, make that waistcoat and patch those trousers, or I'll box your ears. I have killed seven at a blow, slain two giants, led a unicorn captive, and caught a wild boar. Then why should I be afraid of those men standing outside my door?" The men, when they heard the tailor saying these words, were so terrified that they fled as if pursued by a wild army and didn't dare go near him again. So the little tailor was and remained a king all the days of his life.

HANS IN LUCK

HANS had served his master seven years, and at last said to him: "Master, my time is up; I should like to go home and see my mother; so give me my wages." And the master said: "You have been a faithful and good servant, so your pay shall be handsome." Then he gave him a piece of silver that was as big as his head.

Hans took out his pocket handkerchief, put the piece of silver into it, threw it over his shoulder, and jogged off homeward. As he went lazily on, dragging one foot after the other, a man came in sight, trotting along gayly on a capital horse. "Ah!" cried Hans aloud, "what a fine thing it is to ride on horseback! He trips against no stones, spares his shoes, and yet gets on he hardly knows how." The horseman heard this, and said: "Well, Hans, why do you go on foot, then?" "Ah," said he, "I have this heavy load to carry; to be sure it is silver, but it is so heavy that I can't hold up my head, and it hurts my shoulders sadly." "What do you say to changing?" said the horseman; "I will give you my horse, and you shall give me the silver." "With all my heart," said Hans; "but I tell you one thing, — you 'll have a weary task to drag it along." The horseman got off, took the silver, helped Hans up, gave him the bridle into his hands, and said: "When you want to go very fast, you must smack your lips loud, and cry 'Jip.'"

Hans was delighted as he sat on the horse and rode merrily on. After a time he thought he should like to go a little faster, so he smacked his lips and cried "Jip." Away went the horse full gallop; and before Hans knew what he was about he was thrown off, and lay in a ditch by the roadside; and his horse would have run off if a shepherd who was coming by, driving a cow, had not stopped it. Hans soon came to himself, and got up on his legs again. He was sadly vexed and said to the shepherd: "This riding is no joke when a man gets on a beast like this, that stumbles and flings him off as if he would break his neck. However, I am off now once for all: I like your cow a great deal better; one can walk along at one's leisure behind her, and have milk, butter, and cheese every day into the bargain. What would I give to have such a cow!" "Well," said the shepherd, "if you are so fond of her, I will exchange my cow for your horse." "Done!" said Hans merrily. The shepherd jumped upon the horse, and away he rode.

Hans drove off his cow quietly and thought his bargain a very lucky one. "If I have only a piece of bread, I can, whenever I like, eat my butter and cheese with it; and when I am thirsty, I can milk my cow and drink the milk: what can I wish for more?" When he came to an inn, he halted, ate up all his bread, and gave his last penny for a glass of beer: then he drove his cow towards his mother's village: and the heat grew greater as noon came on, till he began to be so hot and parched that his tongue clave to the roof of his mouth. "I can find a cure for this," thought he, "now will I milk my cow and quench my thirst;" so he tied her to the stump of a tree, and held his leathern cap to milk into; but not a drop was to be had.

While he was trying his luck and managing the matter very clumsily, the uneasy beast gave him a kick on the head that knocked him down, and there he lay a long while senseless. Luckily a butcher soon came by, wheeling a pig in a wheelbarrow. "What is the matter with you?" said the butcher, as he helped him up. Hans told him what had happened, and the butcher gave him a flask, saying: " There, drink and refresh yourself; your cow will give you no milk, she is an old beast good for nothing but the slaughter-house." " Alas, alas! " said Hans, " who would have thought it? If I kill her, what would she be good for? I hate cow beef, it is not tender enough for me. If it were a pig, now, one could do something with it; it would, at any rate, make some sausages."

" Well," said the butcher, " to please you I 'll change, and give you the pig for the cow." " Heaven reward you for your kindness! " said Hans, as he gave the butcher the cow, and took the pig off the wheelbarrow, and drove it off, holding it by the string that was tied to its leg.

So on he jogged, and all seemed now to go right with him. The next person he met was a countryman, carrying a fine white goose under his arm. The countryman stopped to ask what o'clock it was; and Hans told him all his luck, and how he had made so many bargains. The countryman said he was going to take the goose to a christening. " Feel," said he, " how heavy it is, and yet it is only eight weeks old. Whoever roasts and eats it, may cut plenty of fat off it, it has lived so well! " " You 're right," said Hans, as he felt it in his hand; " but my pig is heavy, too." Meantime the countryman began to look grave, and shook his head. " Listen, my friend," said he, " your pig may get you into trouble; in the village I have just come from, the squire has had a pig stolen from his sty. I was very much afraid, when I saw you, that you had the squire's pig; it will be hard for you if you are caught, because you will be thrown into the horse-pond."

Poor Hans was badly frightened. " Good man," cried he, " help me out of this scrape; you know this country better than I; take my pig and give me the goose." " I ought to have something into the bargain," said the countryman; " however, I will not be hard upon you, as you are in trouble." Then he took the string in his hand, and drove off the pig by a side path, and Hans went on his way homewards, free from care.

As he came to the last village, he saw a scissors-grinder, working away at his grinding, and singing. Hans watched him for a while, and then said, "You must be well off, master-grinder, you seem to be so happy." "Yes," said the other, "mine is a fine trade; a good grinder always has money in his pocket. But where did you get that splendid goose?" "I did not buy it, but exchanged a pig for it." "And where did you get the pig?" "I gave a cow for it." "And the cow?" "I gave a horse for it." "And the horse?" "I gave a piece of silver as big as my head for that." "And the silver?" "Oh! I worked hard for that seven long years." "You have done well in the world hitherto," said the grinder; "now if you could find money in your pocket whenever you put your hand into it, your fortune would be made." "That is true: but how is that to be done?" "You must turn grinder like me," said the other, "all you want is a grindstone; the rest will come of itself. This one is a little the worse for wear: I would not ask more than the value of your goose for it; — will you buy?" "How can you ask me such a question?" said Hans; "I should be the happiest man in the world if I could always have money in my pocket; what more could I wish for? Take the goose!" "Now," said the grinder, as he gave him a rough stone that lay by his side, "this is an excellent stone; manage it properly, and you can make a rusty nail cut with it."

Hans took the stone and went off with a light heart, and he said to himself: "I must have been born under a lucky star, for everything that I wish for comes to me of itself."

Meantime he began to feel tired, for he had traveled ever since daybreak; he was hungry, too, for he had given away his last penny in his joy at getting the cow. At last he could go no further, and the stone tired him very much; so he dragged himself to the edge of a pond, that he might drink and rest; so he laid the stone carefully by his side on the bank: but as he stooped down to drink, he forgot it, pushed it a little, and down it went into the pond. For a while he watched it sinking in the deep clear water, then sprang up for joy, and again fell upon his knees, and thanked heaven for taking away his only plague, the heavy stone. "How happy am I," cried he: "no one was ever so lucky as I am." Then he got up with a light and merry heart, and went on free from all his troubles, till he reached his mother's house.

THE NOSE

D ID you ever hear the story of the three poor soldiers, who, after having fought hard in the wars, set out on their road home, begging their way as they went?

They had journeyed on a long way, sick at heart with their bad luck at thus being turned loose on the world in their old age, when one evening they reached a deep gloomy wood through which they must pass; night came fast upon them, and they found that they must, however unwillingly, sleep in the woods; so to make all as safe as they could, it was agreed that two should lie down and sleep, while a third sat up and watched lest wild beasts should break in and tear them to pieces; when he was tired, he was to wake one of the others and sleep in his turn, and so on with the third, so as to share the work fairly among them.

The two who were to rest first soon lay down and fell fast asleep, and the other made himself a good fire under the trees and sat down by the side to keep watch. He had not sat long before suddenly up came a little man in a red jacket. "Who's there?" said he. "A friend," said the soldier. "What sort of a friend?"

"An old broken soldier," said the other, "with his two comrades who have nothing left to live on; come, sit down and warm yourself." "Well, my worthy fellow," said the little man, "I will do what I can for you; take this and show it to your comrades in the morning." So he took out an old cloak and gave it to the soldier, telling him that whenever he put it over his shoulders anything that he wished would be fulfilled; then the little man made him a bow and walked away.

The second soldier's turn to watch soon came, and the first laid himself down to sleep; but the second man had not sat by himself long before up came the little man in the red jacket again. The soldier treated him in a friendly way as his comrade had done, and the little man gave him a purse, which he told him was always full of gold, let him draw as much as he would.

Then the third soldier's turn to watch came, and he also had the little man for his guest, who gave him a wonderful horn that drew crowds around it whenever it was played; and made every-one forget his business to come and dance to its beautiful music.

In the morning each told his story and showed his treasure; and as they all liked each other very much and were old friends, they agreed to travel together to see the world, and for a while only to make use of the purse. And thus they spent their time very joyously, till at last they began to be tired of this roving life, and thought they should like to have a home of their own. So the first soldier put his cloak on, and wished for a fine castle. In a moment it stood before their eyes; fine gardens and green lawns spread around it, and flocks of sheep and goats and herds of oxen were grazing about, and out of the gate came a fine coach with three dapple-gray horses to meet them and bring them home.

All this was very well for a time; but it would not do to stay at home always, so they got together all their rich clothes and servants, and ordered their coach with three horses, and set out on a journey to see a neighboring king.

Now this king had an only daughter, and as he took the three soldiers for princes, he gave them a kind welcome. One day as the second soldier was walking with the princess, she saw him with the wonderful purse in his hand. When she asked him what it was, he was foolish enough to tell her; — though indeed it did not much signify, for she was a witch and knew all the wonderful things that the three soldiers brought. Now this princess was very cunning and artful; so she set to work and made a purse so like the soldier's that no one would know one from the other, and then asked him to come and see her, and made him drink some wine that she had got ready for him, till he fell fast asleep. Then she felt in his pocket, and took away the wonderful purse and left the one she had made in its place.

The next morning, the soldiers set out home, and soon after they reached their castle, happening to want some money, they went to their purse for it, and found something indeed in it, but to their great sorrow when they had emptied it, none came in place of what they took. Then the cheat was soon found out; for the second soldier knew where he had been, and how he had told the story to the princess, and he guessed that she had betrayed him. "Alas!" cried he, "poor wretches that we are, what shall we do?" "Oh!" said the first soldier, "let no gray hairs grow for this mishap; I will soon get the purse back."

So he threw his cloak across his shoulders and wished himself in the princess's chamber. There he found her sitting alone, counting the gold that fell around her in a shower from the purse. But the soldier stood looking at her too long, for the moment she saw him she started up and cried out with all her voice: "Thieves! Thieves!" so that the whole court came running in, and tried to seize him. The poor soldier now began to be dreadfully frightened in his turn, and thought it was high time to make the best of his way off; so without thinking of the ready way of traveling that his cloak gave him, he ran to the window, opened it, and jumped out; and unluckily in his haste his cloak caught and was left hanging, to the great joy of the princess, who knew its worth.

The poor soldier made the best of his way home to his comrades on foot and in a very downcast mood; but the third soldier told him to keep up his heart, and took his horn and blew a merry tune.   At the first blast, a countless troop of foot and horse came rushing to their aid, and they set out to make war against their enemy.   Then the king's palace was besieged, and he was told that he must give up the purse and cloak, or not one stone would be left upon another.   And the king went into his daughter's chamber and talked with her; but she said: "Let me try first if I cannot beat them some other way."   So she thought of a cunning scheme to overreach them, and dressed herself as a poor girl with a basket on her arm; and set out by night with her maid, and went into the enemy's camp to sell trinkets.

In the morning, she began to wander about, singing so beautifully that all the tents were emptied, and the soldiers ran round in crowds and thought of nothing but hearing her sing. Amongst the rest, came the soldier to whom the horn belonged, and as soon as she saw him she winked to her maid, who slipped quietly through the crowd and went into his tent, where it hung, and stole it away.   This done, they both returned safely to the palace; the besieging army went away, the three wonderful gifts were left in the hands of the princess, and the three soldiers were as penniless and forlorn as when the little man with the red jacket found them in the wood.

Poor fellows! they began to wonder what they could do now.   "Comrades," at last said the second soldier, who had had the purse, "we had better part; we cannot live together, let each seek his bread as best he can."   So he turned to the right and the other two to the left; for they preferred to travel together.   Then on he went till he came to the wood where they had met with such good luck before.   He walked on a long time, till evening began to fall, when he sat down beneath a tree and soon fell asleep.

In the morning, when he awoke, he was delighted to see that the tree was laden with beautiful apples. He was hungry enough, so he soon plucked and ate first one, then a second, then a third. A strange feeling came over his nose; when he put the apple to his mouth something was in the way. He felt it, and found that it was his nose, which had grown till it hung down on his breast. It did not stop there, but grew and grew. "Heavens!" thought he, "when will it have done growing?" And well might he ask, for by this time it had reached the ground as he sat on the grass, and it kept on growing till he could not bear its weight, or raise himself up; and it seemed as though it would never end, for already it stretched its great length all through the wood.

Meantime his comrades were journeying on, till suddenly one of them stumbled against something. "What can that be?" asked the other. They looked, and could think of nothing that it looked like but a nose. "We will follow it and find the owner," said they; so they traced it till at last they found their poor comrade lying stretched out beneath the apple tree. What could they do? They tried in vain to carry him. They caught a horse that was passing by, and raised him upon its back; but it soon tired of carrying such a load. They sat down in despair, when up came the little man in the red jacket. "Why, how now, friend?" said he, laughing; "well, I must find a cure for you, I see." So he told them to gather a pear from a tree that grew close by, and the nose would come all right again. No time was lost, and the nose was soon brought to its proper size, to the poor soldier's great joy.

"I will do still more for you," said the little man; "take some of those pears and apples with you; whoever eats one of the apples will have his nose grow just as yours did; but if you give him a pear, it will become natural again. Go to the princess and get her to eat some of your apples; her nose will grow twenty times as long as yours did, and you will get what you want of her."

They thanked their old friend heartily for all his kindness, and it was agreed that the poor soldier who had already tried the power of the apple should undertake the task. So he dressed himself as a gardener, and went to the king's palace, and said he had some remarkable apples to sell. Every one that saw them was delighted and wanted to taste them, but he said they were for the princess only; and she soon sent her maid to buy his stock. They were so fine that she soon began eating them, and had already eaten three when she too began to wonder what ailed her nose, for it grew and grew, down to the ground, out of the window, and over the garden, nobody knows where.

Then the king issued a proclamation that whoever would heal this dreadful disease should be richly rewarded. Many tried, but the princess got no relief. And now the old soldier dressed himself very sprucely as a doctor, and said he could cure her; so he chopped up some of the apple, and to punish her a little more gave her a dose, saying he would call to-morrow and see her again. The morrow came, and as, of course, the nose had been growing fast all night, the poor princess was in a dreadful plight. So the doctor chopped up a very little of the pear and gave her, and said he was sure that would do her good, and that he would call again the next day. Next day came, and although the nose was a little smaller, yet it was still bigger than when the doctor first attended her.

Then he thought to himself, " I must frighten this cunning princess a little more before I shall get what I want of her; " so he gave her a little more of the chopped apple, and said he would call on the morrow. The next day the nose was much bigger than before, and the doctor said: " Something is working against my medicine, and is too strong for it; but I know through my art what it is; you have stolen goods about you, and if you do not return them, there is no hope for you." But the princess very stoutly denied this, so the doctor said: " Very well, you may please yourself, but I am sure I am right, and if you do not do as I say, you will die." Then he went to the king and told him how it was. " Daughter," said the king, " send back the cloak, the purse, and the horn that you stole."

So she ordered her maid to fetch all three, and gave them to the doctor, and begged him to give them back to the soldiers. As soon as he had them safe, he gave her a whole pear to eat, and the nose returned to its proper shape. Then the doctor put on the cloak, wished the king and all his court a good day, and was soon with his two brothers, who lived from that time happily at home in their palace, except when they went out in their coach with the three dapple-gray horses.

THE SELFISH SPARROW AND THE HOUSELESS CROWS

A SPARROW once built a nice little house for herself, and lined it well with wool, and protected it with sticks, so that it equally resisted the summer sun and the winter rains. A Crow, who lived close by, had also built a house, but it was not such a good one, being only made of a few sticks laid one above another on the top of a prickly-pear hedge. And so, one day when there was an unusually heavy shower, the Crow's nest was washed away, while the Sparrow's was not at all injured.

Then the Crow and her mate went to the Sparrow, and said, "Sparrow, Sparrow, have pity on us, and give us shelter, for the wind blows, and the rain beats, and the prickly-pear hedge thorns stick into our eyes."

But the Sparrow answered, "I'm cooking the dinner, I cannot let you in now, come again presently."

In a little while, the Crows returned, and said, "Sparrow, Sparrow, have pity on us, and give us shelter, for the wind blows, and the rain beats, and the prickly-pear hedge thorns stick into our eyes." The Sparrow answered, "I'm eating my dinner, I cannot let you in now, come again presently."

The Crows flew away, but in a little while returned, and cried once more, "Sparrow, Sparrow, have pity on us, and give us shelter, for the wind blows, and the rain beats, and the prickly-pear hedge thorns stick into our eyes." The Sparrow replied, "I'm washing the dishes, I cannot let you in now, come again presently."

The Crows waited a while, and then called out, "Sparrow, Sparrow, have pity on us, and give us shelter, for the wind blows, and the rain beats, and the prickly-pear hedge thorns stick into our eyes." But the Sparrow would not let them in, she only answered, "I'm sweeping the floor, I cannot let you in now, come again presently."

Next time the Crows came and cried, "Sparrow, Sparrow, have pity on us and give us shelter, for the wind blows, and the rain beats, and the prickly-pear hedge thorns stick into our eyes," she answered, "I'm making the beds, I cannot let you in now, come again presently." So, on one pretence or another, she refused to help the poor birds.

At last, when she and her children had had their dinner, and she had prepared and put away the dinner for the next day, and had put all the children to bed and gone to bed herself, she cried to the Crows, "You may come in now, and take shelter for the night." The Crows came in, but they were vexed at having been kept out so long in the wind and the rain; and when the Sparrow and her family were all asleep, the one said to the other, "This selfish Sparrow had no pity on us, she gave us no dinner, and would not let us in till she and all her children were comfortably in bed; let us punish her." So the two Crows took all the nice dinner the Sparrow had prepared for herself and her children to eat next day, and flew away with it.

THE WHITE CAT

ONCE upon a time there was a king who had three sons, who were all so clever and brave that he began to be afraid that they would want to reign over the kingdom before he was dead. Now the king, though he felt that he was growing old, did not at all wish to give up the government of his kingdom while he could still manage it very well, so he thought the best way to live in peace would be to divert the minds of his sons by promises which he could always get out of when the time came for keeping them.

So he sent for them all, and after speaking to them kindly he added:

"You will quite agree with me, my dear children, that my great age makes it impossible for me to look after my affairs of state as carefully as I once did. I begin to fear that this may affect the welfare of my subjects, therefore I wish that one of you should succeed to my crown; but in return for such a gift as this it is only right that you should do something for me. Now, as I think of retiring into the country, it seems to me that a pretty, lively, faithful little dog would be very good company for me; so, without any regard for your ages, I promise that the one who brings me the most beautiful little dog shall succeed me at once."

The three princes were greatly surprised by their father's sudden fancy for a little dog, but as it gave the two younger ones a chance they would not otherwise have had of being king, and as the eldest was too polite to make any objection, they accepted the commission with pleasure. They bade forewell to the king, who gave them presents of silver and precious stones and appointed to meet them at the same hour, in the same place, after a year had passed, to see the little dogs they had brought for him.

Then they went together to a castle which was about a league from the city, accompanied by all their particular friends, to whom they gave a grand banquet, and the three brothers promised to be friends always, to share whatever good fortune befell them, and not to be parted by any envy or jealousy; and so they set out, agreeing to meet at the same castle at the appointed time, to present themselves before the king together. Each one took a different road, and the two eldest met with many adventures; but it is about the youngest that you are going to hear. He was young, and gay, and handsome, and knew everything that a prince ought to know; and as for his courage, there was simply no end to it.

Hardly a day passes without his buying several dogs — big and little, greyhounds, mastiffs, spaniels, and lapdogs. As soon as he had bought a pretty one he was sure to see a still prettier, and then he had to get rid of all the others and buy that one, as, being alone, he found it impossible to take thirty or forty thousand dogs about with him. He journey from day to day, no knowing where he was going, until at last, just at nightfall, he reached a great, gloomy forest. He did not know his way, and to make matters worse it began to thunder and the rain poured down. He took the first path he could find, and after walking for a long time he fancied he saw a faint light, and began to hope that he was coming to some cottage where he might find shelter for the night. At length, guided by the light, he reached the door of the most splendid castle he could have imagined. This door was of gold covered with carbuncles, and it was the pure red light which shone from them that had shown him the way through the forest. The walls were of the finest porcelain in all the most delicate colors, and the prince saw that all the stories he had ever read were pictured upon them; but as he was quite terribly wet and the rain still fell in torrents, he could not stay to look about any more, but came back to the golden door. There he saw a deer's foot hanging by a chain of diamonds, and he began to wonder who could live in this magnificent castle.

"They must feel very secure against robbers," he said to himself. "What is to hinder any one from cutting off that chain and digging out those carbuncles and making himself rich for life?"

He pulled the deer's foot, and immediately a silver bell sounded and the door flew open, but the prince could see nothing but numbers of hands in the air, each holding a torch. He was so much surprised that he stood quite still, until he felt himself pushed forward by other hands, so that though he was somewhat uneasy, he could not help going on. With his hand on his sword, to be prepared for whatever might happen, he entered a hall paved with lapis-lazuli, while two lovely voices sang:

> "The hands you see floating above
>   Will swiftly your bidding obey;
> If your heart dreads not conquering love,
>   In this place you may fearlessly stay."

The prince could not believe that any danger threatened him when he was welcomed in this way, as, guided by the mysterious hands, he went toward a door of coral, which opened of its own accord, and he found himself in a vast hall of mother-of-pearl, out of which opened a number of other rooms, glittering with thousands of lights and full of such beautiful pictures and precious things that the prince felt quite bewildered. After passing through sixty rooms the hands that conducted him stopped, and the prince saw a most comfortable-looking arm-chair drawn up close to the chimney-corner. At the same moment the fire lighted itself, and the pretty, soft, clever hands took off the prince's wet, muddy clothes and presented him with fresh ones made of the richest stuffs, all embroidered with gold and emeralds. He could not help admiring everything he saw and the deft way in which the hands waited on him, though they sometimes appeared so suddenly that they made him jump.

When he was quite ready — and I can assure you that he looked very different from the wet and weary prince who had stood outside in the rain and pulled the deer's foot — the hands led him to a splendid room, upon the walls of which were painted the histories of Puss in Boots and a number of other famous cats. The table was laid for supper with two golden plates, and golden spoons and forks, and the sideboard was covered with dishes and glasses of crystal set with precious stones. The prince was wondering who the second place could be for, when suddenly in came about a dozen cats carrying guitars and rolls of music, who took their places at one end of the room, and under the direction of a cat who beat time with a roll of paper began to mew in every imaginable key and to draw their claws across the strings of the guitars, making the strangest kind of music that could be heard. The prince hastily stopped up his ears, but even then the sight of these comical musicians sent him into fits of laughter.

" What funny thing shall I see next? " he said to himself, and instantly the door opened and in came a tiny figure covered by a long black veil. It was conducted by two cats wearing black mantles and carrying swords, and a large party of cats followed, who brought in cages full of rats and mice.

The prince was so much astonished that he thought he must be dreaming, but the little figure came up to him and threw back its veil, and he saw that it was the loveliest little white cat it is possible to imagine. She looked very young and very sad, and in a sweet little voice that went straight to his heart she said to the prince:

"King's Son, you are welcome. The queen of the cats is glad to see you."

"Lady Cat," replied the prince, "I thank you for receiving me so kindly, but surely you are no ordinary pussy-cat? Indeed, the way you speak and the magnificence of your castle prove it plainly."

"King's Son," said the white cat, "I beg you to spare me these compliments, for I am not used to them. But now," she added, "let supper be served and let the musicians be silent, as the prince does not understand what they are saying."

So the mysterious hands began to bring in the supper, and first they put on the table two dishes, one containing stewed pigeons and the other a fricassee of fat mice. The sight of the latter made the prince feel as if he could not enjoy his supper at all; but the white cat seeing this assured him that the dishes intended for him were prepared in a separate kitchen, and he might be certain that they contained neither rats nor mice; and the prince felt so sure that she would not deceive him that he had no more hesitation in beginning. Presently he noticed that on the little paw that was next him the white cat wore a bracelet containing a portrait, and he begged to be allowed to look at it. To his great surprise he found it represented an extremely handsome young man, who was so like himself that it might have been his own portrait! The white cat sighed as he looked at it and seemed sadder than ever, and the prince dared not ask any questions for fear of displeasing her; so he began to talk about other things, and found that she was interested in all the subjects he cared for himself, and seemed to know quite well what was going on in the world. After supper they went into another room, which was fitted up as a theater, and the cats acted and danced for their amusement, and then the white cat said good-night to him, and the hands conducted him into a room he had not seen before, hung with tapestry worked with butterflies' wings of every color. There were mirrors that reached from the ceiling to the floor, and a little white bed with curtains of gauze tied up with ribbons. The prince went to bed in silence, as he did not quite know how to begin a conversation with the hands that waited on him, and in the morning he was awakened by a noise and confusion outside his window, and the hands came and quickly dressed him in hunting costume. When he looked out all the cats were assembled in the courtyard, some leading greyhounds, some blowing horns, for the white cat was going out hunting. The hands led a wooden horse up to the prince and seemed to expect him to mount it, at which he was very indignant; but it was no use for him to object, for he speedily found himself upon its back, and it pranced gayly off with him.

The white cat herself was riding a monkey, which climbed even up to the eagles' nests when she had a fancy for the young eaglets. Never was there a pleasanter hunting party, and when they returned to the castle the prince and the white cat supped together as before, but when they had finished she offered him a crystal goblet, which must have contained a magic draught, for as soon as he had swallowed its contents he forgot everything, even the little dog that he was seeking for the king, and only thought how happy he was to be with the white cat! And so the days passed, in every kind of amusement, until the year was nearly gone. The prince had forgotten all about meeting his brothers, he did not even know what country he belonged to; but the white cat knew when he ought to go back, and one day she said to him:

"Do you know that you have only three days left to look for the little dog for your father, and your brothers have found lovely ones?"

The prince suddenly recovered his memory and cried: "What

can have made me forget such an important thing? My whole fortune depends upon it; and even if I could in such a short time find a dog pretty enough to gain me a kingdom, where should I find a horse who could carry me all that way in three days?" And he began to be very vexed.

But the white cat said to him: "King's Son, do not trouble yourself. I am your friend and will make everything easy for you. You can still stay here for a day, as the good wooden horse can take you to your country in twelve hours."

"I thank you, beautiful Cat," said the prince; "but what good will it do me to get back if I have not a dog to take to my father?"

"See here," answered the white cat, holding up an acorn. "There is a prettier one in this than in the Dog Star!"

"Oh! White Cat dear," said the prince, "how unkind you are to laugh at me now!"

"Only listen," she said, holding the acorn to his ear.

And inside it he distinctly heard a tiny voice say: "Bow-wow!"

The prince was delighted, for a dog that can be shut up in an acorn must be very small indeed. He wanted to take it out and look at it, but the white cat said it would be better not to open the acorn till he was before the king, in case the tiny dog should be cold on the journey. He thanked her a thousand times, and said good-bye quite sadly when the time came for him to set out.

"The days have passed so quickly with you," he said, "I only wish I could take you with me now."

But the white cat shook her head and sighed deeply in answer.

After all, the prince was the first to arrive at the castle where he had agreed to meet his brothers, but they came soon after, and stared in amazement when they saw the wooden horse in the court-yard jumping like a hunter.

The prince met them joyfully, and they began to tell him all their adventures; but he managed to hide from them what he had been doing, and even led them to think that a turnspit dog which he had with him was the one he was bringing for the king. Fond as they all were of one another, the two eldest could not help being glad to think that their dogs certainly had a better chance. The next morning they started in the same chariot. The elder brothers carried in baskets two such tiny, fragile dogs that they hardly dared to touch them. As for the turnspit, he ran after the chariot, and got so covered with mud that one could hardly see what he was like at all. When they reached the palace every one crowded round to welcome them as they went into the king's great hall; and when the two brothers presented their little dogs nobody could decide which was the prettier. They were already arranging between themselves to share the kingdom equally, when the youngest stepped forward, drawing from his pocket the acorn the white cat had given him. He opened it quickly, and there upon a white cushion they saw a dog so small that it could easily have been put through a ring. The prince laid' it upon the ground, and it got up at once and began to dance. The king did not know what to say, for it was impossible that anything could be prettier than this little creature. Nevertheless, as he was in no hurry to part with his crown, he told his sons that, as they had been so successful the first time, he would ask them to go once again, and seek by land and sea for a piece of muslin so fine that it could be drawn through the eye of a needle. The brothers were not very willing to set out again, but the two eldest consented because it gave them another chance, and they started as before. The youngest again mounted the wooden horse and rode back at full speed to his beloved white cat. Every door of the castle stood wide open and every window and turret was illuminated, so it looked more wonderful than before. The hands hastened to meet him and led the wooden horse off to the stable, while he hurried in to find the white cat. She was asleep in a little basket on a white satin cushion, but she very soon started up when she heard the prince, and was overjoyed at seeing him once more.

"How could I hope that you would come back to me, King's Son?" she said. And then he stroked and petted her, and told her of his successful journey, and how he had come back to ask her help, as he believed that it was impossible to find what the king demanded. The white cat looked serious and said she must think what was to be done, but that, luckily, there were some cats in the castle who could spin very well, and if anybody could manage it they could, and she would set them the task herself.

And then the hands appeared carrying torches, and conducted the prince and the white cat to a long gallery which overlooked the river, from the windows of which they saw a magnificent display of fireworks of all sorts; after which they had supper, which the prince liked even better than the fireworks, for it was very late and he was hungry after his long ride. And so the days passed quickly as before. It was impossible to feel dull with the white cat, and she had quite a talent for inventing new amusements — indeed, she was cleverer than a cat has any right to be. But when the prince asked her how it was that she was so wise she only said:

"King's Son, do not ask me; guess what you please. I may not tell you anything."

The prince was so happy that he did not trouble himself at all about the time, but presently the white cat told him that the year was gone, and that he need not be at all anxious about the piece of muslin, as they had made it very well.

"This time," she added, "I can give you a suitable escort"; and on looking out into the courtyard the prince saw a superb chariot of burnished gold, enameled in flame color with a thousand different devices. It was drawn by twelve snow-white horses, harnessed four abreast; their trappings were of flame-colored velvet, embroidered with diamonds. A hundred chariots followed, each drawn by eight horses and filled with officers in splendid uniforms, and a thousand guards surrounded the procession. "Go!" said the white cat, "and when you appear before the king in such state he surely will not refuse you the crown which you deserve. Take this walnut, but do not open it until you are before him; then you will find in it the piece of stuff you asked me for."

"Lovely Blanchette," said the prince, "how can I thank you properly for all your kindness to me? Only tell me that you wish it, and I will give up forever all thought of being king and will stay here with you always."

"King's Son," she replied, "it shows the goodness of your heart that you should care so much for a little white cat who is good for nothing but to catch mice; but you must not stay."

So the prince kissed her little paw and set out. You can imagine how fast he traveled when I tell you that they reached the king's palace in just half the time it had taken the wooden horse to get there. This time the prince was so late that he did not try to meet his brothers at their castle, so they thought he could not be coming and were rather glad of it, and displayed their pieces of muslin to the king proudly, feeling sure of success. And indeed the stuff was very fine and would go through the eye of a very large needle; but the king, who was only too glad to make a difficulty, sent for a particular needle, which was kept among the crown jewels and had such a small eye that everybody saw at once that it was impossible that the muslin should pass through it. The princes were angry and were beginning to complain that it was a trick, when suddenly the trumpets sounded and the youngest prince came in. His father and brothers were quite astonished at his magnificence, and after he had greeted them he took the walnut from his pocket and opened it, fully expecting to find the piece of muslin, but instead there was only

300

a hazel-nut. He cracked it, and there lay a cherry stone. Everybody was looking on, and the king was chuckling to himself at the idea of finding the piece of muslin in a nutshell.

However, the prince cracked the cherry stone, but every one laughed when he saw it contained only its own kernel. He opened that and found a grain of wheat, and in that was a millet-seed. Then he himself began to wonder, and muttered softly:

"White Cat, White Cat, are you making fun of me?"

In an instant he felt a cat's claw give his hand quite a sharp scratch, and hoping that it was meant as an encouragement he opened the millet-seed and drew out of it a piece of muslin four hundred ells long, woven with the loveliest colors and most wonderful patterns; and when the needle was brought it went through the eye six times with the greatest ease! The king turned pale and the other princes stood silent and sorrowful, for nobody could deny that this was the most marvelous piece of muslin that was to be found in the world.

Presently the king turned to his sons and said, with a deep sigh:

"Nothing could console me more in my old age than to realize your willingness to gratify my wishes. Go then once more, and whoever at the end of a year can bring back the loveliest princess shall be married to her, and shall, without further delay, receive the crown, for my successor must certainly be married." The prince considered that he had earned the kingdom fairly twice over, but still he was too well bred to argue about it, so he just went back to his gorgeous chariot, and, surrounded by his escort, returned to the white cat faster than he had come. This time she was expecting him, the path was strewn with flowers, and a thousand braziers were burning scented woods which perfumed the air. Seated in a gallery from which she could see his arrival, the white cat waited for him. "Well, King's Son," she said, "here you are once more, without a crown." "Madam," said he, "thanks to your generosity I have earned one twice over; but the fact is that my father is so loath to part with it that it would be no pleasure to me to take it."

"Never mind," she answered; "it's just as well to try and deserve it. As you must take back a lovely princess with you next time, I will be on the lookout for one for you. In the mean time let us enjoy ourselves; to-night I have ordered a battle between my cats and the river rats, on purpose to amuse you."

So this year slipped away even more pleasantly than the preceding ones. Sometimes the prince could not help asking the white cat how it was she could talk.

"Perhaps you are a fairy," he said. "Or has some enchanter changed you into a cat?"

But she only gave him answers that told him nothing. Days go by so quickly when one is very happy that it is certain the prince would never have thought of its being time to go back, when one evening as they sat together the white cat said to him that if he wanted to take a lovely princess home with him the next day he must be prepared to do as she told him.

"Take this sword," she said, "and cut off my head!"

"I!" cried the prince, "cut off your head! Blanchette darling, how could I do it?"

"I entreat you to do as I tell you, King's Son," she replied.

The tears came into the prince's eyes as he begged her to ask him anything but that — to set him any task she pleased as a proof of his devotion, but to spare him the grief of killing his dear pussy. But nothing he could say altered her determination, and at last he drew his sword, and desperately, with a trembling hand, cut off the little white head. But imagine his astonishment and delight when suddenly a lovely princess stood before him, and, while he was still speechless with amazement, the door opened and a goodly company of knights and ladies entered, each carrying a cat's skin! They hastened with every sign of joy to the princess, kissing her hand and congratulating her on being once more restored to her natural shape. She received them graciously, but after a few minutes begged that they would leave her alone with the prince, to whom she said:

"You see, prince, that you were right in supposing me to be no ordinary cat. My father reigned over six kingdoms. The queen, my mother, whom he loved dearly, had a passion for traveling and exploring, and when I was only a few weeks old she obtained his permission to visit a certain mountain of which she had heard many marvelous tales, and set out, taking with her a number of her attendants. On the way they had to pass near an old castle belonging to the fairies. Nobody had ever been into it, but it was reported to be full of the most wonderful things, and my mother remembered to have heard that the fairies had in their garden such fruits as were to be seen and tasted nowhere else. She began to wish to try for herself, and turned her steps in the direction of the garden. On arriving at the door, which blazed with gold and jewels, she ordered her servants to knock loudly, but it was useless; it seemed as if all the inhabitants of the castle must be asleep or dead. Now, the more difficult it became to obtain the fruit, the more the queen was determined that have it she would. So she ordered that they should bring ladders and get over the wall into the garden, but though the wall did not look very high, and they tied the ladders together to make them very long, it was quite impossible to get to the top.

"The queen was in despair, but as night was coming on she ordered that they should encamp just where they were, and went to bed herself, feeling quite ill, she was so disappointed. In the middle of the night she was suddenly awakened, and saw to her surprise a tiny, ugly old woman seated by her bedside, who said to her:

"'I must say that we consider it somewhat troublesome of your Majesty to insist upon tasting our fruit, but to save you any annoyance, my sisters and I will consent to give you as much as you can carry away on one condition — that is, that you shall give us your little daughter to bring up as our own.'

" ' Ah! my dear madam,' cried the queen, ' is there nothing else that you will take for the fruit? I will give you my kingdoms willingly.'

" ' No,' replied the old fairy, ' we will have nothing but your little daughter. She shall be as happy as the day is long, and we will give her everything that is worth having in Fairyland, but you must not see her again until she is married.'

" ' Though it is a hard condition,' said the queen, ' I consent, for I shall certainly die if I do not taste the fruit, and so I should lose my little daughter either way.'

" So the old fairy led her into the castle, and though it was still the middle of the night, the queen could see plainly that it was far more beautiful than she had been told, which you can easily believe, prince," said the white cat, " when I tell you that it was this castle that we are now in. ' Will you gather the fruit yourself, queen? ' said the old fairy, ' or shall I call it to come to you? '

" ' I beg you to let me see it come when it is called,' cried the queen; ' that will be something quite new.' The old fairy whistled twice, then she cried:

" ' Apricots, peaches, nectarines, cherries, plums, pears, melons, grapes, apples, oranges, lemons, gooseberries, strawberries, raspberries, come! '

" And in an instant they came tumbling in, one over another, and yet they were neither dusty nor spoiled, and the queen found them quite as good as she had fancied them. You see, they grew upon fairy trees.

" The old fairy gave her golden baskets in which to take the fruit away, and it was as much as four hundred mules could carry. Then she reminded the queen of her agreement and led her back to the camp, and next morning she went back to her kingdom; but before she had gone very far she began to repent of her bargain, and when the king came out to meet her she looked so sad that he guessed that something had happened, and asked what was the matter. At first the queen was afraid to tell him, but when, as soon as they reached the palace, five frightful little dwarfs were sent by the fairies to fetch me, she was obliged to confess what she had promised. The king was very angry, and had the queen and myself shut up in a great tower and safely guarded, and drove the little dwarfs out of his kingdom; but the fairies sent a great dragon who ate up all the people he met, and whose breath burned up everything as he passed through the country; and at last, after trying in vain to rid himself of the monster, the king, to save his subjects, was obliged to consent that I should be given up to the fairies. This time they came themselves to fetch me, in a chariot of pearl drawn by sea-horses followed by the dragon, who was led with chains of diamonds. My cradle was placed between the old fairies, who loaded me with caresses, and away we whirled through the air to a tower which they had built on purpose for me. There I grew up surrounded with everything that was beautiful and rare and learning everything that is ever taught to a princess, but without any companions but a parrot and a little dog, who could both talk, and receiving every day a visit from one of the old fairies, who came mounted upon a dragon. One day, however, as I sat at my window I saw a handsome young prince, who seemed to have been hunting in the forest which surrounded my prison, and who was standing and looking up at me. When he saw that I observed him he saluted me with great deference. You can imagine that I was delighted to have some one new to talk to, and in spite of the height of my window our conversation was prolonged till night fell; then my prince reluctantly bade me farewell. But after that he came again many times, and at last I consented to marry him, but the question was how was I to escape from my tower. The fairies always supplied me with flax for my spinning, and by great diligence I made enough cord for a ladder that would reach to the foot of the tower; but, alas! just as my prince was helping me to descend it, the crossest and ugliest of the old fairies flew in. Before he had time to defend himself my unhappy lover was swallowed up by the dragon. As for me, the fairies, furious at having their plans defeated, for they intended me to marry the king of the dwarfs and I utterly refused, changed me into a white cat. When they brought me here I found all the lords and ladies of my father's court awaiting me under the same enchantment, with the people of lesser rank invisible, all but their hands.

"As they laid me under the enchantment the fairies told me all my history, for until then I had quite believed that I was their child, and warned me that my only chance of regaining my natural form was to win the love of a prince who resembled in every way my unfortunate lover."

"And you have won it, lovely princess," interrupted the prince.

"You are indeed wonderfully like him," resumed the princess —"in voice, in features, and everything; and if you really love me my troubles will be at an end."

"And mine too," cried the prince, throwing himself at her feet, "if you will consent to marry me."

"I love you already better than any one in the world," she said; "but now it is time to go back to your father, and we shall hear what he says about it."

So the prince gave her his hand and led her out, and they mounted the chariot together; it was even more splendid than before, and so was the whole company. Even the horses's shoes were of rubies with diamond nails, and I suppose that is the first time such a thing was ever seen.

THE WHITE CAT

As the princess was as kind and clever as she was beautiful, you may imagine what a delightful journey the prince found it, for everything the princess said was charming.

When they came near the castle where the brothers were to meet, the princess got into a chair carried by four of the guards; it was hewn out of one splendid crystal and had silken curtains, which she drew round her that she might not be seen.

The prince saw his brothers walking upon the terrace, each with a lovely princess, and they came to meet him asking if he had also found a wife. He said that he had found something much rarer — a little white cat! At which they laughed very much and asked him if he was afraid of being eaten up by mice in the palace. And then they set out together for the town. Each prince and princess rode in a splendid carriage; the horses were decked with plumes of feathers and glittered with gold. After them came the youngest prince, and last of all the crystal chair, at which everybody looked with admiration and curiosity. When the courtiers saw them coming they hastened to tell the king.

" Are the ladies beautiful? " he asked anxiously.

And when they answered that nobody had ever before seen such lovely princesses he seemed quite annoyed.

However, he received them graciously, but found it impossible to choose between them.

Then turning to his youngest son he said:

" Have you come back alone, after all? "

" Your Majesty," replied the prince, " will find in that crystal chair a little white cat, which has such soft paws and mews so prettily that I am sure you will be charmed with it."

The king smiled and went to draw back the curtains himself, but at a touch from the princess the crystal shivered into a thousand splinters, and there she stood in all her beauty; her fair hair floated over her shoulders and was crowned with flowers, and her softly falling robe was of the purest white. She saluted the king gracefully, while a murmur of admiration rose from all around.

" Sire," she said, " I am not come to deprive you of the throne you fill so worthily. I have already six kingdoms — permit me to bestow one upon you and upon each of your sons. I ask nothing but your friendship and your consent to my marriage with your youngest son; we shall still have three kingdoms left for ourselves."

The king and all the courtiers could not conceal their joy and astonishment, and the marriage of the three princes was celebrated at once. The festivities lasted several months, and then each king and queen departed to their own kingdom and lived happily ever after.

THE CROW AND THE PITCHER

ONCE there was a thirsty crow. She had flown a long way looking for water to drink.

Suddenly she saw a pitcher. She flew down and saw it held a little water, but it was so low in the pitcher that she could not reach it.

"But I must have that water," she cried. "I am too weary to fly farther. What shall I do? I know! I 'll tip the pitcher over."

She beat it with her wings, but it was too heavy. She could not move it.

Then she thought awhile. "I know now! I will break it! Then I will drink the water as it pours out. How good it will taste!"

With beak and claws and wings she threw herself against the pitcher. But it was too strong.

The poor crow stopped to rest. "What shall I do now? I cannot die of thirst with water close by. There must be a way, if I only had wit enough to find it out."

After a while the crow had a bright idea. There were many small stones lying about. She picked them up one by one and dropped them into the pitcher. Slowly the water rose, till at last she could drink it. How good it tasted!

"There is always a way out of hard places," said the crow, "if only you have the wit to find it."

WHY THE SEA IS SALT

ONCE upon a time, long, long ago, there were two brothers, the one rich and the other poor. When Christmas eve came the poor one had not a bite in the house, either of meat or bread; so he went to his brother and begged him, in God's name, to give him something for Christmas Day. It was by no means the first time that the brother had been forced to give something to him, and he was not better pleased at being asked now than he generally was.

" If you will do what I ask you, you shall have a whole ham," said he. The poor one immediately thanked him and promised this.

" Well, here is the ham, and now you must go straight to Dead Man's Hall," said the rich brother, throwing the ham to him.

" Well, I will do what I have promised," said the other, and he took the ham and set off. He went on and on for the livelong day, and at nightfall he came to a place where there was a bright light.

" I have no doubt this is the place," thought the man with the ham. An old man with a long white beard was standing in the outhouse, chopping Yule logs.

" Good-evening," said the man with the ham.

" Good-evening to you. Where are you going at this late hour? " said the man.

" I am going to Dead Man's Hall, if only I am in the right track," answered the poor man.

"Oh! yes, you are right enough, for it is here," said the old man. "When you get inside they will all want to buy your ham, for they don't get much meat to eat there. But you must not sell it unless you can get the hand-mill which stands behind the door for it. When you come out again I will teach you how to stop the hand-mill, which is useful for almost everything."

So the man with the ham thanked the other for his good advice and rapped at the door.

When he got in, everything happened just as the old man had said it would: all the people, great and small, came round him like ants on an ant-hill, and each tried to outbid the other for the ham.

"By rights my old woman and I ought to have it for our Christmas dinner, but since you have set your hearts upon it I must give it up to you," said the man. "But if I sell it I will have the hand-mill which is standing there behind the door."

At first they would not hear to this, and haggled and bargained with the man, but he stuck to what he had said, and the people were forced to give him the hand-mill. When the man came out again into the yard he asked the old wood-cutter how he was to stop the hand-mill, and when he had learned that, he thanked him and set off home with all the speed he could, but did not get there until after the clock had struck twelve on Christmas eve.

"But where in the world have you been?" said the old woman. "Here I have sat waiting hour after hour, and have not even two sticks to lay across each other under the Christmas porridge-pot."

"Oh! I could not come before. I had something of importance to see about, and a long way to go, too; but now you shall just see!" said the man, and then he set the hand-mill on the table and bade it first grind light, then a table-cloth, and then meat, and beer, and everything else that was good for a Christmas eve's supper; and the mill ground all that he ordered. "Bless me!" said the old woman as one thing after another appeared; and she wanted to know where her husband had got the mill from, but he would not tell her that.

"Never mind where I got it. You can see that it is a good one, and the water that turns it will never freeze," said the man. So he ground meat and drink and all kinds of good things to last all Christmas-tide, and on the third day he invited all his friends to come to a feast.

Now, when the rich brother saw all that there was at the banquet and in the house he was both vexed and angry, for he grudged everything his brother had. "On Christmas eve he was so poor that he came to me and begged for a trifle, for God's sake, and now he gives a feast as if he were both a count and a king!" thought he. "But for Heaven's sake tell me where you got your riches from," said he to his brother.

"From behind the door," said he who owned the mill, for he did not choose to satisfy his brother on that point; but later in the evening, when he had taken a drop too much, he could not refrain from telling how he had come by the hand-mill. "There you see what has brought me all my wealth!" said he, and brought out the mill and made it grind first one thing and then another. When the brother saw that, he insisted on having the mill, and after a great deal of persuasion got it; but he had to give $300 for it, and the poor brother was to keep it till the hay-making was over, for he thought, "If I keep it as long as that I can make it grind meat and drink that will last many a long year." During that time you may imagine that the mill did not grow rusty, and when hay-harvest came the rich brother got it, but the other had taken good care not to teach him how to stop it. It was evening when the rich man got the mill home, and in the morning he bade the old woman go out and spread the hay after the mowers, and he would attend to the house himself that day, he said.

So when dinner-time drew near he set the mill on the kitchen table and said: "Grind herrings and milk pottage, and do it both quickly and well."

So the mill began to grind herrings and milk pottage, and first all the dishes and tubs were filled, and then it came out all over the kitchen floor. The man twisted and turned it and did all he could to make the mill stop, but howsoever he turned it and screwed it the mill went on grinding, and in a short time the pottage rose so high that the man was like to be drowned. So he threw open the parlor door, but it was not long before the mill had ground the parlor full too, and it was with difficulty and danger that the man could go through the stream of pottage and get hold of the door-latch. When he got the door open he did not stay long in the room, but ran out, and the herrings and pottage came after him, and it streamed out over both farm and field. Now, the old woman, who was out spreading the hay, began to think dinner was long in coming, and said to the women and the mowers: "Though the master does not call us home, we may as well go. It may be that he finds he is not good at making pottage, and I should do well to help him." So they began to straggle homeward, but when they had got a little way up the hill they met the herrings and pottage and bread, all pouring forth and winding about one over the other, and the man himself in front of the flood. "Would to Heaven that each of you had a hundred stomachs! Take care that you are not drowned in the pottage!" he cried as he went by them as if mischief were at his heels, down to where his brother dwelt. Then he begged him, for God's sake, to take the mill back again, and that in an instant, "for," said he, "if it grind one hour more the whole district will be destroyed by herrings and pottage." But the brother would not take it until the other paid him $300, and that he was obliged to do. Now the poor brother had both the money and the mill again. So it was not long before he had a farm-house much finer than that in which his brother lived, but the mill ground him so much money that he covered it with plates of gold; and the farm-house lay close by the sea-shore, so it shone and glittered far out to sea. Every one who sailed by there now had to put in to visit the rich man in the gold farm-house, and every one wanted to see the wonderful mill, for the report of it spread far and wide, and there was no one who had not heard tell of it.

After a long, long time came also a skipper who wished to see the mill. He asked if it could make salt. "Yes, it could make salt," said he who owned it, and when the skipper heard that he wished with all his might and main to have the mill, let it cost what it might, for, he thought, if he had it he would get off having to sail far away over the perilous sea for freights of salt. At first the man would not hear of parting with it, but the skipper begged and prayed, and at last the man sold it to him, and got many, many thousand dollars for it. When the skipper had got the mill on his back he did not long stay there, for he was so afraid that the man would change his mind, and he had no time to ask how he was to stop it grinding, but got on board his ship as fast as he could.

When he had gone a little way out to sea he took the mill on deck. "Grind salt, and grind both quickly and well," said the skipper. So the mill began to grind salt till it spouted out like water, and when the skipper had got the ship filled he wanted to stop the mill, but whichsoever way he turned it and how much soever he tried it went on grinding, and the heap of salt grew higher and higher, until at last the ship sank. There lies the mill at the bottom of the sea, and still day by day, it grinds on; and that is why the sea is salt.

THE LION IN HIS DEN

A LION who had grown old, and had no more strength to hunt for food, saw that he must get it by cunning. So he crept into a corner of his den, and made believe that he was very sick.

All the animals about came in to take a look at him. As they entered, he snapped them up for his food.

When a good many beasts had been caught in this way, a fox came along.

He did not enter the lion's den, but stood at a little distance from the opening. " How are you to-day, my friend? " asked he.

" Oh, I am very sick," said the lion. " I shall not live long. Come in and see me that I may say farewell to you."

" Ah, no! " said the fox. " I see that all the foot-prints point into your den, and none point out."

THE BOY WHO CRIED "WOLF!"

THERE was once a shepherd-boy who kept his flock at a little distance from the village. Once he thought he would play a trick on the villagers and have some fun at their expense. So he ran toward the village crying out, with all his might:

"Wolf! Wolf! Come and help! The wolves are at my lambs!"

The kind villagers left their work and ran to the field to help him. But when they got there the boy laughed at them for their pains; there was no wolf there.

Still another day the boy tried the same trick, and the villagers came running to help and were laughed at again.

Then one day a wolf did break into the fold and began killing the lambs. In great fright, the boy ran for help. "Wolf! Wolf!" he screamed. "There is a wolf in the flock! Help!"

The villagers heard him, but they thought it was another mean trick; no one paid the least attention, or went near him. And the shepherd-boy lost all his sheep.

That is the kind of thing that happens to people who lie: even when they do tell the truth they will not be believed.

TIT FOR TAT

THERE once lived a Camel and a Jackal who were great friends. One day the Jackal said to the Camel: "I know that there is a fine field of sugar-cane on the other side of the river. If you will take me across, I'll show you the place. This plan will suit me as well as you. You will enjoy the sugar-cane, and I am sure to find many crabs, bones, and bits of fish by the water-side, on which to make a good dinner."

The Camel consented, and swam across the river, taking the Jackal, who could not swim, on his back. When they reached the other side, the Camel went to eat the sugar-cane, and the Jackal ran up and down the river bank devouring all the crabs, bits of fish, and bones he could find.

But being so much smaller an animal, he had made an excellent meal before the Camel had eaten more than two or three mouthfuls; and no sooner had he finished his dinner than he ran round and round the sugar-cane field, yelping and howling with all his might.

The villagers heard him, and thought: "There is a jackal among the sugar-canes; he will be scratching holes in the ground, and spoiling the roots of the plants." And they all went down to the place to drive him away. But when they got there, they found, to their surprise, not only a jackal, but a camel, and drove him from the field and beat him, and beat him, until he was nearly dead.

When they had gone, the Jackal said to the Camel: "We had

better go home." And the Camel said: "Very well; then jump upon my back as you did before."

So the Jackal jumped upon the Camel's back, and the Camel began to re-cross the river. When they had got well into the water, the Camel said: "This is a pretty way in which you have treated me, friend Jackal. No sooner had you finished your own dinner than you must go yelping about the place loud enough to arouse the whole village, and bring all the villagers down to beat me black and blue, and turn me out of the field before I had eaten two mouthfuls! What in the world did you make such a noise for?"

"I don't know," said the Jackal. "It is a habit I have. I always like to sing a little after dinner."

The Camel waded on through the river. The water reached up to his knees — then above them — up, up, up, higher and higher, until he was obliged to swim. Then turning to the Jackal, he said: "I feel very anxious to roll."

"Oh, pray don't! Why do you wish to do so?" asked the Jackal.

"I don't know," answered the Camel. "It is a habit I have. I always like to have a little roll after dinner."

So saying, he rolled over in the water, shaking the Jackal off as he did so. And the Jackal was drowned, but the Camel swam safely ashore.

HERCULES AND THE WAGONER

AS a wagoner was driving a heavy cart through a miry lane, the wheels stuck fast in the clay, and the horses could get no farther.

The man, without making the least effort for himself, dropped on his knees and began calling upon Hercules to come and help him out of his trouble.

"Lazy fellow!" said Hercules, "get up and stir yourself. Urge your horses stoutly, and put your shoulder to the wheel. Heaven helps only those who help themselves."

THE LAMBIKIN

O NCE upon a time there was a wee, wee Lambikin, who frolicked about on his little tottery legs, and enjoyed himself very much.

Now one day he set off to visit his Granny, and was jumping with joy to think of all the good things he should get from her, when whom should he meet but a jackal, who looked at the tender young morsel and said: "Lambikin! Lambikin! I'll EAT YOU!"

But Lambikin only gave a little frisk and said:

> "*To Granny's house I go,*
> *Where I shall fatter grow;*
> *Then you can eat me so.*"

The jackal thought this reasonable, and let Lambikin pass.

By and by he met a vulture, and the vulture, looking hungrily at the tender morsel before him, said: "Lambikin! Lambikin! I'll EAT YOU!"

But Lambikin only gave a little frisk, and said:

> "*To Granny's house I go,*
> *Where I shall fatter grow;*
> *Then you can eat me so.*"

The vulture thought this reasonable, and let Lambikin pass.

By and by he met a tiger, and then a wolf and a dog and

320

an eagle, and all of these, when they saw the tender little morsel, said: "Lambikin! Lambikin! I'll EAT YOU!"

But to all of them Lambikin replied, with a little frisk:

> *"To Granny's house I go,*
> *Where I shall fatter grow;*
> *Then you can eat me so."*

At last he reached his Granny's house, and said, all in a great hurry: "Granny, dear, I've promised to get very fat; so, as people ought to keep their promises, please put me into the corn-bin *at once."*

So his Granny said he was a good boy, and put him into the corn-bin, and there the greedy little Lambikin stayed for seven days, and ate, and ate, and ate, until he could scarcely waddle, and his Granny said he was fat enough for anything, and must go home. But cunning little Lambikin said that would never do, for some animal would be sure to eat him on the way back, he was so plump and tender.

"I'll tell you what you must do," said Master Lambikin, "you must make a little drumikin out of the skin of my little brother who died, and then I can sit inside and trundle along nicely, for I'm as tight as a drum myself."

So his Granny made a nice little drumikin out of his brother's skin, with the wool inside, and Lambikin curled himself up snug and warm in the middle and trundled away gayly. Soon he met with the Eagle, who called out:

> *"Drumikin! Drumikin!*
> *Have you seen Lambikin?"*

And Mr. Lambikin, curled up in his soft, warm nest, replied:

> *"Fallen into the fire, and so will you.*
> *On little Drumikin! Tum-pa, tum-too!"*

"How very annoying!" sighed the eagle, thinking regretfully of the tender morsel he had let slip.

Meanwhile Lambikin trundled along, laughing to himself, and singing:

> "*Tum-pa, tum-too;*
> *Tum-pa, tum-too!*"

Every animal and bird he met asked him the same question:

> "*Drumikin! Drumikin!*
> *Have you seen Lambikin?*"

And to each of them the little slyboots replied:

> "*Fallen into the fire, and so will you.*
> *On little Drumikin! Tum-pa, tum-too!*"
> *Tum-pa, tum-too! tum-pa, tum-too!*"

Then they all sighed to think of the tender little morsel they had let slip.

At last the jackal came limping along, for all his sorry looks as sharp as a needle, and he, too, called out:

> "*Drumikin! Drumikin!*
> *Have you seen Lambikin?*"

And Lambikin, curled up in his snug little nest, replied gayly:

> "*Fallen into the fire, and so will you.*
> *On little Drumikin! Tum-pa —*"

But he never got any further, for the jackal recognized his voice at once, and cried: "Hullo! you've turned yourself inside out, have you? Just you come out of that!"

Whereupon he tore open Drumikin and gobbled up Lambikin.

DIAMONDS AND TOADS

THERE was once upon a time a widow who had two daughters. The eldest was so much like her in the face and humor that whoever looked upon the daughter saw the mother. They were both so disagreeable and so proud that there was no living with them.

The youngest, who was the very picture of her father for courtesy and sweetness of temper, was withal one of the most beautiful girls ever seen. As people naturally love their own likeness, this mother even doted on her eldest daughter, and at the same time had a horrible aversion for the youngest — she made her eat in the kitchen and work continually.

Among other things, this poor child was forced twice a day to draw water above a mile and a half away from the house and bring home a pitcherful of it. One day as she was at this fountain there came to her a poor woman, who begged of her to let her drink.

"Oh! ay, with all my heart, Goody," said this pretty little girl; and rinsing immediately the pitcher, she took up some water from the clearest place of the fountain and gave it to her, holding up the pitcher all the while, that she might drink the easier.

The good woman having drunk said to her:

"You are so very pretty, my dear, so good and so mannerly, that I cannot help giving you a gift." For this was a fairy who had taken the form of a poor country woman to see how far the civility and good manners of this pretty girl would go. " I will give you for gift," continued the fairy, " that at every word you speak there shall come out of your mouth either a flower or a jewel."

When this pretty girl came home her mother scolded at her for staying so long at the fountain.

" I beg your pardon, mamma," said the poor girl, " for not making more haste."

And in speaking these words there came out of her mouth two roses, two pearls, and two diamonds.

" What is it I see there? " said her mother, quite astonished. " I think I see pearls and diamonds come out of the girl's mouth! How happens this, child? "

This was the first time she had ever called her child.

The poor creature told her frankly all the matter, not without dropping out infinite numbers of diamonds.

" In good faith," cried the mother, " I must send my child thither. Come hither, Fanny. Look what comes out of thy sister's mouth when she speaks. Wouldst not thou be glad, my dear, to have the same gift given to thee? Thou hast nothing else to do but go and draw water out of the fountain, and when a certain poor woman asks you to let her drink to give it her very civilly."

" It would be a very fine sight indeed," said this ill-bred minx, " to see me go draw water."

" You shall go, hussy! " said the mother, " and this minute." So away she went, but grumbling all the way, taking with her the best silver tankard in the house.

She was no sooner at the fountain than she saw coming out of the wood a lady most gloriously dressed, who came up to her and asked to drink. This was, you must know, the very fairy who appeared to her sister, but had now taken the air and dress of a princess, to see how far this girl's rudeness would go.

"Am I come hither," said the proud, saucy slut, "to serve you with water, pray? I suppose the silver tankard was brought purely for your ladyship, was it? However, you may drink out of it, if you have a fancy."

"You are not over and above mannerly," answered the fairy, without putting herself in a passion. "Well, then, since you have so little breeding and are so disobliging, I give you for gift that at every word you speak there shall come out of your mouth a snake or a toad."

So soon as her mother saw her coming she cried out:

"Well, daughter?"

"Well, mother?" answered the pert hussy, throwing out of her mouth two vipers and two toads.

"Oh! mercy," cried the mother; "what is it I see? Oh! it is that wretch her sister who has occasioned all this; but she shall pay for it." And immediately she ran to beat her. The poor child fled away from her and went to hide herself in the forest not far from thence.

The king's son, then on his return from hunting, met her, and seeing her so very pretty, asked her what she did there alone and why she cried.

"Alas! sir, my mamma has turned me out of doors."

The king's son, who saw five or six pearls and as many diamonds come out of her mouth, desired her to tell him how that happened. She hereupon told him the whole story; and so the king's son fell in love with her, and considering with himself that such a gift was worth more than any marriage portion, conducted her to the palace of the king his father and there married her.

As for her sister, she made herself so much hated that her own mother turned her off; and the miserable wretch, having wandered about a good while without finding anybody to take her in, went to a corner of the wood and there died.

THE MAGPIE'S NEST

LONG ago, when the world was very young, the birds did not know how to build nests for themselves.

The Magpie was the only bird that knew how to build a nest well. His nest was covered all over, except a hole to go in and out.

The other birds talked a great deal about the wonderful little house which the Magpie could build.

They all wished they might build one just like it for their little birds. So one day two birds of every kind went to see the Magpie.

They said: "Sir Magpie, we have come to learn how to build nests for ourselves and our little birds. We will pay you well if you will show us how."

The Magpie said: "I shall be glad to show you how to build nests. But you must watch everything I do. First, I lay two sticks across each other, so."

"To be sure," said the Crow. "I knew it must begin with two sticks and they should be crossed, of course."

"Then mix some straw and some moss in this way," said the Magpie.

"Oh, yes, certainly," said the Jackdaw. "I guessed that without being taught."

"Then more moss, more straw and feathers, like this," said the Magpie.

THE MAGPIE'S NEST

" Yes, yes," said the Sparrow, " though no builder myself, I knew that was the way to do."

Still the Magpie went on, but the birds acted as if they knew everything he told them.

At last he would tell them no more, though the nest was built up only half way.

" If you knew all about nest-building, then why did you come here to learn it of me? " he said. " You may go and build your own nests. I 'll not tell you how I built mine."

Then away they all flew.

Each bird set to work to build himself a nest.

But when they had built up half way, they stopped, for they did not know how to go on.

So to this day their nests all look like the Magpie's, just cut in two.

THE ELVES AND THE SHOEMAKER

THERE was once a shoemaker who, through no fault of his own, had become so poor that at last he had only leather enough for one pair of shoes. So in the evening he cut out the shoes which he intended to begin upon the next morning, and since he had a good conscience he lay down quietly, said his prayers, and fell asleep.

In the morning he was preparing to sit down to work, when he looked, and there stood the shoes all finished on his table. He was so astonished that he did not know what to say. He took the shoes in his hands to examine them inside and out; and they were so neatly made that not a stitch was out of place, showing that they were done by a master hand.

Very soon a customer came in, and because the shoes pleased him so much he paid more than the ordinary price for them. With this money the shoemaker was able to purchase leather for two pairs of shoes. He cut them out in the evening, and next day was about to go to work with fresh courage; but there was no need for him to work, for the two pairs of shoes stood beautifully finished on his table. Presently customers came in, who paid him so well that he was able to buy leather for four pairs of shoes. The following morning he found the four pairs finished, and so it went on; what he cut out in the evening was finished in the morning, so that he was soon in comfortable circumstances again, and at last was becoming really prosperous.

One evening, not long before Christmas, the shoemaker said

to his wife: "What do you think of staying up to-night to see who it is that lends us the helping hand?"

The wife like the idea; so they lighted a candle and hid themselves in a corner of the room behind some clothes which were hanging there. At midnight came two little naked men, who sat down at the shoemaker's table, took up the work which was cut out, and set to work so nimbly, stitching, sewing, and hammering with their little fingers, that the shoemaker could not take his eyes off them. They did not stop till everything was finished and the shoes stood ready on the table; then they ran quickly away.

The next day the wife said to her husband: " The little men have made us rich, and we must show them how grateful we are. They must be almost frozen, running about with nothing on. I 'll tell you what we 'll do; I will make them little shirts, and coats, and vests, and trousers, and knit them stockings, and you shall make each of them a pair of shoes."

The shoemaker was pleased with this plan, and on Christmas eve, when everything was ready, they laid out the presents on the table instead of the usual work; but there was no leather to be seen, only these charming little clothes.

At first they were astonished, and then perfectly delighted. With the greatest speed they put on and smoothed down the pretty clothes, singing:

> " Now we are boys so fine to see,
> Why should we longer cobblers be? "

Then they danced and skipped, and leaped over chairs and benches. At last they danced out at the door. From this time on they came no more; but the shoemaker prospered as long as he lived, and succeeded in all his undertakings.

WHY THE BEAR IS STUMPY-TAILED

ONE day the Bear met the Fox, who came slinking along with a string of fish he had stolen.

"Whence did you get those?" asked the Bear.

"Oh! my Lord Bruin, I've been out fishing and caught them," said the Fox.

So the Bear had a mind to learn to fish, too, and bade the Fox tell him how to set about it.

"Oh! it's an easy thing for you," answered the Fox, "and soon learned. You've only got to go upon the ice, and cut a hole and stick your tail down into it; and so you must go on holding it there as long as you can. You're not to mind if your tail smarts a little; that's when the fish bite. The longer you hold it there the more fish you'll get; and then all at once out with it, with a cross pull sideways, and with a strong pull, too."

Yes; the Bear did as the Fox had said, and held his tail a long, long time down in the hole, till it was fast frozen in. Then he pulled it out with a cross pull, and it snapped short off. That's why Bruin goes about with a stumpy tail to this very day.

THE UGLY DUCKLING

IT was lovely summer weather in the country, and the golden corn, the green oats, and the haystacks in the meadows looked beautiful. On a sunny slope stood a pleasant old farmhouse, close by a deep river. Under some big burdock leaves on the bank sat a duck on her nest, waiting for her young brood to hatch; she was beginning to get tired of her task, for the little ones were a long time coming out of their shells.

At length one shell cracked, and then another, and from each egg came a living creature that lifted its head and cried, " Peep, peep." " Quack, quack," said the mother, and then they all quacked as well as they could, and looked about them on every side at the large green leaves. Their mother allowed them to look as much as they liked, because green is good for their eyes.

" How large the world is," said the young ducks, when they found how much more room they had now than when they were inside the egg-shell.

" Do you imagine this is the whole world? " asked the mother; " wait till you have seen the garden; it stretches far beyond that to the parson's field, but I have never ventured so far. Are you all out? " she continued, rising; " no, I declare, the largest egg lies there still. I wonder how long this is to last, I am quite tired of it "; and she seated herself again on the nest.

" Well, how are you getting on? " asked an old duck who paid her a visit.

" One egg is not hatched yet," said the duck, " it will not

break. But just look at all the others, are they not the prettiest little ducklings you ever saw?"

"Let me see the egg that will not hatch," said the old duck; "I have no doubt it is a turkey's egg. I was persuaded to hatch some once and after all my care and trouble with the young ones, they were afraid of the water. I quacked and clucked, but all to no purpose. I could not get them to venture in. Let me look at the egg. Yes, that is a turkey's egg; take my advice, leave it where it is, and teach the other children to swim."

"I think I will sit on it a little while longer," said the duck. "I have sat so long already, a few days will be nothing."

"Please yourself," said the old duck, and she went away.

At last the large egg hatched, and a young one crept forth crying, "Peep, peep." It was very large and ugly. The duck stared at it, and exclaimed, "It is very large and not like the others. I wonder if it really is a turkey. We shall soon find out when we go to the water. It must go in, if I have to push it in myself."

On the next day, the weather was delightful, and the sun shone brightly on the green burdock leaves, so the mother duck took her young brood down to the water, and jumped in with a splash. "Quack, quack," cried she, and one after another the little ducklings jumped in. The water closed over their heads, but they came up again in an instant, and swam about quite prettily with their legs paddling under them as easily as possible, and the ugly duckling swam with them.

"Oh," said the mother, "that is not a turkey; how well he used his legs and how upright he holds himself! He is my own child, and he is not so ugly after all if you look at him properly. Quack, quack! come with me now, I will take you to the farm-yard, but you must keep close to me, or you may be trodden upon; and, above all, beware of the cat."

The ducklings did as they were bid, and, when they came

to the yard, the other ducks stared and said: " Look, here comes another brood, as if there were not enough already! And what a queer looking object one of them is; we don't want him here," and then one flew at him and bit him in the neck.

" Let him alone," said his mother; " he is not doing any harm."

" Yes, but he is too big and ugly," said the spiteful duck, " and therefore he must be turned out."

They soon got to feel at home in the farmyard; but the poor duckling that had crept out of his shell last of all and looked so ugly, was bitten and pushed and made fun of, not only by the ducks, but by all the poultry.

" He is too big," they all said, and the turkey cock, who had been born into this world with spurs, and fancied himself really an emperor, puffed himself out and flew at the duckling, and became quite red in the head with passion, so that the poor little thing did not know where to go, and was quite miserable because he was so ugly and laughed at by the whole farmyard. So it went on from day to day, till it got worse and worse. The poor duckling was driven about by every one; even his brothers and sisters were unkind to him, and would say: " Ah, you ugly creature, I wish that cat would get you," and his mother said she wished he had never been born. The ducks pecked him, the chickens beat him, and the girl who fed the poultry kicked him. So at last he ran away, frightening the little birds in the hedge as he flew over the palings.

" They are afraid of me because I am so ugly," he said. So he closed his eyes and flew still farther, until he came out on a large moor, inhabited by wild ducks. Here he remained the whole night, feeling very tired and sorrowful.

In the morning, when the wild ducks rose in the air, they stared at their new comrade. " What sort of a duck are you? " they all said, coming round him.

He bowed to them and was as polite to them as he could be, but he did not reply to their question. "You are exceedingly ugly," said the wild duck, "but that will not matter if you do not marry into our family."

Poor thing! All he wanted was to stay among the rushes, and find something to eat and drink.

After he had been on the moor two days, some men came to shoot the birds there. How they terrified the poor duckling! He hid himself among the reeds, and lay quite still, when suddenly a dog came running by him, and went splash into the water without touching him.

"Oh," sighed the duckling, "how thankful I am for being so ugly; even a dog will not bite me."

It was late in the day before all became quiet, but even then the poor young thing did not dare to move. He waited for several hours, and then after looking carefully around him, hastened away from the moor as fast as he could. He ran over field and meadow till a storm arose and he could hardly struggle against it. Towards evening, he reached a poor little cottage. The duckling was so tired that he could go no farther; he sat down by the cottage, and then he noticed that there was a hole near the bottom of the door, large enough for him to slip through, which he did very quietly and got shelter for the night.

A woman, a tom-cat, and a hen lived in this cottage. The tom-cat whom his mistress called, "My little son," was a great favorite; he could raise his back and purr, and could even throw out sparks from his fur if it were stroked the wrong way. The hen had very short legs, so she was called, "Chickie short-legs." She laid good eggs, and her mistress loved her as if she had been her own child. In the morning the strange visitor was discovered, and the tom-cat began to purr and the hen to cluck.

"What is that noise about?" said the old woman, looking round the room, but her sight was not very good; therefore, when she saw the duckling, she thought it must be a fat duck that had strayed away from home. "Oh, what a prize!" she exclaimed, "I hope it is not a drake, for then I will have some duck's eggs. I must wait and see." So the duckling was allowed to remain on trial for three weeks, but there were no eggs.

Now the tom-cat was the master of the house, and the hen was the mistress, and they always said: "We and the world," for they believed themselves to be half the world, and the better half, too. The duckling thought that others might hold a different opinion on the subject, but the hen would not listen to such doubts. "Can you lay eggs?" she asked. "No." "Then have the goodness to hold your tongue." "Can you raise your back or purr, or throw out sparks?" said the tom-cat. "No." "Then you have no right to express an opinion when sensible people are speaking." So the duckling sat in a corner, feeling very low-spirited, till the sunshine and fresh air came into the room through the open door, and then he began to feel such a longing for a swim on the water, that he could not help telling the hen.

"What an absurd idea," said the hen, "you have nothing else to do, therefore you have foolish fancies. If you could purr or lay eggs, they would pass away."

"But it is delightful to swim about on the water," said the duckling, "and so refreshing to feel it close over your head, while you dive down to the bottom."

"Delightful, indeed!" said the hen; "why, you must be crazy! Ask the cat, he is the cleverest animal I know. Ask him how he would like to swim about on the water, or to dive under it, for I will not speak of my own opinion; ask our mistress, the old woman, there is no one in the world more clever than she is. Do you think she would like to swim, or to let the water close over her head?"

"You don't understand me," said the duckling.

"We don't understand you? Who can understand you, I wonder? Do you consider yourself more clever than the cat, or the woman? I will say nothing of myself. Don't imagine such nonsense, child, and thank your good fortune that you have been received here. Are you not in a warm room, and in society from which you may learn something? But you are a chatterer, and your company is not very agreeable. Believe me, I speak only for your good. I may tell you unpleasant truths, but that is a proof of my friendship. I advise you, therefore, to lay eggs, and learn to purr as quickly as possible."

"I believe I must go out into the world again," said the duckling.

"Yes, do," said the hen. So the duckling left the cottage, and soon found water on which he could swim and dive, but he was avoided by all other animals because he was so ugly.

Autumn came, and the leaves in the forest turned to orange and gold; then, as winter approached, the wind caught them as they fell and whirled them in the cold air. The clouds, heavy with hail and snowflakes, hung low in the sky, and the raven stood on the ferns, crying, "Croak, croak." It made one shiver with cold to look at him. All this was very sad for the poor little duckling.

One evening, just as the sun set, amid bright clouds, there came a large flock of beautiful birds out of the bushes. The duckling had never seen any like them before. They were swans, and they curved their graceful necks, while their soft plumage shone with dazzling whiteness. They uttered a singular cry as they spread their glorious wings and flew away from those cold regions to warmer countries across the sea. As they mounted higher and higher in the air, the ugly duckling felt a strange sensation as he watched them. He whirled himself in the water like a wheel, stretched out his neck towards them, and uttered a cry so strange that it frightened himself. Could he ever forget those beautiful happy birds; and when at last they were out of his sight, he dived under the water, and rose again almost beside himself with excitement. He knew not the names of these birds, nor where they had flown, but he felt towards them as he had never felt for any other bird in the world. He was not envious of these beautiful creatures, but he wished to be as lovely as they. Poor ugly creature, how gladly he would have lived even with the ducks, had they only given him encouragement. The winter grew colder and colder, he was obliged to swim about on the water to keep it from freezing, but every night the space on which he swam became smaller and smaller. At length it froze so hard that the ice in the water cracked as he moved, and the duckling had to paddle with his legs as well as he could, to keep the space from closing up. He became exhausted at last, and lay still and helpless, frozen fast in the ice.

Early in the morning, a peasant, who was passing by, saw what had happened. He broke the ice in pieces with his wooden shoe, and carried the duckling home to his wife. The warmth revived the poor little creature; but when the children wanted to play with him, the duckling thought they would do him some harm; so he started up in terror, fluttered into the milk-pan, and splashed the milk about the room. Then the woman clapped her hands, which frightened him still more. He flew first into the butter-cask, then into the meal-tub, and out again. What a condition he was in! The woman screamed, and struck at him with the tongs; the children laughed and screamed, and tumbled over each other, in their efforts to catch him; but luckily he escaped. The door stood open; the poor creature could just manage to slip out among the bushes, and lie down quite exhausted in the newly fallen snow.

It would be very sad, were I to relate all the misery and privations which the poor little duckling endured during the hard winter; but when it had passed, he found himself lying one morning in a moor, amongst the rushes. He felt the warm sun shining, and heard the lark singing, and saw that all around was beautiful spring. Then the young bird felt that his wings were strong, as he flapped them against his sides, and rose high into the air. They bore him onwards, until he found himself in a large garden, before he well knew how it had happened. The apple trees were in full blossom, and the fragrant elders bent their long green branches down to the stream which wound round a smooth lawn. Everything looked beautiful, in the freshness of early spring. From a thicket close by, came three beautiful white swans, rustling their feathers, and swimming lightly over the smooth water. The duckling remembered the lovely birds, and felt more strangely unhappy than ever.

"I will fly to these royal birds," he exclaimed, "and they will kill me, because I am so ugly, and dare to approach them; but it does not matter: better be killed by them than pecked by the ducks, beaten by the hens, pushed about by the girl who feeds the poultry, or starved with hunger in the winter."

Then he flew to the water, and swam towards the beautiful swans. The moment they espied the stranger, they rushed to meet him with outstretched wings.

"Kill me," said the poor bird; and he bent his head down to the surface of the water, and awaited death.

But what did he see in the clear stream below? His own image; no longer a dark, gray bird, ugly and disagreeable to look at, but a graceful and beautiful swan; and the great swans swam round the new-comer, and stroked his neck with their beaks, as a welcome.

Into the garden, presently came some little children, and threw bread and cake into the water.

"See," cried the youngest, "there is a new one"; and the rest were delighted, and ran to their father and mother, dancing and clapping their hands, and shouting joyously. "There is another swan come, a new one!"

Then they threw more bread and cake into the water, and said: "The new one is the most beautiful of all; he is so young and pretty." And the old swans bowed their heads before him.

Then he felt quite ashamed, and hid his head under his wing; for he did not know what to do, he was so happy, and yet not at all proud. He had been persecuted and despised for his ugliness, and now he heard them say he was the most beautiful of all the birds. Even the elder tree bent down its boughs into the water before him, and the sun shone warm and bright. Then he rustled his feathers, curved his slender neck, and cried joyfully, from the depths of his heart: "I never dreamed of such happiness as this, while I was an ugly duckling."

THE FIELD MOUSE AND THE TOWN MOUSE

A FIELD Mouse had a friend who lived in a house in town. Now the Town Mouse was asked by the Field Mouse to dine with him, and out he went and sat down to a meal of corn and wheat.

"Do you know, my friend," said he, "that you live a mere ant's life out here? Why, I have all kinds of things at home; come and enjoy them."

So the two set off for town, and there the Town Mouse showed his beans and meal, his dates, too, his cheese and fruit and honey. And as the Field Mouse ate, drank, and was merry, he thought how rich his friend was, and how poor he was himself.

But as they ate, a man all at once opened the door, and the mice were in such fear that they ran into a crack.

Then, when they would eat some nice figs, in came a maid to get a pot of honey or a bit of cheese; and when they saw her, they hid in a hole.

Then the Field Mouse would eat no more, but said to the Town Mouse: "Do as you like, my good friend; eat all you want, have your fill of good things, but you are always in fear of your life. As for me, poor mouse, who have only corn and wheat, I will live on at home, in no fear of any one."

THE SIX COMRADES

THERE was once a man who had served bravely in the wars, and when they were ended he received his discharge and three florins, which was all he had to face the world with.

"This is mean treatment!" said he. "But wait a bit; if only I can get hold of the right people, the king shall be made to give me the treasures of the whole kingdom."

So, full of wrath, he went into the forest, where he came across a man who had just uprooted six trees as if they had been corn-stalks.

"Wilt thou be my servant and travel with me?" said our hero.

"Yes," replied the man; "but first I must take home these few fagots to my mother," and lifting the bundle on his shoulder, he carried it away.

Then he returned to his master, who said: "We two shall be a match for all the world."

Now, when they had journeyed for a little space they met a huntsman, who was on his knees taking aim with his gun.

And the master said: "Tell me, huntsman, what it is you are going to shoot."

And the man answered: "Two miles off there is a fly sitting on a branch of an oak tree, whose left eye I intend to shoot out."

"Come with me!" said the master; "we three shall be a match for all the world."

The huntsman was quite willing, and he came with him, and they soon arrived at seven windmills whose sails were whirling round at tremendous speed, although there was not a breath of wind to stir a leaf on the trees.

Then said the master: " I cannot think what it is that drives the windmills, for there is not the slightest breeze." But going on farther with his servants for about two miles, they saw a man sitting on a tree, puffing out his cheeks and blowing. So the master said:

" My good fellow, what are you doing up there? "

" Oh," replied the man, " there are seven windmills two miles from here; just look how I am sending them around."

" Come with me! " cried the master; " we four shall be a match for all the world."

So the blower climbed down and accompanied him, and presently they came upon a man who was standing on one leg, for he had unbuckled the other and it was lying on the ground by his side. Then the master said:

" I suppose you want to make yourself more comfortable while resting? "

" No," said the man; " I am a runner, and in order not to race over the ground too quickly, I have unbuckled my leg, for, if I were to run with both, I should go faster than any bird flies."

" Come with me! " said the master; " we five shall be a match for the whole world."

The five comrades all started off together, and soon they met a man who had on a hat, which he wore tilted on one side of his head.

Then said the master: " Manners, my friend, manners. Don't wear your hat like that, but put it on properly; you look like a simpleton."

" I dare not do it," returned the man, " for if I did, there would come such a fearful frost that every bird in the sky would freeze and fall dead upon the ground."

"Come with me!" said the master; "we six shall be a match for all the world."

Then the six companions came to a city where the king had proclaimed that whoever should run in a race with his daughter and be victorious might become her husband, but if he lost the race he would also lose his head.

This was told to our hero, who said: "I will make my servant run for me."

Then the king answered: "Then must thou also forfeit thine own life as well as thy servant's, for both heads must be sacrificed if the race be lost."

When the conditions were agreed upon, and everything was arranged, the master buckled on the runner's other leg, saying: "Now, be as nimble as you can, and don't fail to win."

Now, the wager was that whoever was the first to bring water from a distant spring should be the winner.

The runner received the pitcher, as did also the king's daughter, and they both began to run at the same moment; but when the Princess had run a little way the runner was quite out of sight, and it seemed as if there had only been a rushing of the wind. In a very short time he reached the well, so he drew up the water to fill his pitcher and turned back.

But when he was half way home, he was overcome with fatigue, so he put the pitcher down, stretched himself on the ground, and fell asleep. He made a pillow of a horse's skull, which was lying close by, thinking that, as it was so hard, he would very soon wake up again.

In the meantime, the king's daughter, who was a splendid runner and ran better than many a man, reached the spring and hurried back with her pitcher of water. Suddenly, she saw the runner lying asleep on the wayside; she was overjoyed at this, and exclaimed: "The enemy is given into my hands!" Then, emptying his pitcher, she ran on as fast as she could.

Now, all would have been lost if by great good fortune the huntsman had not been standing on one side of the castle towers and had seen everything with his sharp eyes.

Said he: "The king's daughter shall be no match for us if I can help it." So, loading his gun, he aimed so true that he shot away the horse's skull from under the runner's head without harming him in the least.

This awakened the runner, who, springing up, saw in a flash that his pitcher had been emptied, and that the king's daughter was already far ahead of him.

However, he did not lose courage, but ran back swiftly to the well, drew up fresh water, filled his pitcher, and was back again full ten minutes sooner than the king's daughter.

"See what I can do," cried he, "when I really use my legs; what I did before could scarcely be called running."

The king was displeased, and so was his daughter, that a common discharged soldier should have won the race; so they consulted with each other how they could rid themselves of him, together with his five comrades.

Then the king said to his daughter: "Do not be afraid, my child, for I have found a way to prevent their coming back."

So he said to the six companions: "You must now eat, drink, and be merry." Saying which, he led them to a room that had an iron floor and iron doors, and even the windows were secured with iron bars.

In this apartment there was a table covered with the most delicious appetizing dishes; and the king said: "Now come in and sit down and enjoy yourselves."

Directly they were all inside he had the doors locked and bolted. This done, the king sent for the cook, and commanded him to light a fire underneath the room, until the iron should become red-hot.

The heat soon became so great that the six comrades guessed that the king wished to suffocate them.

But the man with the hat set it straight on his head, and immediately a frost fell on everything, and all the heat vanished, while the meats on the dishes began to freeze.

When the king believed they had all perished in the heat he ordered the doors opened, and there stood all the six men safe and sound.

They said they would like very much to come out and warm themselves, for the cold had been so intense that the meat had frozen on their plates.

Then the king commanded why the cook had not obeyed his commands.

But the cook pointed to the tremendous fire that was still burning, and the king saw that he could not harm the six comrades in this way.

In despair the king began to cast about in his mind for some other way to rid himself of his unwelcome guests; so he commanded the master to be sent before him.

"If you will give up all claim to my daughter," said he, "you shall have as much gold as you can wish for."

"Indeed, your Majesty, if you will only give me as much as my servant can carry, I will no more demand your daughter."

This pleased the king very much, and the master said that he would return in fourteen days to take away the gold.

Thereupon the master ordered all the tailors in the kingdom to sew him a sack of such a size that it would take fourteen days to make it. When it was finished he sent the strong man, who uprooted the trees, with the sack on his shoulder to the king.

So the king ordered a ton of gold to be fetched, which required sixteen men to carry; but the strong man took it up in one hand and said: "Why don't you bring more at a time? This scarcely covers the bottom of the sack."

So the king sent again and again for all his treasures to be brought, and the strong man threw it all into the sack, which was yet not half full.

"Bring me more!" he cried, "these few crumbs won't fill it."

Therefore they were obliged to bring seven thousand wagons laden with gold to the palace; these the strong man pushed into his sack, together with the oxen which were yoked to the wagons.

At last when everything that could possibly be found had been put in, he said: "Well, I must finish this; even if the sack is n't quite full, it's all the easier to tie it up."

Saying which, he lifted it on his back and went off with his companions.

When the king saw how this one man was carrying off all the wealth of his kingdom, he flew into a great passion and ordered all his cavalry to pursue the six comrades, commanding them to take away the sack from the strong man.

The two regiments soon overtook the six men and shouted to them: "Halt! You are our prisoners. Put down that sack of gold, or we will cut you to pieces."

"What is this you are saying?" asked the blower coolly. "We are your prisoners? Aha! First you must have a little dance together up in the air."

Then he puffed out his cheeks and blew the two regiments up into the air.

Some were blown away on the one side of the mountains, and some disappeared in the blue distance on the other.

A sergeant cried for mercy: he had nine wounds, and was a brave fellow and did not deserve such a disgrace. So the blower blew gently after him, which brought him back to the ground without hurting him.

"Now go home," said the blower, "and tell the king that

he may send any number of horsemen after us, but I will blow them all into the air."

When the king received this message he said: "Let the fellows go! They will meet with their deserts."

So the six comrades brought home the wealth of the kingdom which they divided, and lived happily to the end of their days.

ALADDIN AND THE WONDERFUL LAMP

THERE once lived a poor tailor, who had a son called Aladdin, a careless, idle boy who would do nothing but play all day long in the streets with little idle boys like himself. This so grieved the father that he died, yet in spite of his mother's tears and prayers Aladdin did not mend his ways. One day, when he was playing in the streets as usual, a stranger asked him his age and if he was not the son of Mustapha the tailor. "I am, sir," replied Aladdin; "but he died a long while ago." On this the stranger, who was a famous African magician, fell on his neck and kissed him, saying: "I am your uncle and knew you from your likeness to my brother. Go to your mother and tell her I am coming." Aladdin ran home and told his mother of his newly found uncle. "Indeed, child," she said, "your father had a brother, but I always thought he was dead." She prepared supper and bade Aladdin seek his uncle, who came laden with wine and fruit. He presently fell down and kissed the place where Mustapha used to sit, bidding Aladdin's mother not to be surprised at not having seen him before, as he had been forty years out of the country. He then turned to Aladdin and asked him his trade, at which the boy hung his head, while his mother burst into tears. On learning that Aladdin was idle and would learn no trade, he offered to take a shop for him and stock it with merchandise. Next day he bought Aladdin a fine suit of clothes and took him all over the city, showing him the sights, and brought him home at nightfall to his mother, who was overjoyed to see her son so fine.

ALADDIN'S LAMP

Next day the magician led Aladdin into some beautiful gardens a long way outside the city gates. They sat down by a fountain and the magician pulled a cake from his girdle, which he divided between them. They then journeyed onward till they almost reached the mountains. Aladdin was so tired that he begged to go back, but the magician beguiled him with pleasant stories and led him on in spite of himself. At last they came to two mountains divided by a narrow valley. "We will go no farther," said the false uncle. "I will show you something wonderful; only do you gather up sticks while I kindle a fire."

When it was lit the magician threw on it a powder he had about him, at the same time saying some magical words. The earth trembled a little and opened in front of them, disclosing a square flat stone with a brass ring in the middle to raise it by. Aladdin tried to run away, but the magician caught him and gave him a blow that knocked him down. "What have I done, uncle?" he said piteously; whereupon the magician said more kindly: "Fear nothing, but obey me. Beneath this stone lies a treasure which is to be yours, and no one else may touch it, so you must do exactly as I tell you."

At the word treasure Aladdin forgot his fears and grasped the ring as he was told, saying the names of his father and grandfather. The stone came up quite easily and some steps appeared. "Go down," said the magician. "At the foot of those steps you will find an open door leading into three large halls. Tuck up your gown and go through them without touching anything, or you will die instantly. These halls lead into a garden of fine fruit trees. Walk on till you come to a niche in a terrace where stands a lighted lamp. Pour out the oil it contains and bring it to me." He drew a ring from his finger and gave it to Aladdin, bidding him prosper.

Aladdin found everything as the magician had said, gathered some fruit off the trees, and having got the lamp arrived at the mouth of the cave. The magician cried out in a great hurry: "Make haste and give me the lamp." This Aladdin refused to do until he was out of the cave. The magician flew into a terrible passion, and throwing some more powder on to the fire, he said something and the stone rolled back into its place.

The magician left Persia forever, which plainly showed that he was no uncle of Aladdin's, but a cunning magician, who had read in his magic books of a wonderful lamp which would make him the most powerful man in the world. Though he alone knew where to find it, he could only receive it from the hand of another. He had picked out the foolish Aladdin for this purpose, intending to get the lamp and kill him afterward.

For two days Aladdin remained in the dark, crying and lamenting. At last he clasped his hands in prayer, and in so doing rubbed the ring, which the magician had forgotten to take from him. Immediately an enormous and frightful genie rose out of the earth, saying: "What wouldst thou with me? I am the slave of the ring and will obey thee in all things." Aladdin fearlessly replied, "Deliver me from this place!" whereupon the earth opened and he found himself outside. As soon as his eyes could bear the light he went home, but fainted on the threshold. When he came to himself he told his mother what had passed and showed her the lamp and the fruits he had gathered in the garden, which were in reality precious stones. He then asked for some food. "Alas! child," she said, "I have nothing in the house, but I have spun a little cotton and will go and sell it." Aladdin bade her keep her cotton, for he would sell the lamp instead. As it was very dirty she began to rub it, that it might fetch a higher price. Instantly a hideous genie appeared and asked what she would have. She fainted away, but Aladdin, snatching the lamp, said boldly: "Fetch me something to eat!" The genie returned with a silver bowl, twelve silver plates containing rich meats, two silver cups, and two bottles of wine. Aladdin's mother, when she came to herself, said: "Whence comes this splendid feast?" "Ask not, but eat," replied Aladdin. So they sat at breakfast till it was dinner-time, and Aladdin told his mother about the lamp. She begged him to sell it and have nothing to do with devils. "No," said Aladdin. "Since chance hath made us aware of its virtues, we will use it, and the ring likewise, which I shall always wear on my finger." When they had eaten all the genie had brought Aladdin sold one of the silver plates, and so on until none was left. He then had recourse to the genie, who gave him another set of plates, and thus they lived for many years.

One day Aladdin heard an order from the Sultan proclaimed that every one was to stay at home and close his shutters while the princess, his daughter, went to and from the bath. Aladdin was seized by a desire to see her face, which was very difficult, as she always went veiled. He hid himself behind the door of the bath and peeped through a chink. The princess lifted her veil as she went in, and looked so beautiful that Aladdin fell in love with her at first sight. He went home so changed that his mother was frightened. He told her he loved the princess so deeply that he could not live without her, and meant to ask her in marriage of her father. His mother, on hearing this, burst out laughing, but Aladdin at last prevailed upon her to go before the sultan and carry his request. She fetched a napkin and laid in it the magic fruits from the enchanted garden, which sparkled and shone like the most beautiful jewels. She took these with her to please the sultan, and set out, trusting in the lamp. The grand vizier and the lords of council had just gone in as she entered the hall and placed herself in front of the sultan. He took no notice of her. She went every day for a week and stood in the same place. When the council broke up on the sixth day the sultan said to his vizier: " I see a certain woman in the audience-chamber every day carrying something in a napkin. Call her next time, that I may find out what she wants." Next day, at a sign from the vizier, she went up to the foot of the throne and remained kneeling till the sultan said to her: " Rise, good woman, and tell me what you want." She hesitated, so the sultan sent away all but the vizier and bade her speak freely, promising to forgive her beforehand for anything she might say. She then told him of her son's violent love for the princess. " I prayed him to forget her," she said, " but in vain. He threatened to do some desperate deed if I refused to go and ask your Majesty for the hand of the princess. Now I pray you to forgive not me alone, but my son Aladdin." The sultan asked her kindly what she had in the napkin, whereupon she unfolded the jewels and presented them. He was thunderstruck, and turning to the vizier said: " What sayest thou? Ought I not to bestow the princess on one who values her at such a price?" The vizier, who wanted her for his own son, begged the sultan to withhold her for three months, in the course of which he hoped his son would contrive to make him a richer present. The sultan granted this, and told Aladdin's mother that though he consented to the marriage, she must not appear before him again for three months.

Aladdin waited patiently for nearly three months, but after two had elapsed his mother, going into the city to buy oil, found every one rejoicing and asked what was going on. " Do you not know," was the answer, " that the son of the grand vizier is to marry the sultan's daughter to-night?" Breathless, she ran and told Aladdin, who was overwhelmed at first, but presently bethought him of the lamp. He rubbed it, and the genie appeared, saying: " What is thy will?" Aladdin replied: " The sultan, as thou knowest, has broken his promise to me, and the vizier's son is to have the princess. My command is that to-night you bring hither the bride and bridegroom." " Master, I obey," said the genie. Aladdin then went to his chamber, where, sure enough, at midnight the genie transported the bed containing the vizier's son and the princess. " Take this new-married man," he said, "and put him outside in the cold, and return at day-break." Whereupon the genie took the vizier's son out of bed, leaving Aladdin with the princess. "Fear nothing," Aladdin said to her. "You are my wife, promised to me by your unjust father, and no harm shall come to you." The princess was too frightened to speak, and passed the most miserable night of her life, while Aladdin lay down beside her and slept soundly. At the appointed hour the genie fetched in the shivering bridegroom, laid him in his place, and transported the bed back to the palace.

Presently the sultan came to wish his daughter good-morning. The unhappy vizier's son jumped up and hid himself, while the princess would not say a word and was very sorrowful. The sultan sent her mother to her, who said: "How comes it, child, that you will not speak to your father? What has happened?" The princess sighed deeply, and at last told her mother how, during the night, the bed had been carried into some strange house, and what had passed there. Her mother did not believe her in the least, but bade her rise and consider it an idle dream.

The following night exactly the same thing happened, and next morning, on the princess' refusing to speak, the sultan threatened to cut off her head. She then confessed all, bidding him ask the vizier's son if it were not so. The sultan told the vizier to ask his son, who owned the truth, adding that, dearly as he loved the princess, he had rather die than go through another such fearful night, and wished to be separated from her. His wish was granted, and there was an end of feast and rejoicing.

When the three months were over Aladdin sent his mother to remind the sultan of his promise. She stood in the same place as before, and the sultan, who had forgotten Aladdin, at once remembered him and sent for her. On seeing her poverty the sultan felt less inclined than ever to keep his word, and asked his vizier's advice, who counseled him to set so high a value on the princess that no man living could come up to it. The sultan then turned to Aladdin's mother, saying: " Good woman, a sultan must remember his promises, and I will remember mine, but your son must first send me forty basins of gold brimful of jewels, carried by forty black slaves, led by as many white ones, splendidly dressed. Tell him that I await his answer." The mother of Aladdin bowed low and went home, thinking all was lost. She gave Aladdin the message, adding: " He may wait long enough for your answer! " " Not so long, mother, as you think," her son replied. " I would do a great deal more than that for the princess." He summoned the genie, and in a few moments the eighty slaves arrived and filled up the small house and garden. Aladdin made them set out to the palace, two and two, followed by his mother. They were so richly dressed, with such splendid jewels in their girdles, that every one crowded to see them and the basins of gold they carried on their heads. They entered the palace and, after kneeling before the sultan, stood in a half-circle round the throne with their arms crossed, while Aladdin's mother presented them to the sultan. He hesitated no longer, but said: " Good woman, return and tell your son that I wait for him with open arms." She lost no time in telling Aladdin, bidding him make haste. But Aladdin first called the genie. " I want a scented bath," he said, " a richly embroidered habit, a horse surpassing the sultan's, and twenty slaves to attend me. Besides this, six slaves, beautifully dressed, to wait on my mother; and lastly, ten thousand pieces of gold in ten purses." No sooner said than done. Aladdin mounted his horse and passed through the streets, the slaves strewing gold as they went. Those who had played with him in his childhood knew him not, he had grown so handsome. When the sultan saw him he came down from his throne, embraced him, and led him into a hall where a feast was spread, intending to marry him to the princess that very day. But Aladdin refused, saying, " I must build a palace fit for her," and took his leave. Once home, he said to the genie: " Build me a palace of the finest marble, set with jasper, agate, and other precious stones. In the middle you shall build me a large hall with a dome, its four walls of massive gold and silver, each side having six windows, whose lattices, all except one which is to be left unfinished, must be set with diamonds and rubies. There must be stables and horses and grooms and slaves. Go and see about it!"

The palace was finished by next day, and the genie carried him there and showed him all his orders faithfully carried out, even to the laying of a velvet carpet from Aladdin's palace to the sultan's. Aladdin's mother then dressed herself carefully and walked to the palace with her slaves, while he followed her on horseback. The sultan sent musicians with trumpets and cymbals to meet them, so that the air resounded with music and cheers. She was taken to the princess, who saluted her and treated her with great honor. At night the princess said good-bye to her father and set out on the carpet for Aladdin's palace, with his mother at her side and followed by the hundred slaves. She was charmed at the sight of Aladdin, who ran to receive her. "Princess," he said, " blame your beauty for my boldness if I have displeased you." She told him that, having seen him, she willingly obeyed her father in this matter. After the wedding had taken place Aladdin led her into the hall, where a feast was spread, and she supped with him, after which they danced till midnight.

Next day Aladdin invited the sultan to see the palace. On entering the hall with the twenty-four windows, with their rubies, diamonds, and emeralds, he cried: "It is a world's wonder! There is only one thing that surprises me. Was it by accident that one window was left unfinished?" "No, sir, by design," returned Aladdin. "I wished your Majesty to have the glory of finishing this palace." The sultan was pleased and sent for the best jewelers in the city. He showed them the unfinished window and bade them fit it up like the others. "Sir," replied their spokesman, "we cannot find jewels enough." The sultan had his own fetched, which they soon used, but to no purpose, for in a month's time the work was not half-done. Aladdin, knowing that their task was vain, bade them undo their work and carry the jewels back, and the genie finished the window at his command. The sultan was surprised to receive his jewels again, and visited Aladdin, who showed him the window finished. The sultan embraced him, the envious vizier meanwhile hinting that it was the work of enchantment.

Aladdin had won the hearts of the people by his gentle bearing. He was made captain of the sultan's armies and won several battles for him, but remained modest and courteous as before, and lived thus in peace and content for several years.

But far away in Africa the magician remembered Aladdin, and by his magic arts discovered that Aladdin, instead of perishing miserably in the cave, had escaped and had married a princess, with whom he was living in great honor and wealth. He knew that the poor tailor's son could only have accomplished this by means of the lamp, and traveled night and day till he reached the capital of China, bent on Aladdin's ruin. As he passed through the town he heard people talking everywhere about a marvelous palace. "Forgive my ignorance," he said. "What is this palace you speak of?" "Have you not heard of Prince Aladdin's palace," was the reply, "the greatest wonder of the world? I will direct you if you have a mind to see it." The magician thanked him who spoke, and having seen the palace knew that it had been raised by the genie of the lamp and became half-mad with rage. He determined to get hold of the lamp and again plunge Aladdin into the deepest poverty.

Unluckily, Aladdin had gone a-hunting for eight days, which gave the magician plenty of time. He bought a dozen copper lamps, put them into a basket, and went to the palace, crying,

"New lamps for old!" followed by a jeering crowd. The princess, sitting in the hall of twenty-four windows, sent a slave to find out what the noise was about, who came back laughing, so that the princess scolded her. "Madam," replied the slave, "who can help laughing to see an old fool offering to exchange fine new lamps for old ones?" Another slave, hearing this, said: "There is an old one on the cornice there which he can have." Now, this was the magic lamp, which Aladdin had left there, as he could not take it out hunting with him. The princess, not knowing its value, laughingly bade the slave take it and make the exchange. She went and said to the magician: "Give me a new lamp for this." He snatched it and bade the slave take her choice, amid the jeers of the crowd. Little he cared, but left off crying his lamps, and went out of the city gates to a lonely place, where he remained till nightfall, when he pulled out the lamp and rubbed it. The genie appeared, and at the magician's command carried him, together with the palace and the princess in it, to a lonely place in Africa.

Next morning the sultan looked out of the window toward Aladdin's palace and rubbed his eyes, for it was gone. He sent for the vizier and asked what had become of the palace. The vizier looked out too and was lost in astonishment. He again put it down to enchantment, and this time the sultan believed him and sent thirty men on horseback to fetch Aladdin in chains. They met him riding home, bound him, and forced him to go with them on foot. The people, who loved him, followed, armed, to see that he came to no harm. He was carried before the sultan, who ordered the executioner to cut off his head. The executioner made Aladdin kneel down, bandaged his eyes, and raised his scimitar to strike. At that instant the vizier, who saw that the crowd had forced their way into the courtyard and were scaling the walls to rescue Aladdin, called to the executioner to stay his hand. The people, indeed, looked so threatening that the sultan gave way and ordered Aladdin to be unbound, and pardoned him in the sight of the crowd.

Aladdin now begged to know what he had done. " False wretch! " said the sultan, " come hither," and showed him from the window the place where his palace had stood. Aladdin was so amazed that he could not say a word. " Where is your palace and my daughter? " demanded the sultan. " For the first I am not so deeply concerned, but my daughter I must have, and you must find her or lose your head." Aladdin begged for forty days in which to find her, promising if he failed to return and suffer death at the sultan's pleasure. His prayer was granted, and he went forth sadly from the sultan's presence.

For three days he wandered about like a madman, asking every one what had become of his palace, but they only laughed and pitied him. He came to the banks of a river and knelt down to say his prayers before throwing himself in. In so doing he rubbed the magic ring he still wore. The genie he had seen in the cave appeared and asked his will. " Save my life, genie," said Aladdin, " and bring my palace back." " That is not in my power," said the genie. " I am only the slave of the ring; you must ask him of the lamp." " Even so," said Aladdin, " but thou canst take me to the palace and set me down under my dear wife's window." He at once found himself in Africa, under the window of the princess, and fell asleep out of sheer weariness.

He was awakened by the singing of the birds, and his heart was lighter. He saw plainly that all his misfortunes were owing to the loss of the lamp, and vainly wondered who had robbed him of it.

That morning the princess rose earlier than she had done since she had been carried into Africa by the magician, whose company she was forced to endure once a day. She treated him so harshly that he dared not live there altogether. As she was dressing, one of her women looked out and saw Aladdin. The princess ran and opened the window, and at the noise she made Aladdin looked up. She called to him to come to her, and great was the joy of these lovers at seeing each other again. After he had kissed her Aladdin said: "I beg of you, princess, in God's name, before we speak of anything else, for your own sake and mine, tell me what has become of an old lamp I left on the cornice in the hall of twenty-four windows when I went hunting." "Alas!" she said, "I am the innocent cause of our sorrows," and told him of the exchange of the lamp. "Now I know," cried Aladdin, "that we have to thank the African magician for this! Where is the lamp?" "He carries it about with him," said the princess. "I know, for he pulled it out of his breast to show me. He wishes me to break my faith with you and marry him, saying that you were beheaded by my father's command. He is forever speaking ill of you, but I only reply by my tears. If I persist, I doubt not he will use violence."

Aladdin comforted her and left her for a while. He changed clothes with the first person he met in the town, and having bought a certain powder returned to the princess, who let him in by a little side door. "Put on your most beautiful dress," he said to her, "and receive the magician with smiles, leading him to believe that you have forgotten me. Invite him to sup with you and say you wish to taste the wine of his country. He will go for some, and while he is gone I will tell you what to do." She listened carefully to Aladdin, and when he left her arrayed herself gayly for the first time since she left China. She put on a girdle and head-dress of diamonds, and seeing in a glass that she was more beautiful than ever, received the magician, saying, to his great amazement: "I have made up my mind that Aladdin is dead and that all my tears will not bring him back to me, so I am resolved to mourn no more, and have therefore invited you to sup with me; but I am tired of the wines of China, and would fain taste those of Africa."

The magician flew to his cellar, and the princess put the powder Aladdin had given her into her cup. When he returned she asked him to drink her health in the wine of Africa, handing him her cup in exchange for his, as a sign she was reconciled to him. Before drinking the magician made her a speech in praise of her beauty, but the princess cut him short, saying: "Let us drink first, and you shall say what you will afterward." She set her cup to her lips and kept it there, while the magician drained his to the dregs and fell back lifeless. The princess then opened the door to Aladdin and flung her arms round his neck; but Aladdin put her away, bidding her leave him, as he had more to do. He then went to the dead magician, took the lamp out of his vest, and bade the genie carry the palace and all in it back to China. This was done, and the princess in her chamber only felt two little shocks, and little thought she was at home again.

The sultan, who was sitting in his closet mourning for his lost daughter, happened to look up, and rubbed his eyes, for there stood the palace as before! He hastened thither, and Aladdin received him in the hall of the twenty-four windows, with the princess at his side. Aladdin told him what had happened and showed him the dead body of the magician, that he might believe. A ten days' feast was proclaimed, and it seemed as if Aladdin might now live the rest of his life in peace; but it was not to be.

The African magician had a younger brother, who was, if possible, more wicked and more cunning than himself. He traveled to China to avenge his brother's death, and went to visit a pious woman called Fatima, thinking she might be of use to him. He changed clothes with her, colored his face like hers, put on her veil, and murdered her, that she might tell no tales. Then he went toward the palace of Aladdin, and all the people, thinking he was the holy woman, gathered round him, kissing his hands and begging his blessing. When he got to the palace there was such a noise going on round him that the princess bade her slave look out of the window and ask what was the matter. The slave said it was the holy woman, curing people by her touch of their ailments, whereupon the princess, who had long desired to see Fatima, sent for her. On coming to the princess the magician offered up a prayer for her health and prosperity. When he had done the princess made him sit by her and begged him to stay with her always. The false Fatima, who wished for nothing better, consented, but kept his veil down for fear of discovery. The princess showed him the hall and asked him what he thought of it. "It is truly beautiful," said the false Fatima. "In my mind it wants but one thing." "And what is that?" said the princess. "If only a roc's egg," replied he, "were hung up from the middle of this dome, it would be the wonder of the world."

After this the princess could think of nothing but the roc's egg, and when Aladdin returned from hunting he found her in a very ill humor. He begged to know what was amiss, and she told him that all her pleasure in the hall was spoiled for the want of a roc's egg hanging from the dome. "If that is all," replied Aladdin, "you shall soon be happy." He left her and rubbed the lamp, and when the genie appeared commanded him to bring a roc's egg. The genie gave such a loud and terrible shriek that the hall shook. "Wretch!" he cried, "is it not enough that I have done everything for you but you must command me to bring my master and hang him up in the midst of this dome? You and your wife and your palace deserve to be burned to ashes, but that this request does not come from you, but from the brother of the African magician, whom you destroyed. He is now in your palace disguised as the holy woman — whom he murdered. He it was who put that wish into your wife's head. Take care of yourself, for he means to kill you." So saying, the genie disappeared.

Aladdin went back to the princess, saying his head ached, and requesting that the holy Fatima should be fetched to lay her hands on it. But when the magician came near, Aladdin, seizing his dagger, pierced him to the heart. "What have you done?" cried the princess. "You have killed the holy woman!" "Not so," replied Aladdin, "but a wicked magician," and told her of how she had been deceived.

After this Aladdin and his wife lived in peace. He succeeded the sultan when he died and reigned for many years, leaving behind him a long line of kings.

ONE, TWO, THREE

ONE, two, buckle my shoe;
   Three, four, shut the door;
   Five, six, pick up sticks;
Seven, eight, lay them straight;
Nine, ten, a good fat hen;
Eleven, twelve, who will delve?
Thirteen, fourteen, maids a-courting;
Fifteen, sixteen, maids a-kissing;
Seventeen, eighteen, maids a-waiting?
Nineteen, twenty, my stomach's empty.
Pray, dame, give me some supper.

HISTORY OF FIVE LITTLE PIGS

SHOWING THE ADVENTURES OF

One Little Pig who went to Market,
Of a Second Little Pig who stayed at Home,
Of a Third Little Pig who got Roast Beef,
Of a Fourth Little Pig who had None, and
Of a Fifth Little Pig who cried " Wee! Wee! Wee! "
All the way home.

IF children wish to lead a happy life, they must try to become wise and good, and the sure way to do so is to be obedient to their parents and teachers, to be kind and gentle towards each other, and always ready to help those who cannot help themselves. The story of the Five Little Pigs shows how foolish and wicked it is to neglect the words of a parent, and also shows that those who do act as they are told get a great many other nice things as well as roast beef, and are consequently very happy.

The First Little Pig

There was once a family of five little pigs, and Mrs. Pig, their mother, loved them all very dearly. Some of these little pigs were very good, and took a great deal of pains to please their mother. But the best of all was the eldest pig. He was so useful and active that his mother and all his brothers called him Mr. Pig. He was a fine, strong, broad-backed fellow, with a large smiling face, and very long brown ears. One day his mother told him to go to market with the donkey and cart filled with vegetables. She told him to be very careful with Rusty — for that was the donkey's name — as he had a very bad temper. The cart was soon filled, and Rusty having been put in harness, away went Mr. Pig to market at a gallop.

Rusty went on very well for about a mile and a half, but then his bad temper began to show itself. First he drew himself up on his hind legs, then he fixed his fore legs firmly on the ground, and began kicking away at the front of the cart.

When he had quite tired himself out he made a great noise with his mouth and nostrils, and came to a standstill. All the coaxing and whipping that Mr. Pig gave him could not induce him to move a step. Mr. Pig saw a number of little pigs playing in a field by the roadside, so he went up to them and asked them to assist him.

A rope was tied in front of Rusty, and the little pigs dragged him and the cart along, while Mr. Pig gave Rusty a good whipping from behind.

At last all the kind little pigs, who were so willing to assist Mr. Pig, were tired out. One by one they were forced to quit their hold of the rope, till at last poor Mr. Pig found himself alone, and at a long distance from the market.

As perverse Rusty would not drag the cart, Mr. Pig took him out of the shafts, and sat down by the roadside, thinking what he should do. But he knew he would never get to market in that way.

So he started up, and placing himself in the shafts, pulled away by himself, and being a very strong and brave pig, he went along in this manner till within sight of the market-place.

When he got there, all the big and little pigs began to laugh at him. They called Mr. Pig a great many names, saying what a fool he was to drag his cart to market, instead of making his donkey do so. But they did not laugh so loudly when Mr. Pig told them all his struggles on the road; some of them went so far as to curl their tails in anger at the bad conduct of Rusty. Mr. Pig lost no time in selling off all his cart-load of vegetables.

Very soon after, Rusty came trotting into the market-place with his ears thrown forward, and eyeing with a deal of seeming pleasure the empty cart. Mr. Pig at first thought of giving lazy Rusty a sound whipping, but he thought also how much he was wanted at home, and as Rusty seemed willing to take his place in the cart, he thought it would be better to start for home without delay. So after embracing Rusty, he again placed him in the shafts, and away trotted the donkey as briskly as if nothing had occurred. When he got home, he told Mrs. Pig all his story, and she patted him on the back, and called him her best and most worthy son.

So you see there are two things to be learned from the conduct of the sapient Mr. Pig, and the way he managed his business. The first is, that we should never give in when we encounter a difficulty, but should set our wits to work to find a remedy, as Mr. Pig did when Rusty refused to go; and the second is, that it is better to make up a quarrel than to continue angry. For if Mr. Pig had not made friends with Rusty, he would have had to drag his cart home himself, and what a heavy job that would have been, when he was tired with his day's work!

THE SECOND LITTLE PIG

This little pig wanted very much to go with his eldest brother, the steady Mr. Pig, to market, and because his mother would not allow him to do so, he cried very much. But he was such a naughty pig, and so fond of mischief, that Mrs. Pig knew it would not be safe to trust him so far from home. She had to go to the miller's to buy some flour, for she wanted to make some nice cakes for Mr. Pig and his four brothers. Before she went out, she told this little pig to keep up a good fire to bake the cakes by when she came home. But when he was left alone, instead of learning his lessons, he began to tease the cat.

He pulled her ears, and put her paws on the bars of the grate, and did many cruel things, such as only so bad a little pig would think of. Then he dressed up Miss Fan in his mother's cloak and cap, and put a pipe in her mouth. After this he found his mother's birch which he made Fan hold in her paw. When he was tired of thus playing, he got the bellows, which had for a very long time been a puzzle to him. He could not tell how it was that the wind came from the pipe, and also where the wind came from. So he thought he would see the inside of the bellows, and judge for himself. Upon this he took a knife and cut right through the leather portion, quite spoiling it.

When he had done so, he could not find out at all what he wanted to know, so he began to cry. He thought he would amuse himself with his brother's toys, so he took down his brother's large kite, and big drum, and splendid horse with black and white spots on its back. But he soon got tired of merely playing with them, and then his habits of mischief began to show themselves. He forced the drum sticks through the parchments of the big drum, tore off the flowing tail of the kite, and broke one of the hind legs of the spotted horse, after which he pulled off its head from its body.

This very naughty pig after this went to the cupboard and finding out his mother's jam-pots, half emptied most of them. He did not even wait to look for a spoon, but forcing his paws into the jam, ate it in this way. Even this was not enough mischief for him. Taking the poker, he made it red-hot, and with it burnt more than ten great holes in the hearth-rug, and also burnt holes in his mother's fine new carpet. When his mother came home from the miller's with the flour, she sat down by the fire, and being very tired soon fell asleep. No sooner had she done so, than this bad little pig, getting a long handkerchief, tied her in her chair. But it was not very long before she awoke: very quickly she found out all the mischief that this little pig had been doing.

She soon saw all the damage he had done to his brother's playthings; quickly, too, she brought out her thickest, heaviest birch. The naughty little pig ran all round the room, and cried and begged his mother to forgive him.

But all this did not avail him in the least: his mother took him by the ear, and applied the birch to his back and sides till they tingled and smarted in such a way that he did not forget in a long time.

I am sure you will think that this little pig was rightly served for being so naughty, for only think how many things he might have done while his mother was away, if he had only been good.

He might have learnt part of the alphabet, or repeated over the pence table to himself while he attended to the cakes, or have made a net to keep the sparrows from the cherry tree, or have done half a hundred useful things; but instead of all this, the cross-grained pig must needs get into mischief. Oh, it was very bad!

THE THIRD LITTLE PIG

This little pig who had roast beef was a very good and careful little fellow. He gave his mother scarcely any trouble, and like his eldest brother, Mr. Pig, took a pleasure in doing what she bade him.

Here you see him sitting down; with a clean face and well washed hands, to some nice roast beef. His brother, who was idle and would not learn his lessons, is crying on a stool in the corner, with a dunce's cap on. And this is the reason why the good little pig had roast beef, while his brother, the idle pig, had none. He sat down quietly in the corner while he learned his lesson; having gone over it many times, saying one line after another to himself, he asked his mother to hear him repeat it. And he did so from the first line to the very last, without a single mistake. Mrs. Pig stroked him on the ears and forehead and called him a good little pig. After this he asked her to allow him to assist her in making the tea. He brought everything she wanted, and lifted off the tea-kettle from the fire without spilling a drop either on his toes or the carpet.

By-and-by he went out, after asking his mother's permission, to have a game with his hoop. He had not gone far, when he saw an old blind pig who, with his hat in his hand, was crying at the loss of his dog. That naughty dog had broken the string by which his master held him, and had run away. He felt in his pocket and found he had a half-penny, and this he gave to the poor old pig, like a kind and thoughtful little pig as he was.

Not very long after this he saw a great, strong, spiteful pig, who wore a cap on his head, beating one of his little brothers. Going up to the big pig, he told him what a shame it was that he should so ill-treat a poor little pig so much smaller than himself, who had done him no harm. The stupid great pig did not seem quite able to make out what this wise pig said to him, but he ran off. His poor little brother had been knocked down and bruised, and one of his eyes was very red and swollen; so he took out his handkerchief and tied it over his brother's face. Then he, in the most careful and tender manner, lead the beaten little pig home to his mother's house.

He placed one of his paws under his own arm, and so they went along. They were a long time getting home, for the poor pig who had been treated so badly was lame, and cried a great deal with the pain his eyes caused him.

But when they got home the careful little pig made him some nice hot mutton broth, and took it up to his bed for him to sip it. It was for such good, kind, thoughtful conduct as this that his mother almost every week gave this little pig roast beef.

And every day for a fortnight, so long as the poor little ill-used pig continued to suffer from his hurts, this good little pig visited him every day, and never came without bringing him a present of some kind or other. Sometimes it was a part of a turnip, or a bit of peeled mangold-wurzel, or some other light delicacy; sometimes a bunch of flowers to smell at with his poor little pale nose; and when poor piggie got better, our good-natured little friend brought him a bit of his own roast beef, and contented himself with half a portion, which was better than if he had eaten it all himself.

THE FOURTH LITTLE PIG

Unlike his brother, the little pig who had roast beef, this was a most perverse and wilful little pig. No wonder, then, that while his good brother had roast beef, he had none. His mother had set him to learn his lesson, but no sooner had she gone out into the garden, than he tore his book to pieces. He took the poker and forced the leaves through the bars of the grate, and held the poker in his hand till they were all burnt, laughing all the time.

When his mother came back, he did not let her know what he had done. But when she had fallen asleep, he ran off into the streets to play with the other idle little pigs, such as himself.

He was very fond of jumping over the backs of little pigs. Sometimes when the other little pig would refuse to allow him to jump over his back, or would not lend him his top, he would beat the poor pig in a spiteful way. And so it would happen that a number of the little pigs he had so ill-treated would fall upon him together, as you will see. Not having a ball of his own to play with, he thought he would take one away from a weak little pig who could not resist. But very shortly two of the bigger brothers of the little pig he had so robbed came up and gave him a sound beating. When they had done so they ran off and left him crying. He felt quite sorry, now that it was too late, that he had not stayed at home and read over and learned his lessons. He was afraid to go home, too, though he felt very tired and hungry. So he strayed about till it was quite dark and cold, and having lost his cap, he caught a cold in his head. Mrs. Pig at home was quite angry at first at his running away, so she went in search of him, as did also Mr. Pig and his brothers. It was very late indeed when they found him, and a great distance from home, for in his terror and fright he had lost his way, and he was put to bed: the doctor came to see him, and left a lot of very nasty physic which he had to take. He was in much pain, and had to lie in bed for more than a week, which never would have happened had he stayed at home and learned his lessons, instead of running off after destroying his books. And this is why he had no roast beef given to him.

Now you see this little pig was much worse off than the one I told you about just now, who was beaten by the spiteful pig, and to whom the little pig who had roast beef was so kind. For that pig had been unjustly beaten, and therefore had a right to be pitied by his friends, whereas this one had brought all his misfortunes upon himself. And it is much easier to bear a misfortune when we can say " it cannot be helped," than when we are obliged to acknowledge that it was our own fault as this little pig, sitting up in bed, and taking his nasty, bitter medicine, was compelled to do.

THE FIFTH LITTLE PIG

One day, in the summer-time, Mrs. Pig told all her sons, the five little pigs, that they might go into the country for a whole day. Mr. Pig, the eldest son, asked his brothers whether they would rather spend the day with him, or enjoy it alone, each one by himself. They all agreed to go with him, but one, this little pig that you see crying " Wee! wee! wee! " all the way home.

This little pig bought a new fishing-rod and tackle, and he was anxious to try to fish for the first time. He had made up his mind to fish in a stream that was close by, and so he said he would spend his holiday by himself.

" Very well," said Mrs. Pig, " but you must not go into Farmer Grumpey's grounds, for he is a very severe man, and he carries a great heavy whip."

The little pig told his mother that he did not intend to fish in this farmer's part of the river. Away he went; but he had told his mother a story — he did intend to go into Farmer Grumpey's grounds. When he got there he threw his line into the water, and watched the float for a long time. After a while he saw it bobbing about under the water, and very soon after he dragged an immense fish to land. Piggy took him up into his arms, and started towards home with him; but he soon found the fish was too heavy to be carried in that way, so he tried to drag him along by a string, but even this he found too troublesome a task. So he sat down at the foot of a tree, greatly perplexed in his mind as to what he should do next, biting his nails, and trying to think of some plan by which he might be able to get the fish along. He had only been thus thinking a short time, when he fancied he heard a noise like a growling of a dog, and looking round, to his great terror he discovered it to be nothing less than the gruff voice of Farmer Grumpey himself, who was making toward him with his heavy whip in his hand, shouting out and threatening Piggy with terrible punishment as soon as he should get near him; so he jumped up, caught the great fish in his arms, and ran off as fast as he could. Farmer Grumpey ran too, cracking his whip and shouting out, followed by one of his men. Piggy saw that they were overtaking him, so he dropped his fish and ran faster. But it was no use: poor Piggy was caught by the strong and rough farmer, who said he would cut his back for fishing in his grounds without his consent. So he laid his strong whip over Piggy's back for some time, after which this poor Piggy ran off crying " Wee! wee! wee-e-e!!! " all the way home. So now you have heard the story of these five little pigs. You may learn by it that those who are kind to others, and industrious, and good-natured, are sure to find friends and be esteemed, while the idle and ill-natured make themselves hated and despised. I should not forget to mention that I have heard that the idle pig, who had to wear a dunce's cap, became quite an altered character, and indeed grew so clever, that he came up to London at last, and made a great name as " Toby, the learned pig." But I only give this as a report.

THE STORY OF THE THREE LITTLE PIGS

"Once upon a time when pigs spoke rhyme
And monkeys chewed tobacco,
And hens took snuff to make them tough
And ducks went quack, quack, quack, O!"

THERE was an old sow with three little pigs, and as she had not enough to keep them, she sent them out to seek their fortune. The first that went off met a man with a bundle of straw, and said to him: "Please, man, give me that straw to build me a house." Which the man did, and the little pig built a house with it.

Presently came along a wolf, and knocked at the door, and said: "Little pig, little pig, let me come in." To which the pig answered: "No, no, by the hair of my chiny chin chin." The wolf then answered to that: "Then I 'll huff and I 'll puff, and I 'll blow your house in." So he huffed, and he puffed, and he blew his house in, and ate up the little pig.

The second little pig met a man with a bundle of furze and said: "Please, man, give me that furze to build a house." Which the man did, and the pig built his house.

Then along came the wolf, and said: "Little pig, little pig, let me come in." "No, no, by the hair of my chiny chin chin." "Then I 'll puff, and I 'll huff, and I 'll blow your house in."

So he huffed, and he puffed, and he puffed, and he huffed, and at last he blew the house down, and he ate up the little pig.

The third little pig met a man with a load of bricks, and said: "Please, man, give me those bricks to build a house with."

So the man gave him the bricks, and he built his house with them. So the wolf came, as he did to the other little pigs, and said:

"Little pig, little pig, let me come in." "No, no, by the hair of my chiny chin chin." "Then I'll huff, and I'll puff, and I'll blow your house in."

Well, he huffed, and he puffed, and he huffed, and he puffed, and he puffed, and he huffed; but he could NOT get the house down. When he found that he could not, with all his huffing and puffing, blow the house down, he said:

"Little pig, I know where there is a nice field of turnips."

"Where?" said the little pig.

"Oh, in Mr. Smith's home-field, and if you will be ready to-morrow morning I will call for you, and we will go together, and get some for dinner."

"Very well," said the little pig, "I will be ready. What time do you mean to go?"

"Oh, at six o'clock."

Well, the little pig got up at five, and got the turnips before the wolf came (which he did about six), and said:

"Little pig, are you ready?"

The little pig said: "Ready! I have been and come back again, and got a nice potful for dinner."

The wolf felt very angry at this, but thought that he would be up to the little pig somehow or other, so he said: "Little pig, I know where there is a nice apple tree."

"Where?" said the pig.

"Down at Merry-garden," replied the wolf, "and if you will not deceive me I will come for you at five o'clock to-morrow and get some apples."

Well, the little pig bustled up the next morning at four o'clock, and went off for the apples, hoping to get back before the wolf came; but he had farther to go, and had to climb the tree, so that just as he was coming down from it, he saw the wolf coming, which, as you may suppose, frightened him very much. When the wolf came up he said:

" Little pig, what! are you here before me? Are they nice apples? "

" Yes, very," said the little pig. " I will throw you down one."

And he threw it so far, that, while the wolf was gone to pick it up, the little pig jumped down and ran home. The next day the wolf came again, and said to the little pig:

" Little pig, there is a fair at Shanklin this afternoon. Will you go? "

" Oh, yes," said the little pig, " I will go. What time shall you be ready? "

" At three," said the wolf. So the little pig went off before the time as usual, and got to the fair, and bought a butter-churn, which he was going home with, when he saw the wolf coming. Then he could not tell what to do. So he got into the churn to hide, and by so doing turned it round, and it rolled down the hill with the pig in it, which frightened the wolf so much, that he ran home without going to the fair. He went to the little pig's house, and told him how frightened he had been by a great round thing which came down the hill past him. Then the little pig said:

" Hah, I frightened you, then. I had been to the fair and bought a butter-churn, and when I saw you, I got into it, and rolled down the hill."

Then the wolf was very angry indeed, and declared he *would* eat up the little pig, and that he would get down the chimney after him. When the little pig saw what he was about, he hung on the pot full of water, and made up a blazing fire, and, just as the wolf was coming down, took off the cover, and in fell the wolf; so the little pig put on the cover again in an instant, boiled him up, and ate him for supper, and lived happy ever afterwards.

JACK THE GIANT KILLER

IN the reign of the famous King Arthur there lived near the Land's End of England, in the county of Cornwall, a worthy farmer who had an only son named Jack. Jack was a bold boy; he took pleasure in hearing or reading stories of wizards, conjurers, giants, and fairies, and used to listen eagerly while his father talked of the great deeds of the brave knights of King Arthur's Round Table.

When Jack was sent to take care of the sheep and oxen in the fields, he used to amuse himself with planning battles, sieges, and the means to conquer or surprise a foe. He did not care much for the common sports of children; but hardly any one could equal him at wrestling, or if he met with a match for himself in strength, his skill and courage always made him the victor.

In those days there lived on St. Michael's Mount of Cornwall, which rises out of the sea at some distance from the mainland, a huge giant. He was eighteen feet high and three yards round, and his fierce and savage looks were the terror of all his neighbors. He dwelt in a gloomy cavern on the very top of the mountain, and used to wade over to the mainland in search of his prey.

When he came near, the people left their houses; and after he had feasted upon their cattle, he would throw half a dozen oxen upon his back, and tie three times as many sheep and hogs round his waist, and so march back to his own abode.

The giant had done this for many years, and the coast of Cornwall was greatly hurt by his thefts, when Jack boldly resolved to destroy him. He therefore took a horn, shovel, pick-ax, and a dark lantern, and early in a long winter's evening he swam to the Mount. There he set to work at once, and before morning he had dug a pit twenty-two feet deep, and almost as many feet broad. He covered it over with sticks and straw, and strewed some of the earth over these, to make it look just like solid ground. He then put his horn to his mouth, and blew such a loud and long tantivy, that the giant awoke and came toward Jack, roaring like thunder:

"You saucy villain, you shall pay dearly for breaking my rest; I will broil you for my breakfast."

He had scarcely spoken these words when coming one step farther he tumbled headlong into the pit, and his fall shook the very mountain.

"O ho, Mr. Giant!" said Jack, looking into the pit, "have you found your way so soon to the bottom? How is your appe-tite now? Will nothing serve you for breakfast this cold morn-ing but broiling Jack?"

The giant now tried to arise, but Jack struck him a blow on the crown of the head with his pickax, which killed him at once. Jack then made haste back to rejoice his friends with the news of the giant's death. When the justices of Cornwall heard of this valiant action, they sent for Jack, and declared that he should always be called Jack the Giant Killer; and they also gave him a sword and belt, upon which was written in letters of gold:

"This is the valiant Cornishman
Who slew the Giant Cormoran."

The news of Jack's great deeds soon spread over the western parts of England; and another giant, called Old Blunderbore, vowed to have revenge on Jack if it ever should be his fortune to get him into his power. This giant kept an enchanted castle in the midst of a lonely wood.

JACK THE GIANT KILLER

About four months after the death of Cormoran, as Jack was taking a journey into Wales, he passed through this very wood; and as he was weary, he sat down to rest by the side of a pleasant fountain, and there he fell into a deep sleep. The giant came to the fountain for water just at this time, and found Jack there; and as the lines on Jack's belt showed who he was, the giant lifted him up and laid him gently upon his shoulder to carry him to his castle. But as he passed through the thicket, the rustling of the leaves waked Jack, who was sadly afraid when he found himself in the clutches of Blunderbore.

Yet this was nothing to his fright soon after; for when they reached the castle, he beheld the floor covered all over with the skulls and bones of men and women. The giant locked Jack up in a large room, while he went to fetch another giant who lived in the same wood to enjoy a dinner off Jack's flesh with him. While he was away Jack heard dreadful shrieks, groans, and cries from many parts of the castle, and soon after he heard a mournful voice repeat these lines:

> " Haste, valiant stranger, haste away,
> Lest you become the giant's prey.
> On his return he 'll bring another
> Still more savage than his brother:
> A horrid, cruel monster, who,
> Before he kills, will torture you.
> Oh, valiant stranger! haste away,
> Or you 'll become these giants' prey."

This warning was so shocking to poor Jack that he was ready to go mad. He ran to the window, and saw the two giants coming along, arm in arm. This window was right over the gates of the castle.

" Now," thought Jack, " either my death or freedom is at hand."

There were two strong cords in the room; Jack made a

large noose with a slip-knot at the ends of both these, and as the giants were coming through the gates, he threw the ropes over their heads. He then made the other ends fast to a beam in the ceiling, and pulled with all his might till he had almost strangled them. When he saw that they were both quite black in the face and had not the least strength left, he drew his sword and slid down the ropes. He then killed the giants, and thus saved himself from a cruel death. Jack next took a great bunch of keys from the pocket of Blunderbore and went into the castle again. He made a strict search through all the rooms, and in them found three ladies tied up by the hair of their heads and almost starved to death. They told him their husbands had been killed by the giants, who had condemned them to be starved to death.

"Ladies," said Jack, " I have put an end to the monster and his wicked brother; and I give you this castle and all the riches it contains to make you some amends for the dreadful pains you have felt."

He then very politely gave them the keys of the castle, and went farther on his journey to Wales. As Jack had not taken any of the giant's riches for himself, and so had very little money of his own, he thought it best to travel as fast as he could. At length he lost his way, and when night came on he was in a lonely valley between two lofty mountains, where he walked about for some hours without seeing any dwelling place, so he thought himself very lucky at last in finding a large and handsome house.

He went up to it boldly and knocked loudly at the gate, when, to his great terror and surprise, there came forth a monstrous giant with two heads. He spoke to Jack very civilly, for he was a Welsh giant, and all the mischief he did was by private and secret malice, under the show of friendship and kindness. Jack told him that he was a traveler who had lost his way, on which the huge monster made him welcome, and led him into a room

where there was a good bed to pass the night in. Jack took off
his clothes quickly; but, though he was so weary, he could not
go to sleep. Soon after this he heard the giant walking backward and forward in the next room, and saying to himself:

> "Though here you lodge with me this night,
>   You shall not see the morning light;
>   My club shall dash your brains out quite."

"Say you so?" thought Jack. "Are these your tricks upon
travelers? But I hope to prove myself as cunning as you."

Then getting out of bed, he groped about the room, and at
last found a large, thick billet of wood, which he laid in his own
place in the bed, and then hid himself in a dark corner of the
room.

In the middle of the night the giant came with his great club
and struck many heavy blows on the bed, in the very place where
Jack had laid the billet; and then he went back to his own room,
thinking all Jack's bones were broken. Early in the morning
Jack put a bold face upon the matter, and walked into the giant's
room to thank him for his lodging.

The giant started when he saw him, and he began to stammer
out: "Oh, dear me! Is it you? Pray, how did you sleep last
night? Did you see or hear anything in the dead of night?"

"Nothing worth speaking of," said Jack, carelessly. "A rat,
I believe, gave me three or four slaps with his tail, and disturbed
me a little; but I soon went to sleep again."

The giant wondered more and more at this; yet he did not
answer a word, but went to bring two great bowls of hasty-
pudding for their breakfast. Jack wished to make the giant believe that he could eat as much as himself; so he contrived to
button a leathern bag inside his coat, and slipped the hasty-
pudding into this bag, while he seemed to put it into his mouth.

When breakfast was over, he said to the giant: "Now I will

show you a fine trick; I can cure all wounds with a touch; I could cut off my head one minute, and the next put it sound again on my shoulders. You shall see an example."

He then took hold of the knife, ripped up the leathern bag, and all the hasty-pudding tumbled out upon the floor.

"Ods splutter hur nails!" cried the Welsh giant, who was ashamed to be outdone by such a little fellow as Jack; "hur can do that hurself."

So he snatched up the knife, plunged it into his stomach, and in a moment dropped down dead.

As soon as Jack had thus tricked the Welsh monster, he went farther on his journey; and a few days after he met with King Arthur's only son, who had his father's leave to travel into Wales to deliver a beautiful lady from the power of a wicked magician, who held her in his enchantments. When Jack found that the young prince had no servants with him, he begged leave to attend him; and the prince at once agreed to this, and gave Jack many thanks for his kindness. The prince was a handsome, polite, and brave knight, and so good-natured that he gave money to everybody he met.

At length he gave his last penny to an old woman, and then turned to Jack and said: "How shall we be able to get food for ourselves the rest of our journey?"

"Leave that to me, sir," said Jack. "I will provide for my prince."

Night now came on, and the prince began to grow uneasy at thinking where they should lodge.

"Sir," said Jack, "be of good heart; two miles farther there lives a large giant, whom I know well. He has three heads, and will fight five hundred men, and make them fly before him."

"Alas!" replied the king's son, "we had better never have been born than meet with such a monster."

"My lord, leave me to manage him, and wait here, in quiet till I return."

The prince now staid behind, while Jack rode on at full speed; and when he came to the gates of the castle, he gave a loud knock.

The giant, with a voice like thunder, roared out: "Who is there?"

And Jack made answer and said: "No one but your poor nephew Jack."

"Well," said the giant, "what news, nephew Jack?"

"Dear uncle," said Jack, "I have heavy news."

"Pooh!" said the giant; "what heavy news can come to me? I am a giant with three heads; and can fight five hundred men, and make them fly before me."

"Alas!" said Jack, "here is the king's son, coming with two thousand men to kill you and to destroy the castle and all that you have."

"Oh, Jack," said the giant, "this is heavy news, indeed! But I have a large cellar under ground, where I will hide myself, and you shall lock, bolt, and bar me in, and keep the keys till the king's son is gone."

Now when Jack had made the giant fast in the vault, he went back and fetched the prince to the castle. They both made themselves merry with the wine and other dainties that were in the house. So that night they rested very pleasantly, while the giant lay trembling and shaking with fear in the cellar under ground. Early in the morning Jack gave the king's son gold and silver out of the giant's treasure, and set him three miles forward on his journey. Then Jack went to let his uncle out of the hole, who asked Jack what he should give him as a reward for saving his castle.

"Why, good uncle," said Jack, "I desire nothing but the old coat and cap, with the old rusty sword and slippers, which are hanging at your bed's head."

Then said the giant: " You shall have them; and pray keep them for my sake, for they are things of great use: the coat will keep you invisible, the cap will give you knowledge, the sword cut through anything, and the shoes are of vast swiftness. These may be useful to you in all times of danger; so take them with all my heart."

Jack gave many thanks to the giant, and then set off to the prince. When he had come up with the king's son, they soon arrived at the dwelling of the beautiful lady, who was under the power of a wicked magician. She received the prince very politely, and made a noble feast for him; and when it was ended, she rose and, wiping her mouth with a fine handkerchief, said: " My lord, you must submit to the custom of my palace; to-morrow morning I command you to tell me on whom I bestow this handkerchief, or lose your head."

She then went out of the room. The young prince went to bed very mournful; but Jack put on his Cap of Knowledge, which told him that the lady was forced by the power of enchantment to meet the wicked magician every night in the middle of the forest. Jack now put on his Coat of Darkness, and his Shoes of Swiftness, and was there before her. When the lady came, she gave the handkerchief to the magician. Jack with his Sword of Sharpness, at one blow, cut off his head; the enchantment was then ended in a moment, and the lady was restored to her former virtue and goodness.

She was married to the prince on the next day, and soon after went back with her royal husband and a great company to the court of King Arthur, where they were received with loud and joyful welcomes; and the valiant hero Jack, for the many great exploits he had done for the good of his country, was made one of the Knights of the Round Table. As Jack had been so lucky in all his adventures, he resolved not to be idle for the future, but still to do what services he could for the honor of the king and the nation. He therefore humbly begged his Majesty to furnish him with a horse and money, that he might travel in search of new and strange exploits.

" For," said he to the king, " there are many giants yet living in the remote parts of Wales, to the great terror and distress of your Majesty's subjects; therefore if it please you, sire, to favor me in my design, I will soon rid your kingdom of these giants and monsters in human shape."

Now when the king heard this offer, and began to think of the cruel deeds of these blood-thirsty giants and savage monsters, he gave Jack everything proper for such a journey. After this Jack took leave of the king, the prince, and all the knights, and set off, taking with him his Cap of Knowledge, his Sword of Sharpness, his Shoes of Swiftness, and his Invisible Coat, the better to perform the great exploits that might fall in his way.

He went along over high hills and lofty mountains, and on the third day he came to a large wide forest through which his road led. He had hardly entered the forest, when on a sudden he heard very dreadful shrieks and cries. He forced his way through the trees, and saw a monstrous giant dragging along by the hair of their heads a handsome knight and his beautiful lady. Their tears and cries melted the heart of honest Jack to pity and compassion; he alighted from his horse, and tying him to an oak tree, put on his Invisible Coat, under which he carried his Sword of Sharpness.

When he came up to the giant, he made several strokes at him, but could not reach his body, on account of the enormous height of the terrible creature; but he wounded his thighs in several places; and at length, putting both hands to his sword, and aiming with all his might, he cut off both the giant's legs just below the garter; and the trunk of his body tumbling to the ground, made not only the trees shake, but the earth itself tremble with the force of his fall.

Then Jack, putting his foot upon his neck, exclaimed: " Thou barbarous and savage wretch, behold I come to execute upon thee the just reward for all thy crimes "; and instantly killed him, whilst the noble knight and the virtuous lady were both joyful spectators of his sudden death and their deliverance. The courteous knight and his fair lady not only returned Jack hearty thanks for their deliverance, but also invited him to their house, to refresh himself after his dreadful encounter, and also to receive a reward for his good services.

"No," said Jack, "I cannot be at ease till I find out the den that was the monster's habitation."

The knight on hearing this grew very sorrowful, and replied: "Noble stranger, it is too much to run a second hazard. This monster lived in a den under yonder mountain, with a brother of his, more fierce and cruel than himself. Therefore, if you should go thither, and perish in the attempt, it would be a heart-breaking thing to me and my lady; so let me persuade you to go with us, and desist from any further pursuit."

"Nay," answered Jack, "if there be another, even if there were twenty, I would shed the last drop of blood in my body before one of them should escape my fury. When I have finished this task, I will come and pay my respects to you." So when they told him where to find them again, he got on his horse and went after the dead giant's brother.

Jack had not gone a mile and a half before he came in sight of the mouth of the cavern; and nigh the entrance of it he saw waiting for his brother the other giant, sitting on a huge block of fine timber, with a knotted iron club lying by his side. His eyes looked like flames of fire, his face was grim and ugly, and his cheeks seemed like two flitches of bacon; the bristles of his beard seemed to be thick rods of iron wire, and his long locks of hair hung down upon his broad shoulders like curling snakes. Jack got down from his horse, and turned him into a thicket;

then he put on his Coat of Darkness, and drew a little nearer to behold this figure, and said softly: "O monster! are you there? It will not be long before I shall take you fast by the beard."

The giant all this while could not see him, by reason of his Invisible Coat, so Jack came quite close to him and struck a blow at his head with his Sword of Sharpness; but he missed his aim, and only cut off his nose, which made the giant roar like loud claps of thunder. And though he rolled his glaring eyes round on every side, he could not see who had given him the blow; yet he took up his iron club, and began to lay about him like one that was mad with pain and fury.

"Nay," said Jack, "if this be the case I will kill you at once." So saying, he slipped nimbly behind him, and jumping upon the block of timber, as the giant rose from it, he stabbed him in the back, when after a few howls he dropped down dead. Jack cut off his head, and sent it, together with an account of all his exploits, with the head of his brother, whom he had killed in the forest, to King Arthur, by a wagon which he hired for that purpose. When Jack had thus killed these two monsters, he went into their cave in search of their treasure. He passed through many turnings and windings, which led him to a room paved with freestone. At the end of it was a boiling caldron, and on the right hand stood a large table where the giants used to dine. He then came to a window that was secured with iron bars, through which he saw a number of wretched captives, who cried out when they saw Jack:

"Alas! alas! young man, you are come to be one among us in this horrid den."

"I hope," said Jack, "you will not stay here long; but pray tell me what is the meaning of your being here at all?"

"Alas!" said one poor old man, "I will tell you, sir. We are persons that have been taken by the giants who hold this cave, and are kept till they choose to keep a feast, then one of us is to be killed and cooked to please their taste. It is not long since they took three for that purpose."

" Well," said Jack, " I have given them such a dinner that it will be long enough before they have any more."

The captives were amazed at his words. " You may believe me," said Jack; " for I have killed them both with the edge of the sword, and have sent their great heads to the court of King Arthur as marks of my success."

To show them that what he said was true, he unlocked the gate, and set them all free. Then he led them to the great room, placed them round the table, and set before them two quarters of beef, with bread and wine, upon which they feasted to their fill. When supper was over, they searched the giants' coffers, and Jack divided the store in them among the captives, who thanked him for their escape. The next morning they set off to their homes, and Jack went to the house of the knight, whom he had left with his lady not long before. It was just at the time of sunrise that Jack mounted his horse to proceed on his journey.

He arrived at the knight's house, where he was received with the greatest joy by the thankful knight and his lady, who, in honor of Jack's exploits, gave a grand feast, to which all the nobles and gentry were invited.

When the company were assembled, the knight declared to them the great deeds of Jack, and gave him, as a mark of respect, a fine ring on which was engraved the picture of the giant dragging the knight and the lady by the hair, with this motto round it:

" Behold in dire distress were we,
    Under a giant's fierce command;
  But gained our lives and liberty
    From valiant Jack's victorious hand."

Among the guests then present were five aged gentlemen, who were fathers to some of those captives who had been freed by Jack from the dungeon of the giants. As soon as they heard that he was the person who had done such wonders, they pressed round him with tears of joy, to return him thanks for the happiness he had brought to them. After this the bowl went round and every one drank to the health and long life of the gallant hero. Mirth increased, and the hall was filled with peals of laughter and joyful cries. But, on a sudden, a herald, pale and breathless, with haste and terror, rushed into the midst of the company and told them that Thundel, a savage giant with two heads, had heard of the death of his two kinsmen and was come to take his revenge on Jack, and that he was now within a mile of the house, the people flying before him like chaff before the wind.

At this news the very boldest of the guests trembled; but Jack drew his sword and said: " Let him come, I have a rod for him also. Pray, ladies and gentlemen, do me the favor to walk into the garden, and you shall soon behold the giant's defeat and death."

To this they all agreed, and heartily wished him success in his dangerous attempt. The knight's house stood in the middle of a moat, thirty feet deep and twenty wide, over which lay a drawbridge. Jack set men to work to cut the bridge on both sides, almost to the middle, and then dressed himself in his Coat of Darkness, and went against the giant with his Sword of Sharpness. As he came close to him, though the giant could not see him for his Invisible Coat, yet he found some danger was near, which made him cry out:

"Fa, fe, fi, fo, fum,
I smell the blood of an Englishman;
Let him be alive, or let him be dead,
I 'll grind his bones to make me bread."

" Say you so, my friend? " said Jack, " you are a monstrous miller indeed."

" Art thou," cried the giant, " the villain that killed my kins-men? Then I will tear thee with my teeth and grind thy bones to powder! "

" You must catch me first," said Jack; and throwing off his Coat of Darkness, and putting on his Shoes of Swiftness he began to run, the giant following him like a walking castle, mak-ing the earth shake at every step.

Jack led him round and round the walls of the house, that the company might see the monster; and to finish the work Jack ran over the drawbridge, the giant going after him with his club. But when the giant came to the middle where the bridge had been cut on both sides, the great weight of his body made it break, and he tumbled into the water and rolled about like a large whale. Jack now stood by the side of the moat, and laughed and jeered at him, saying: " I think you told me you would grind my bones to powder; when will you begin? "

The giant foamed at both his horrid mouths with fury, and plunged from side to side of the moat; but he could not get out to have revenge on his little foe. At last Jack ordered a cart rope to be brought to him. He then drew it over his two heads, and by the help of a team of horses dragged him to the edge of the moat, where he cut off the monster's heads; and before he either ate or drank he sent them both to the court of King Arthur. He then went back to the table with the company, and the rest of the day was spent in mirth and good cheer.

After staying with the knight for some time, Jack grew weary of such an idle life, and set out again in search of new adventures. He went over hills and dales without meeting any, till he came to the foot of a very high mountain. Here he knocked at the door of a small and lonely house, and an old man, with a head as white as snow, let him in.

" Good father," said Jack, " can you lodge a traveler who has lost his way? "

"Yes," said the hermit, "I can, if you will accept such fare as my poor house affords."

Jack entered, and the old man set before him some bread and fruit for his supper.

When Jack had eaten as much as he chose, the hermit said: "My son, I know you are the famous conqueror of giants; now on the top of this mountain is an enchanted castle, kept by a giant named Galligantus, who, by the help of a vile magician, gets many knights into his castle, where he changes them into the shape of beasts.

"Above all, I lament the hard fate of a duke's daughter, whom they seized as she was walking in her father's garden, and brought thither through the air in a chariot drawn by two fiery dragons, and turned her into the shape of a deer.

"Many knights have tried to destroy the enchantment and deliver her; yet none have been able to do it, by reason of two fiery griffins who guard the gate of the castle, and destroy all who come nigh. But as you, my son, have an Invisible Coat, you may pass by them without being seen; and on the gates of the castle you will find engraved some words which tell by what means the enchantment may be broken."

Jack promised that in the morning, at the risk of his life, he would break the enchantment; and after a sound sleep he arose early, put on his Invisible Coat, and got ready for the attempt.

When he had climbed to the top of the mountain, he saw the two fiery griffins; but he passed between them without the least fear of danger, for they could not see him because of his Invisible Coat.

On the castle gate he found a golden trumpet, under which were written these lines:

"Whoever can this trumpet blow,
Shall cause the giant's overthrow."

As soon as Jack had read this, he seized the trumpet and blew a shrill blast, which made the gates to fly open, and the very castle itself to tremble. The giant and the conjuror now knew that their wicked course was at an end, and they stood biting their thumbs and shaking with fear.

Jack, with his Sword of Sharpness, soon killed the giant, and the magician was then carried away by a whirlwind; and all the knights and beautiful ladies who had been changed into birds and beasts returned to their proper shapes. The castle vanished away like smoke, and the head of the giant Galligantus was sent to King Arthur. The knights and ladies rested that night at the old man's hermitage, and next day they set out for the court. Jack then went up to the king, and gave his Majesty an account of all his fierce battles.

Jack's fame had spread through the whole country; and at the king's desire the duke gave him his daughter in marriage, to the joy of all the kingdom. After this the king gave him a large estate, on which he and his lady lived the rest of their days in joy and content.

I DON'T CARE

I SHALL go this way," said a young black colt, who was out on the moor.

"No, no," said a horse who was close by. "You must stay on the moor."

"Why?" asked the colt.

"I cannot tell you," said the horse. "I have been told to stay by an old horse, and I shall do so."

"I don't care," said the young colt, and off he ran down the road.

By and by he met an old mare at an inn door.

"Why are you here?" asked she.

"I have come out for a bit of fun," said the colt.

"But you should not do so," said the mare. "You are not fit to go out in the world. You have no shoes."

"I don't care," said the colt, and he kicked up his heels to show that he did not mind what the old mare said. But the mare said no more.

Then he went on down the road, as fast as he could run.

He met a mule with a pack on his back. The mule shook his head when he saw the Colt.

": You should not be here," he said. "You have come from off the moor, I know. The town is close by."

"I don't care," said the colt. And on he ran right through the town. He had not been in a town in all his life, and the noise, and the sight of all the men, and carts, and cars made him feel quite crazy. He ran here and there, while men and boys ran to catch him, and threw stones and sticks, and cried out at him, up and down all the streets.

At last, in a great sheet of glass, he saw what he thought was a young colt, and he ran up to ask it what he should do, and how he could get back to the moor. Of course it was not a colt, but his own self that he saw in the glass.

The glass cut him when he dashed at it, and he fell down. And then he was caught.

"Why, that is my young colt from off the moor!" said a man, who just then came up. "These are his little games, are they? He must have a log of wood tied to his feet so he cannot run away again."

So he was led back to the moor, with his head cut, and his feet all sore, and there he had to stump from place to place with a great log tied to his feet. But he did not say, "I don't care" any more.

TITTY MOUSE TATTY MOUSE

ONCE upon a time Titty Mouse and Tatty Mouse both lived in a house.

Titty Mouse went a-leasing, and Tatty Mouse went a-leasing.

So they both went a-leasing.

Titty Mouse leased an ear of corn, and Tatty Mouse leased an ear of corn.

So they both leased an ear of corn.

Titty Mouse made a pudding, and Tatty Mouse made a pudding.

So they both made a pudding.

And Tatty Mouse put her pudding into the pot to boil, but when Titty went to put hers in the pot, it tumbled over and scalded her to death.

Then Tatty sat down and wept.

Then a three-legged stool said: "Tatty, why do you weep?"

"Titty's dead," said Tatty, "and so I weep."

Then said the stool: "I'll hop"; so the stool hopped.

Then a broom in the corner said: "Stool, why do you hop?"

"Oh!" said the stool, "Titty's dead, and Tatty weeps, and so I hop."

Then said the broom: "I'll sweep"; so the broom began to sweep.

Then said the door: "Broom, why do you sweep?"

" Oh! " said the broom, " Titty 's dead, and Tatty weeps, and the stool hops, and so I sweep."

Then said the door: " I 'll jar "; so the door jarred.

Then said the window, " Door, why do you jar? "

" Oh! " said the door, Titty 's dead, and Tatty weeps, and the stool hops, and the broom sweeps, and so I jar."

Then said the window: " I 'll creak "; so the window creaked.

Now, there was an old form outside the house, and when the window creaked, the form said: " Window, why do you creak? "

" Oh! " said the window, " Titty 's dead, and Tatty weeps, and the stool hops, and the broom sweeps, the door jars, and so I creak."

Then said the old form: " I 'll run round the house "; then the old form ran round the house.

Now, there was a fine large walnut tree growing by the cottage, and the tree said to the form, " Form, why do you run round the house? "

" Oh," said the form, " Titty 's dead, and Tatty weeps, and the stool hops, and the broom sweeps, the door jars, and the window creaks, and so I run round the house."

Then said the walnut tree: " I 'll shed my leaves "; so the walnut tree shed all its beautiful green leaves.

Now, there was a little bird perched on one of the boughs of the tree, and when all the leaves fell, it said: " Walnut tree, why do you shed your leaves? "

" Oh! " said the tree, " Titty 's dead, and Tatty weeps, the stool hops, and the broom sweeps, the door jars, and the window creaks, the old form runs round the house, and so I shed my leaves."

Then said the little bird: " I 'll moult all my feathers "; so he moulted all his pretty feathers.

Now, there was a little girl walking below, carrying a jug of milk for her brothers' and sisters' supper, and when she saw the poor little bird moult all its feathers, she said: "Little bird, why do you moult all your feathers?"

"Oh!" said the little bird, "Titty's dead, and Tatty weeps, the stool hops, and the broom sweeps, the door jars, and the window creaks, the old form runs round the house, the walnut tree sheds its leaves, and so I moult all my feathers."

Then said the little girl: "I'll spill the milk"; so she dropped the pitcher and spilt the milk.

Now, there was an old man just by on the top of a ladder thatching a rick, and when he saw the little girl spill the milk, he said: "Little girl, what do you mean by spilling the milk? Your little brothers and sisters must go without their supper."

Then said the little girl: "Titty's dead and Tatty weeps, the stool hops, and the broom sweeps, the door jars, and the window creaks, the old form runs round the house, the walnut tree sheds all its leaves, the little bird moults all its feathers, and so I spilt the milk."

"Oh!" said the old man, "then I'll tumble off the ladder and break my neck"; so he tumbled off the ladder and broke his neck.

And when the old man broke his neck, the great walnut tree fell down with a crash, and upset the old form and house, and the house falling knocked the window out, and the window knocked the door down, and the door upset the broom, the broom upset the stool, and poor little Tatty Mouse was buried beneath the ruins.

THE STORY OF THE HOUSE THAT JACK BUILT

THIS is the house that Jack built.

This is the malt
That lay in the house that Jack built.

This is the rat,
That ate the malt
That lay in the house that Jack built.

This is the cat,
That killed the rat,
That ate the malt
That lay in the house that Jack built.

This is the dog,
That worried the cat,
That killed the rat,
That ate the malt
That lay in the house that Jack built.

This is the cow with the crumpled horn,
That tossed the dog,
That worried the cat,
That killed the rat,
That ate the malt
That lay in the house that Jack built.

THE HOUSE THAT JACK BUILT

This is the maiden all forlorn,
That milked the cow with the crumpled horn,
That tossed the dog,
That worried the cat,
That killed the rat,
That ate the malt
That lay in the house that Jack built.

This is the man all tattered and torn,
That kissed the maiden all forlorn,
That milked the cow with the crumpled horn,
That tossed the dog,
That worried the cat,
That killed the rat,
That ate the malt
That lay in the house that Jack built.

This is the priest all shaven and shorn,
That married the man all tattered and torn,
That kissed the maiden all forlorn,
That milked the cow with the crumpled horn,
That tossed the dog,
That worried the cat,
That killed the rat,
That ate the malt
That lay in the house that Jack built.

This is the cock that crowed in the morn,
That waked the priest all shaven and shorn,
That married the man all tattered and torn,
That kissed the maiden all forlorn,
That milked the cow with the crumpled horn,
That tossed the dog,
That worried the cat,

That killed the rat,
That ate the malt
That lay in the house that Jack built.

This is the farmer sowing his corn,
That kept the cock that crowed in the morn,
That waked the priest all shaven and shorn,
That married the man all tattered and torn,
That kissed the maiden all forlorn,
That milked the cow with the crumpled horn,
That tossed the dog,
That worried the cat,
That killed the rat,
That ate the malt
That lay in the house that Jack built.

DICK WHITTINGTON AND HIS CAT[1]

IN the reign of the famous King Edward the Third of England
lived a little boy called Dick Whittington. His father and
mother dying when he was very young, he was left a ragged
little fellow running about a country village.

As poor Dick was not old enough to work, he was very badly
off, getting but little for his dinner and sometimes nothing at
all for his breakfast; for the people who lived in the village were
very poor themselves, and could not spare him much more than
the parings of potatoes, and now and then a hard crust.

Dick Whittington was a very poor boy, but he was also a
very sharp boy, and he was always listening to whatever was
talked about. On Sunday he was sure to get near the farmers,
talking in the churchyard before the clergyman had come; and
once a week you might see him leaning against the sign-post of
the village, where people stopped as they came from the next
market town; and when the barber's shop door was open, there
he was, all attention to what the gossipy customers were telling.
In this manner Dick heard many strange things about the great
city of London; for the simple country people of that day thought
that the London folk were all fine gentlemen and ladies, and that
the streets were paved with gold.

One day a large wagon, drawn by eight horses with bells at
their heads, passed through the village while Dick was standing

[1] Sir Richard Whittington was a real character. He was one of London's commercial princes
and was thrice her lord mayor. He died early in the fifteenth century.

by the sign-post. He thought that the wagon must be going to the fine town of London; so he took courage, and asked the wagoner to let him walk with him by the side of the wagon. As soon as the wagoner heard that Dick had neither father nor mother, and saw by his ragged clothes that he could not well be worse off than he was, he told him that he might go. So they set off together.

Nobody knows how little Dick contrived to get meat and drink on the road, nor how he could walk so far, — for it was a long way, — nor what he did at night for a place to lie down and sleep in. Perhaps some good-natured people in the towns that he passed through, when they saw that he was a poor ragged boy, gave him something to eat; and perhaps the wagoner allowed him to get into the wagon at night and take a nap. However, Dick got safely to London, where he was in such a hurry to see the fine streets paved all over with gold that he did not even stay to thank the kind wagoner, but ran off as fast as his legs could carry him through many of the streets, thinking every moment to come to those that were paved with gold. Dick, who had seen a guinea three times in his own little village, remembered what a deal of money it brought in change; and he thought he had nothing to do but to take up some little bits of the pavement, when he would have as much money as he could wish for.

Poor Dick ran till he was tired, and had quite forgotten his friend, the wagoner; but at last finding it grow dark, and that there was everywhere nothing but dirt instead of gold, he sat down in a dark corner, and cried himself to sleep. Dick was all night in the streets. The next morning, being very hungry, he got up and wandered about, asking everybody he met to give him a halfpenny to keep him from starving. Only two or three persons gave him a halfpenny; so the poor boy was soon quite weak and faint for want of food.

At last a good-natured-looking gentleman saw how hungry

he looked. "Why don't you go to work, my lad?" said he to Dick.

"That I would," answered Dick, "but I don't know how to get any work."

"If you are willing," said the gentleman, "come along with me"; and so saying he took him to a hay-field. In this field Dick worked briskly and lived merrily till the hay was all made. Soon, however, he found himself as badly off as before; and again being almost starved, he laid himself down at the door of Mr. Fitzwarren, a rich merchant. Here he was soon seen by the cook, an ill-tempered creature, who called out to him: —

"What business have you there, you lazy rogue? There is nothing else these days but beggars. If you don't take yourself away, we will see how you will like a sousing of some dish-water I have here that is hot enough to make you jump."

Just at this time Mr. Fitzwarren himself came home to dinner, and when he saw a dirty, ragged boy lying at the door, he said to him: "Why do you lie there, my lad? You seem old enough to work; I am afraid you are lazy."

"No, indeed, sir," said Dick to him, "that is not the case, for I would work with all my heart; but I don't know anybody, and I believe I am very sick for want of food."

"Poor fellow," answered Mr. Fitzwarren, "get up, and let us see what ails you."

Dick now tried to rise, but was obliged to lie down again, being too weak to stand; for he had not eaten anything for three days, and was no longer able to run about and beg halfpence of people in the streets. So the kind merchant ordered him to be taken into the house, and a good dinner given to him, and that he should do what dirty work he was able for the cook.

Little Dick would have lived very happily in this good family if it had not been for the ill-natured cook, who was finding fault and scolding him from morning till night; and besides, she was so fond of basting that when she had not roast meat to baste she would be basting poor Dick.

At last her ill usage of him was told to Miss Alice, Mr. Fitzwarren's daughter, who asked the ill-tempered creature if it was not a shame to use a little forlorn boy so cruelly, and said she should certainly be turned away if she did not treat him kindly. But though the cook was so ill-tempered, the footman was quite different; he had lived in the family many years, and was an elderly man and very kind-hearted; he had once a little son of his own who died when about the age of Dick, so he could not help feeling pity for the poor boy, and sometimes gave him a halfpenny to buy gingerbread or a top, for tops were cheaper at that time than they are now.

The footman was very fond of reading, and used often in the evening to entertain the other servants, when they had done their work, with some amusing book. Little Dick took great pleasure in hearing this good man, which made him wish very much to learn to read too; so the next time the footman gave him a halfpenny he bought a little book with it, and, with the footman's help, Dick soon learned his letters, and afterward learned to read.

About this time Miss Alice was going out one morning for a walk, and the footman happened to be out of the way, so as little Dick had a suit of good clothes that Mr. Fitzwarren gave him to go to church in on Sundays he was told to put them on and walk behind her.

As they went along, Miss Alice saw a poor woman with one child in her arms and another on her back; she pulled out her purse and gave the woman some money, but as she was putting it into her pocket again she dropped it on the ground and walked on. It was lucky that Dick was behind and saw what she had done; he picked up the purse and gave it to her again.

Another time when Miss Alice was sitting with the window

open, and amusing herself with a favorite parrot, it suddenly flew away to the branch of a high tree, where all the servants were afraid to venture after it. As soon as Dick heard of this he pulled off his coat and climbed up the tree as nimbly as a squirrel, and after a great deal of trouble, for Poll hopped about from branch to branch, he caught her and brought her down safe to his mistress. Miss Alice thanked him, and liked him ever after for this.

The ill-humored cook was now a little kinder; but besides her ugliness Dick had another hardship to get over. His bed stood in a garret where there were so many holes in the floor and the walls that every night he was waked in his sleep by the rats and mice, which often ran over his face and made such a noise that he sometimes thought the walls were tumbling down about him. One day a gentleman, who came to see Mr. Fitz-warren, required his shoes to be cleaned; Dick took great pains to make them shine, and the gentleman gave him a penny. With this he thought he would buy a cat; so the next day, seeing a little girl with a cat under her arm, he went up to her and asked if she would let him have it for a penny. The girl said she would, with all her heart, for her mother had more cats than she could keep. She told him, besides, that this one was a very good mouser.

Dick hid his cat in the garret, and always took care to carry a part of his dinner to her. In a short time he had no more trouble from the rats and mice, and slept as soundly as he could wish.

Soon after this his master had a ship ready to sail, and as he thought it right that all his servants should have some chance for good fortune as well as himself, he called them into the parlor and asked them what they would send out to be sold to the natives. They all had something that they were willing to venture except poor Dick, who had neither money nor goods, and so could send nothing at all. For this reason he did not come into the parlor with the rest, but Miss Alice guessed what was the matter, and ordered him to be called in. She then said she would lay down some money for him from her own purse, but her father told her this would not do, for Dick must send something of his own.

When poor Dick heard this, he said he had nothing but a cat, which he bought for a penny that was given him.

"Fetch your cat then, my good boy," said Mr. Fitzwarren, "and let her go."

Dick went upstairs and brought down his Puss, and with tears in his eyes gave her to the captain, for he said he should now be kept awake all night again by the rats and mice. All the company laughed at Dick's odd venture, and Miss Alice, who felt pity for the poor boy, gave him some halfpence to buy another cat.

This, and many other marks of kindness shown him by Miss Alice, made the ill-tempered cook jealous of poor Dick, and she began to use him more cruelly than ever, and always made fun of him for sending his cat to sea. She asked him if he thought his cat would sell for as much money as would buy a stick to beat him.

At last poor little Dick could not bear this usage any longer, and he thought he would run away from his place; so he packed up his few things and set out very early in the morning on Allhallows' Day, which is the first of November.

He walked as far as Holloway and there sat down on a stone, which to this day is called Whittington's Stone, and began to think which road he should take. While he was thinking what he could do, the bells of Bow Church, which at that time were only six, began to ring, and he fancied their sounds seemed to say to him:

"Turn again Whittington,
Lord Mayor of London."

WHITTINGTON AND HIS CAT

"Lord Mayor of London!" said he to himself. "Why, to be sure, I would put up with almost anything now to be lord mayor of London, and ride in a fine coach when I grow to be a man! Well, I will go back and think nothing of all the cuffing and scolding of the old cook if I am to be lord mayor of London at last."

Dick went back, and was lucky enough to get into the house and set about his work before the old cook came downstairs.

The ship with the cat on board was a long time at sea, and was at last driven by the winds on a part of the coast of Barbary, where the only people are Moors, whom the English had never known before. The people of this country came in great numbers to see the sailors, who were all of a different color from themselves, and treated them very civilly; and when they became better acquainted, were very eager to buy the fine things with which the ship was laden. When the captain saw this, he sent patterns of the best things he had to the king of the country, who was so much pleased with them that he sent for the captain and his chief mate to be brought to the palace.

Here they were placed, as is the custom of the country, on rich carpets, marked with gold and silver flowers. The king and queen were seated at the upper end of the room; and a number of dishes of the greatest rareties were brought in for dinner. But before they had been set on the table a minute a vast number of rats and mice rushed in and helped themselves from every dish, throwing the gravy and pieces of the meat all about the room. The captain wondered very much at this, and asked the king's servants if these vermin were not very unpleasant.

"Oh! yes," they said, "and the king would give half his riches to get rid of them; for they not only waste his dinner, as you see, but disturb him even in his bedroom, so that for fear of them he is obliged to be watched while he is asleep."

The captain was ready to jump for joy when he heard this.

He thought of poor Dick's cat, and told the king he had a creature on board his ship that would kill all the rats and mice.

The king was still more glad than the captain. "Bring this creature to me," said he, "and if it can do what you say, I will give you your ship full of gold for her."

The captain, to make quite sure of his good luck, answered, that she was such a clever cat for catching rats and mice that he could hardly bear to part with her; but that to oblige his Majesty he would fetch her.

"Run, run," said the queen, "for I long to see the dear creature that will do us such a service."

Away ran the captain to the ship while another dinner was got ready. He took Puss under his arm, and came back to the palace soon enough to see the table covered with rats and mice again, and the second dinner likely to be lost in the same way as the first. When the cat saw them, she did not wait for bidding, but jumped out of the captain's arms, and in a few moments laid almost all the rats and mice dead at her feet. The rest of them, in a fright, scampered away to their holes.

The king and queen were quite charmed to get rid so easily of such plagues; for ever since they could remember they had not had a comfortable meal by day or any quiet sleep by night. They desired that the creature who had done them so great a kindness might be brought for them to look at.

On this the captain called out, "Puss, Puss," and the cat ran up to him and jumped upon his knee. He then held her out to the queen, who started back, and was afraid to touch a creature that was able to kill so many rats and mice; but when she saw how gentle the cat seemed, and how glad she was at being stroked by the captain, she ventured to touch her too, saying all the time, "Poot, Poot," for she could not speak English. At last the queen took Puss on her lap, and by degrees became quite free with her, till Puss purred herself to sleep.

When the king had seen the actions of Mistress Puss, he bought the captain's whole ship's cargo, and afterwards gave him a great deal of gold besides, which was worth still more, for the cat. The captain then took leave of the king and queen and the great persons of their court, and with all his ship's crew set sail with a fair wind for England, and after a happy voyage arrived safe at London.

One morning when Mr. Fitzwarren had just come into his counting-house, and had seated himself at the desk, somebody came tap, tap, tap, at the door.

"Who is there?" said Mr. Fitzwarren.

"A friend," answered some one, opening the door, when who should it be but the captain and mate of the ship just arrived from the coast of Barbary. They were followed by several men carrying a vast number of pieces of gold that had been paid him by the king of Barbary for the ship's cargo. They then told the story of the cat, and showed the rich present the king had sent to Dick for her, upon which the merchant called out to his servants: —

> "Go fetch him, we will tell him of the same,
> Pray call him Mr. Whittington by name."

Mr. Fitzwarren now showed himself to be really a good man; for when some of his clerks said so great a treasure was too much for such a boy as Dick, he answered: "God forbid that I should keep the value of a single penny from him! It is all his own, and he shall have every farthing's worth of it to himself."

He then sent for Dick, who at that time happened to be scouring the cook's kettles, and was quite dirty; so that he wanted to excuse himself from going to his master by saying that the great nails in his shoes would spoil the fine polished floor.

Mr. Fitzwarren, however, made him come in, and ordered a chair to be set for him; so that poor Dick thought they were making fun of him, as the servants often did in the kitchen, and began to beg his master not to play tricks with a poor simple boy, but to let him go down again to his work.

"Indeed, Mr. Whittington," said the merchant, "we are all quite in earnest with you, and I most heartily rejoice in the news these gentlemen have brought you; for the captain has sold your cat to the king of Barbary, and brought you in return for her more riches than I possess in the whole world; and I wish you may long enjoy them!"

Mr. Fitzwarren then told the men to open the great treasure they had brought with them, and he said: " Mr. Whittington has now nothing to do but to put it in some place of safety."

Poor Dick hardly knew how to behave himself for joy; he begged his master to take what part of it he pleased, since he owed it all to his kindness.

"No, no," answered Mr. Fitzwarren, "this is all your own, and I have no doubt you will use it well."

Dick next asked his mistress, and then Miss Alice, to accept a part of his good fortune; but they would not, and at the same time told him that his success afforded them great pleasure.

But the poor fellow was too kind-hearted to keep it all to himself; so he made a handsome present to the captain, the mate, and every one of the sailors, and afterwards to his good friend the footman, and the rest of Mr. Fitzwarren's servants, and even to the ill-natured old cook. After this Mr. Fitzwarren advised him to send for proper tradesmen, and get himself dressed like a gentleman; and told him he was welcome to live in his house till he could provide himself with a better.

When Whittington's face was washed, his hair curled, his hat cocked, and he was dressed in a nice suit of clothes, he was as handsome and genteel as any young man who visited at Mr. Fitzwarren's; so that Miss Alice, who had been so kind to him, and thought of him with pity, now looked upon him as fit to be her sweetheart; and the more so, no doubt, because Whittington was now always thinking what he could do to oblige her, and making her the prettiest presents that could be. Mr. Fitzwarren soon saw their love for each other, and proposed to join them in marriage; and to this they both readily agreed. A day for the wedding was soon fixed; and they were attended to church by the lord mayor, the court of aldermen, the sheriffs, and a great number of the richest merchants in London, whom they afterwards treated with a very fine feast.

History tells us that Mr. Whittington and his lady lived in great splendor and were very happy. They had several children. He was sheriff of London in the year 1360, and several times afterwards lord mayor; the last time he entertained King Henry the Fifth on his Majesty's return from the famous battle of Agincourt.

In this company the king, on account of Whittington's gallantry, said: "Never had prince such a subject"; and when Whittington was told this at the table, he answered: "Never had subject such a king." Going with an address from the city on one of the king's victories, he received the honor of knighthood.

Sir Richard Whittington supported many poor people; he built a church and also a college, with a yearly allowance to poor scholars, and near it raised a hospital. The figure of Sir Richard Whittington, with his cat in his arms, carved in stone, was to be seen till the year 1780 over the archway of the old prison of Newgate that stood across Newgate Street. The following epitaph was written on the tomb of Sir Richard and Lady Whittington, and continued perfect till destroyed by the fire in London:

" Here lies Sir Richard Whittington, thrice mayor,
And his dear wife, a virtuous, loving pair;

Him fortune raised to be beloved and great
By the adventure only of a cat.
Let none that read it of God's love despair,
Who trust in Him, He will of them take care;
But growing rich, choose humbleness, not pride,
Let these dead virtuous persons be your guide."

ALI BABA; OR, THE FORTY THIEVES

IN a town in Persia there dwelt two brothers, one named
Cassim, the other Ali Baba. Cassim was married to a rich
wife and lived in plenty, while Ali Baba had to maintain his
wife and children by cutting wood in a neighboring forest and
selling it in the town. One day, when Ali Baba was in the forest,
he saw a troop of men on horseback coming toward him in a cloud
of dust. He was afraid they were robbers and climbed into a tree
for safety. When they came up to him and dismounted he counted
forty of them. They unbridled their horses and tied them to
trees. The finest man among them, whom Ali Baba took to be
their captain, went a little way among the bushes and said,
"Open, sesame!"[1] so plainly that Ali Baba heard him. A door
opened in the rocks, and having made the troop go in, he followed
them and the door shut again of itself. They stayed some time
inside, and Ali Baba, fearing they might come out and catch him,
was forced to sit patiently in the tree. At last the door opened
again and the forty thieves came out. As the captain went in
last he came out first, and made them all pass by him; he then
closed the door, saying: "Shut, sesame!" Every man bridled
his horse and mounted, the captain put himself at their head, and
they returned as they came.

Then Ali Baba climbed down and went to the door concealed
among the bushes, and said, "Open, sesame!" and it flew open.
Ali Baba, who expected a dull, dismal place, was greatly surprised to find it large and well lighted and hollowed by the hand

[1] Sesame is a kind of grain.

of man in the form of a vault, which received the light from an opening in the ceiling. He saw rich bales of merchandise — silk, stuff-brocades, all piled together, and gold and silver in heaps, and money in leather purses. He went in and the door shut behind him. He did not look at the silver, but brought out as many bags of gold as he thought his asses, which were browsing outside, could carry, loaded them with the bags, and hid it all with fagots. Using the words " Shut, sesame! " he closed the door and went home.

Then he drove his asses into the yard, shut the gates, carried the money-bags to his wife, and emptied them out before her. He bade her keep the secret, and he would go and bury the gold. " Let me first measure it," said his wife. " I will go borrow a measure of some one, while you dig the hole." So she ran to the wife of Cassim and borrowed a measure. Knowing Ali Baba's poverty, the sister was curious to find out what sort of grain his wife wished to measure, and artfully put some suet at the bottom of the measure. Ali Baba's wife went home and set the measure on the heap of gold, and filled it and emptied it often, to her great content. She then carried it back to her sister, without noticing that a piece of gold was sticking to it, which Cassim's wife perceived directly her back was turned. She grew very curious, and said to Cassim when he came home: " Cassim, your brother is richer than you. He does not count his money, he measures it." He begged her to explain this riddle, which she did by showing him the piece of money and telling him where she found it. Then Cassim grew so envious that he could not sleep, and went to his brother in the morning before sunrise. " Ali Baba," he said, showing him the gold piece, " you pretend to be poor and yet you measure gold." By this Ali Baba perceived that through his wife's folly Cassim and his wife knew their secret, so he confessed all and offered Cassim a share. " That I expect," said Cassim; " but I must know where to find the treasure, otherwise I will discover all and you will lose all." Ali Baba, more out of kindness than fear, told him of the cave and the very words to use. Cassim left Ali Baba, meaning to be beforehand with him and get the treasure for himself. He rose early next morning and set out with ten mules loaded with great chests. He soon found the place and the door in the rock. He said, " Open, sesame! " and the door opened and shut behind him. He could have feasted his eyes all day on the treasures, but he now hastened to gather together as much of it as possible; but when he was ready to go he could not remember what to say for thinking of his great riches. Instead of " sesame " he said " Open, barley! " and the door remained fast. He named several different sorts of grain, all but the right one, and the door still stuck fast. He was so frightened at the danger he was in that he had as much forgotten the word as if he had never heard it.

About noon the robbers returned to their cave and saw Cassim's mules roving about with great chests on their backs. This gave them the alarm: they drew their sabers and went to the door, which opened on their captain's saying, " Open, sesame! " Cassim, who had heard the trampling of their horses' feet, resolved to sell his life dearly, so when the door opened he leaped out and threw the captain down. In vain, however, for the robbers with their sabers soon killed him. On entering the cave they saw all the bags laid ready, and could not imagine how any one got in without knowing their secret. They cut Cassim's body into four quarters and nailed them up inside the cave, in order to frighten any one who should venture in, and went away in search of more treasure.

As night drew on Cassim's wife grew very uneasy, and ran to her brother-in-law and told him where her husband had gone. Ali Baba did his best to comfort her, and set out to the forest in search of Cassim. The first thing he saw on entering the cave was his dead brother. Full of horror, he put the body on one of his asses and bags of gold on the other two, and covering all with some fagots, returned home. He drove the two asses laden with gold into his own yard, and led the other to Cassim's house. The door was opened by the slave Morgiana, whom he knew to be both brave and cunning. Unloading the ass, he said to her: "This is the body of your master, who has been murdered, but whom we must bury as though he had died in his bed. I will speak with you again, but now tell your mistress I am come." The wife of Cassim, on learning the fate of her husband, broke out into cries and tears, but Ali Baba offered to take her to live with him and his wife if she would promise to keep his counsel and leave everything to Morgiana; whereupon she agreed and dried her eyes.

Morgiana, meanwhile, sought an apothecary and asked him for some lozenges. "My poor master," she said, "can neither eat nor speak, and no one knows what his distemper is." She carried home the lozenges and returned next day weeping, and asked for an essence only given to those just about to die. Thus, in the evening, no one was surprised to hear the wretched shrieks and cries of Cassim's wife and Morgiana, telling every one that Cassim was dead. The day after Morgiana went to an old cobbler near the gates of the town who opened his stall early, put a piece of gold in his hand, and bade him follow her with his needle and thread. Having bound his eyes with a handkerchief, she took him to the room where the body lay, pulled off the bandage, and bade him sew the quarters together, after which she covered his eyes again and led him home. Then they buried Cassim, and Morgiana his slave followed him to the grave, weeping and tearing her hair, while Cassim's wife stayed at home uttering lamentable cries. Next day she went to live with Ali Baba, who gave Cassim's shop to his eldest son.

The forty thieves, on their return to the cave, were much astonished to find Cassim's body gone and some of their moneybags. "We are certainly discovered," said the captain, "and shall be undone if we cannot find out who it is that knows our secret. Two men must have known it; we have killed one, we must now find the other. To this end one of you who is bold and artful must go into the city dressed as a traveler, and discover whom we have killed, and whether men talk of the strange manner of his death. If the messenger fails he must lose his life, lest we be betrayed." One of the thieves started up and offered to do this, and after the rest had highly commended him for his bravery he disguised himself, and happened to enter the town at daybreak, just by Baba Mustapha's stall. The thief bade him goodday, saying: " Honest man, how can you possibly see to stitch at your age?" " Old as I am," replied the cobbler, " I have very good eyes, and you will believe me when I tell you that I sewed a dead body together in a place where I had less light than I have now." The robber was overjoyed at his good fortune, and giving him a piece of gold, desired to be shown the house where he stitched up the dead body. At first Mustapha refused, saying that he had been blindfolded; but when the robber gave him another piece of gold he began to think he might remember the turnings if blindfolded as before. This means succeeded; the robber partly led him and was partly guided by him right in front of Cassim's house, the door of which the robber marked with a piece of chalk. Then, well pleased, he bade farewell to Baba Mustapha and returned to the forest. By and by Morgiana, going out, saw the mark the robber had made, quickly guessed that some mischief was brewing, and fetching a piece of chalk marked two or three doors on each side, without saying anything to her master or mistress.

The thief, meantime, told his comrades of his discovery. The captain thanked him and bade him show him the house he had marked. But when they came to it they saw that five or six of the houses were chalked in the same manner. The guide was so confounded that he knew not what answer to make, and when they returned he was at once beheaded for having failed. Another robber was dispatched, and having won over Baba Mustapha, marked the house in red chalk; but Morgiana being again too clever for them, the second messenger was put to death also. The captain now resolved to go himself, but, wiser than the others, he did not mark the house, but looked at it so closely that he could not fail to remember it. He returned, and ordered his men to go into the neighboring villages and buy nineteen mules and thirty-eight leather jars, all empty except one, which was full of oil. The captain put one of his men, fully armed, into each, rubbing the outside of the jars with oil from the full vessel. Then the nineteen mules were loaded with thirty-seven robbers in jars and the jar of oil, and reached the town by dusk. The captain stopped his mules in front of Ali Baba's house and said to Ali Baba, who was sitting outside for coolness: " I have brought some oil from a distance to sell at to-morrow's market, but it is now so late that I know not where to pass the night, unless you will do me the favor to take me in." Though Ali Baba had seen the captain of the robbers in the forest, he did not recognize him in the disguise of an oil merchant. He bade him welcome, opened his gates for the mules to enter, and went to Morgiana to bid her prepare a bed and supper for his guest. He brought the stranger into his hall, and after they had supped went again to speak to Morgiana in the kitchen, while the captain went into the yard under pretense of seeing after his mules, but really to tell his men what to do. Beginning at the first jar and ending at the last, he said to each man: " As soon as I throw some stones from the window of the chamber where I lie, cut the jars open with your knives and come out, and I will be with you in a trice." He returned to the house, and Morgiana led him to his chamber. She then told Abdallah, her fellow-slave, to set on the pot to make some broth for her master, who had gone to bed. Meanwhile her lamp went out, and she had no more oil in the house. "Do not be uneasy," said Abdallah; "go into the yard and take some out of those jars." Morgiana thanked him for his advice, took the oil pot, and went into the yard. When she came to the first jar the robber inside said softly: "Is it time?"

Any other slave but Morgiana, on finding a man in the jar instead of the oil she wanted, would have screamed and made a noise; but she, knowing the danger her master was in, bethought herself of a plan, and answered quietly: "Not yet, but presently." She went to all the jars, giving the same answer, till she came to the jar of oil. She now saw that her master, thinking to entertain an oil merchant, had let thirty-eight robbers into his house. She filled her oil pot, went back to the kitchen, and having lit her lamp, went again to the oil jar and filled a large kettle full of oil. When it boiled she went and poured enough oil into every jar to stifle and kill the robber inside. When this brave deed was done she went back to the kitchen, put out the fire and the lamp, and waited to see what would happen.

In a quarter of an hour the captain of the robbers awoke, got up, and opened the window. As all seemed quiet he threw down some little pebbles which hit the jars. He listened, and as none of his men seemed to stir he grew uneasy and went down into the yard. On going to the first jar and saying: "Are you asleep?" he smelled the hot boiled oil and knew at once that his plot to murder Ali Baba and his household had been discovered. He found all the gang were dead, and missing the oil out of the last jar became aware of the manner of their death. He then forced the lock of a door leading into a garden, and climbing over several walls made his escape. Morgiana heard and saw all this, and rejoicing at her success went to bed and fell asleep.

At daybreak Ali Baba arose, and seeing the oil jars there still, asked why the merchant had not gone with his mules. Morgiana bade him look in the first jar and see if there was any oil. Seeing a man he started back in terror. "Have no fear," said Morgiana; "the man cannot harm you: he is dead." Ali Baba, when he had recovered somewhat from his astonishment, asked what had become of the merchant. "Merchant!" said she; "he is no more a merchant than I am!" and she told him the whole story, assuring him that it was a plot of the robbers of the forest, of whom only three were left, and that the white and red chalk marks had something to do with it. Ali Baba at once gave Morgiana her freedom, saying that he owed her his life. They then buried the bodies in Ali Baba's garden, while the mules were sold in the market by his slaves.

The captain returned to his lonely cave, which seemed frightful to him without his lost companions, but firmly resolved to avenge them by killing Ali Baba. He dressed himself carefully and went into the town, where he took lodgings in an inn. In the course of a great many journeys to the forest he carried away many rich stuffs and much fine linen, and set up a shop opposite that of Ali Baba's son. He called himself Cogia Hassan, and as he was both civil and well dressed he soon made friends with Ali Baba's son, and through him with Ali Baba, whom he was continually asking to sup with him. Ali Baba, wishing to return his kindness, invited him into his house and received him smiling, thanking him for his kindness to his son. When the merchant was about to take his leave Ali Baba stopped him, saying: "Where are you going, sir, in such haste? Will you not stay and sup with me?" The merchant refused, saying that he had a reason; and on Ali Baba's asking him what that was he replied: "It is, sir, that I can eat no victuals that have any salt in them." "If that is all," said Ali Baba, "let me tell you that there shall be no salt in either the meat or the bread that we eat to-night." He went to give this order to Morgiana, who was much surprised. "Who is this man," she said, "who eats no salt with his meat?" "He is an honest man, Morgiana," returned her master; "therefore do as I bid you." But she could not withstand a desire to see this strange man, so she helped Abdallah to carry up the dishes, and saw in a moment that Cogia Hassan was the robber captain and carried a dagger under his garment. "I am not surprised," she said to herself, "that this wicked man, who intends to kill my master, will eat no salt with him; but I will hinder his plans."

She sent up the supper by Abdallah, while she made ready for one of the boldest acts that could be thought on. When the dessert had been served, Cogia Hassan was left alone with Ali Baba and his son, whom he thought to make drunk and then to murder them. Morgiana meanwhile, put on a head-dress like a dancing-girl's, and clasped a girdle round her waist, from which hung a dagger with a silver hilt, and said to Abdallah: "Take your tabor, and let us go and divert our master and his guest." Abdallah took his tabor and played before Morgiana until they came to the door, where Abdallah stopped playing and Morgiana made a low courtesy. "Come in, Morgiana," said Ali Baba, "and let Cogia Hassan see what you can do"; and turning to Cogia Hassan he said: "She's my slave and my housekeeper." Cogia Hassan was by no means pleased, for he feared that his chance of killing Ali Baba was gone for the present; but he pretended great eagerness to see Morgiana, and Abdallah began to play and Morgiana to dance. After she had performed several dances she drew her dagger and made passes with it, sometimes pointing it at her own breast, sometimes at her master's, as if it were part of the dance. Suddenly, out of breath, she snatched the tabor from Abdallah with her left hand, and holding the dagger in her right, held out the tabor to her master. Ali Baba and his son put a piece of gold into it, and Cogia Hassan, seeing that she was coming to him, pulled out his purse to make her a present, but while he was putting his hand into it Morgiana plunged the dagger into his heart.

"Unhappy girl!" cried Ali Baba and his son, "what have you done to ruin us?" "It was to preserve you, master, not to ruin you," answered Morgiana. "See here," opening the false merchant's garment and showing the dagger; "see what an enemy you have entertained! Remember, he would eat no salt with you, and what more would you have? Look at him! he is both the false oil merchant and the captain of the forty thieves."

Ali Baba was so grateful to Morgiana for thus saving his life that he offered her to his son in marriage, who readily consented, and a few days after the wedding was celebrated with great splendor. At the end of a year Ali Baba, hearing nothing of the two remaining robbers, judged they were dead and set out to the cave. The door opened on his saying, "Open, sesame!" He went in, and saw that nobody had been there since the captain left it. He brought away as much gold as he could carry and returned to town. He told his son the secret of the cave, which his son handed down in his turn, so the children and grandchildren of Ali Baba were rich to the end of their lives.

RUMPELSTILTZKIN; OR, THE MILLER'S DAUGHTER

THERE was once upon a time a poor miller who had a very beautiful daughter. Now, it happened one day that he had an audience with the king, and in order to appear a person of some importance he told him that he had a daughter who could spin straw into gold. "Now that's a talent worth having," said the king to the miller. "If your daughter is as clever as you say, bring her to my palace to-morrow and I'll put her to the test." When the girl was brought to him he led her into a room full of straw, gave her a spinning-wheel and spindle, and said: "Now set to work and spin all night till dawn, and if by that time you haven't spun the straw into gold you shall die." Then he closed the door behind him and left her alone inside.

So the poor miller's daughter sat down and didn't know what in the world she was to do. She hadn't the least idea of how to spin straw into gold, and became at last so miserable that she began to cry. Suddenly the door opened and in stepped a tiny little man and said: "Good-evening, Miss Miller-maid. Why are you crying so bitterly?" "Oh!" answered the girl, "I have to spin straw into gold and haven't a notion how it's done." "What will you give me if I spin it for you?" asked the manikin. "My necklace," replied the girl. The little man took the necklace, sat himself down at the wheel, and whir! whir! whir! the wheel went round three times and the bobbin was full. Then he put on another, and whir! whir! whir! the wheel went round

423

three times, and the second too was full; and so it went on till the morning, when all the straw was spun away and all the bobbins were full of gold.

As soon as the sun rose the king came, and when he perceived the gold he was astonished and delighted, but his heart only lusted more than ever after the precious metal. He had the miller's daughter put into another room full of straw, much bigger than the first, and bade her, if she valued her life, spin it all into gold before the following morning. The girl did n't know what to do and began to cry; then the door opened as before, and the tiny little man appeared and said: " What 'll you give me if I spin the straw into gold for you? " " The ring from my finger," answered the girl. The manikin took the ring, and whir! round went the spinning-wheel again, and when morning broke he had spun all the straw into glittering gold. The king was pleased beyond measure at the sight, but his greed for gold was still not satisfied, and he had the miller's daughter brought into a yet bigger room full of straw, and he said: " You must spin all this away in the night; but if you succeed this time you shall become my wife." " She's only a miller's daughter, it's true," he thought; " but I could n't find a richer wife if I were to search the whole world over." When the girl was alone the little man appeared for the third time and said: " What 'll you give me if I spin the straw for you once again? " " I 've nothing more to give," answered the girl. " Then promise me when you are queen to give me your first child." " Who knows what may n't happen before that? " thought the miller's daughter; and besides, she saw no other way out of it, so she promised the manikin what he demanded, and he set to work once more and spun the straw into gold. When the king came in the morning and found everything as he had desired, he straightway made her his wife, and the miller's daughter became a queen.

When a year had passed a beautiful son was born to her, and

she thought no more of the little man, till all of a sudden one day he stepped into her room and said: " Now give me what you promised." The queen was in a great state, and offered the little man all the riches in her kingdom if he would only leave her the child. But the manikin said: " No, a living creature is dearer to me than all the treasure in the world." Then the queen began to cry and sob so bitterly that the little man was sorry for her and said: " I 'll give you three days to guess my name, and if you find it out in that time you may keep your child."

Then the queen pondered the whole night over all the names she had ever heard, and sent a messenger to scour the land and to pick up far and near any names he should come across. When the little man arrived on the following day she began with Kasper, Melchior, Belshazzar, and all the other names she knew, in a string, but at each one the manikin called out: " That 's not my name." The next day she sent to inquire the names of all the people in the neighborhood, and had a long list of the most uncommon and extraordinary for the little man when he made his appearance. " Is your name, perhaps, Sheepshanks, Crook-shanks, Spindleshanks? " but he always replied: " That 's not my name." On the third day the messenger returned and announced: " I have not been able to find any new names, but as I came upon a high hill round the corner of the wood, where the foxes and hares bid each other good-night, I saw a little house, and in front of the house burned a fire, and round the fire sprang the most grotesque little man, hopping on one leg and crying:

> " ' To-morrow I brew, to-day I bake,
> And then the child away I 'll take;
> For little deems my royal dame
> That Rumpelstiltzkin is my name! ' "

You may imagine the queen's delight at hearing the name, and when the little man stepped in shortly afterward and asked:

" Now, my lady queen, what's my name? " she asked first: " Is your name Conrad? " " No." " Is your name Harry? " " No." " Is your name, perhaps, Rumpelstiltzkin? " " Some demon has told you that! some demon has told you that! " screamed the little man, and in his rage drove his right foot so far into the ground that it sank in up to his waist; then in a passion he seized the left foot with both hands and tore himself in two.

LITTLE TOTTY

A FARMER'S wife who had no children went one day to a fairy, who appeared as an old woman, and begged her to give her a baby. "Even a very tiny one would make me happy," she said. The fairy laughed, and gave her a barley-corn, telling her to put it in a flower-pot, and she would see what would happen. The woman obeyed, and the very next day she saw that a beautiful tulip bud was standing on its tall stalk in the pot. The woman, delighted, kissed the golden leaves; the bud opened, and inside it she found a lovely baby only half as long as a thumb. She called her "Totty."

The woman made a walnut-shell her cradle; the bed was of violets, the coverlet was a rose leaf. As Totty grew bigger her mother seated her on a large tulip leaf floating on water in a plate, and Totty rowed herself from side to side with two oars made of white horse hairs. One night a toad jumped through the bedroom window and saw Totty sleeping. "She will make a lovely wife for my son," she said; so she took up the cradle and carried it to the pond, where she put it on a great lily leaf. Totty cried bitterly when she woke and found herself there, but the toad made her weave rushes for the household linen when she should be married to Tadpole, her son. The fishes in the pond were very sorry for her, so they bit the stem of the leaf through, and it floated down the stream.

Totty tied a white butterfly, that flew down to her, to the leaf with her girdle, and felt very happy, as he drew her leaf

427

along far from the toad and her son. But one day a cockchafer saw her and fell in love with her. He seized her by her waist and flew with her into a tree, but his friends said she was very ugly, and the cockchafer believed them, and told Totty he did not now care for her; but he flew down with her, and left her on a daisy in the wood. Totty lived there all the summer; but when the winter came she was cold and hungry, and she begged the field-mouse to take her in. The mouse was kind to her, but she wanted her to marry the old mole, who often visited her, and Totty did not like to live in the dark, underground home of the great mole. She cried bitterly about it. But the mouse insisted. "Obey me," she said, "or I will bite you. The mole is rich; look at his fur, it is splendid!" Now, during the winter, Totty had found a poor swallow almost dead with cold, and she had taken him barley-corns, and covered him up warmly, and saved his life; in the spring he had flown off. Summer came and went, and at last the mouse would wait no longer for the marriage; she fixed Totty's wedding-day with the mole, and the poor girl went out of the door to look for the last time at the setting sun, and stood there crying quietly.

By and by she heard "Tweet, tweet," quite near to her, and saw her friend the swallow on a branch close by her. He asked her why she wept, and she told him. "Get on my back," he said, "and I will take you away from the cruel mouse." Totty joyfully did as he told her, and the swallow flew fast away over land and sea, till he put her down on a large white flower like a convolvulus, and she saw standing in it a little man with a gold crown on his head. He was very little bigger than Totty, and was the King of the Flower Fairies. He asked Totty to marry him; she said "Yes," and he made her his Queen.

LAZY JACK

ONCE upon a time there was a boy whose name was Jack, and he lived with his mother upon a dreary common. They were very poor, and the old woman made her living by spinning; but Jack was so lazy that he would do nothing but bask in the sun in hot weather, and sit by the fire in the winter time. His mother could not persuade him to do anything for her, and was obliged at last to tell him that if he did n't begin to work for his food, she would turn him out to get his living as he could.

This threat at length aroused Jack, and he went out and hired himself to a farmer for a penny; but as he was coming home, never having had any money in his possession before, he lost it in passing over a brook. "You foolish boy," said his mother, "you should have put it in your pocket."

"I 'll do so another time," said Jack.

The next day Jack went out again, and hired himself to a cow keeper, who gave him a jar of milk for his day's pay. Jack took the jar and put it into the large pocket of his coat, spilling it all long before he reached home. "Dear me!" said the old woman, "you should have carried it on your head."

"I 'll do so another time," said Jack.

The following day Jack hired himself again to a farmer, who agreed to give him a cream cheese for his services. In the evening Jack took the cheese, and went home with it on his head. By the time he got home the cheese was completely spoiled, part of it being lost and part matted with his hair. "You foolish boy," said his mother, "you should have carried it very carefully in your hands."

"I 'll do so another time," said Jack.

The day after this Jack went out and hired himself to a baker, who would give him nothing for his work but a large black cat. Jack took the cat, and began carrying it very carefully in his hands, but in a short time pussy scratched him so that he had to let it go. When he got home his mother said to him: "You foolish boy, you should have tied it with a string, and dragged it along after you."

"I 'll do so another time," said Jack.

The next day Jack hired himself to a butcher, who rewarded him with a shoulder of mutton. Jack took the mutton, tied it to a string and trailed it along after him in the dirt, so that by the time he got home it was completely spoiled. His mother was by this time quite out of patience with him, for the next day was Sunday, and she was obliged to content herself with cabbage for her dinner. "You foolish boy," said she, "you should have carried it on your shoulder."

"I 'll do so another time," said Jack.

On the Monday Jack went and hired himself once more to a cattle keeper, who gave him a donkey for his trouble. Although Jack was very strong, he found some difficulty in hoisting the donkey on his shoulders, but at last he accomplished it and began walking home with his prize. Now, it happened that in the course of his journey there lived a rich man with his only daughter, a beautiful girl, but unfortunately deaf and dumb: she had never laughed in her life, and the doctor said she never would recover till some one made her laugh. Many had tried without success, and at last the father, in despair, offered her in marriage to the first man who could make her laugh. This young lady happened to be looking out of the window when Jack was passing with the donkey on his shoulders, with its legs sticking up in the air, and the sight was so comical and strange that she burst into a great fit of laughter, and immediately recovered her speech and hearing. Her father was overjoyed, and fulfilled his promise by marrying her to Jack, who was thus made a rich man. They lived in a large house, and Jack's mother lived happily with them until she died.

TOM TIT TOT

ONCE upon a time there was a woman, and she baked five pies. And when they came out of the oven, they were so overbaked the crust was too hard to eat. So she said to her daughter:

"Daughter, put those pies on the shelf, and leave them there a little, and they 'll come again." She meant, you know, that the crust would get soft.

But the girl said to herself: "Well, if they 'll come again, I 'll eat them now." And she set to work and ate them all.

When supper time came the woman said: "Go and get one of those pies. I dare say the crust is soft now."

The girl went and looked and found nothing but the dishes. So she came back and said: "No, they are not soft yet."

"Not any of them?" said the mother.

"Not any of them," said the daughter.

"Well, whether they are soft or not," said the mother, "I 'll have one for supper."

"But you can't, if they are not soft," said the girl.

"But I can," said she. "Go and bring the best of them."

"Best or worst," said the girl, "I 've eaten them all up, so you can't have any."

Well, the woman was wholly beaten, and she took her spinning to the door to spin, and as she spun she sang:

"My daughter has eaten five, five pies to-day,
My daughter has eaten five, five pies to-day."

The king was coming down the street, and he heard her sing, but what she sang he could n't hear, so he stopped and said:

"What were you singing, my good woman?"

The woman was ashamed to let him hear what her daughter had been doing, so she sang instead:

> "My daughter has spun five, five skeins to-day,
> My daughter has spun five, five skeins to-day."

"My stars!" said the king, "I've never heard of any one who could do that."

Then he said: "Look here, I want a wife, and I'll marry your daughter. But," said he, "eleven months out of the year, she shall have all she wants to eat, and all the gowns she likes to get, and all the company she likes to have; but the last month of the year she must spin five skeins every day, and, if she does n't, I shall kill her."

"All right!" said the woman; for she thought what a grand marriage that was. And as for the five skeins, when the time came, there would be plenty of ways of getting out of it, and very likely he would forget about it.

So they were married. And for eleven months the girl had all the food she liked to eat, and all the gowns she liked to wear, and all the company she wished to have.

But when the twelfth month drew near, she began to think about the skeins, and to wonder if he remembered them. But not a word did he say about them, and she thought he had forgotten.

However, the last day of the last month, he took her to a room she had never seen before. There was nothing in it but a spinning-wheel and a stool.

And he said: "Now, my dear, you'll be shut in here to-morrow with some food and some flax, and if you have n't spun five skeins by night, off will go your head."

With that he left her.

She was very much frightened, — she had always been such a lazy girl that she had n't even learned how to spin, and what was she to do to-morrow with no one to help her? She sat down on a stool in the kitchen and cried.

Suddenly she heard a knocking on the door, and on opening it saw a small black thing with a long tail. It looked up at her curiously, and said:

" What are you crying for? "

" What 's that to you? " she said.

" Never mind," it said; " but tell me why you are crying."

" It won't do me any good if I do," said she.

" How do you know? " it said, and twirled its tail around.

" Well," she said, " it won't do any harm if it does no good "; so she told it about the pies, and the skeins, and everything.

" This is what I 'll do," said the little black thing, " I 'll come to your window every morning, and take the flax, and bring it back spun at night."

" What 's your pay? " said she.

It looked out of the corner of its eyes, and said: " I 'll give you three guesses every night to guess my name, and if you have n't guessed it before the month is up, you shall be mine."

Well, she thought she would be sure to guess its name before the month was up, and so she said:

" All right! I 'll agree."

" All right! " it said; and how it twirled its tail.

The next day her husband took her into the room, and there was the flax and the day's food.

" Now there 's the flax," he said, " and if it is n't spun by to-night, off goes your head." And then he went out and locked the door.

He had hardly gone when there was a knocking against the window, and on opening it, there was the little old thing sitting on the ledge.

"Where's the flax?" it said.

"Here it is," said she, and gave it to him.

When evening came there was a knocking against the window. She opened it, and there was the little old thing with five skeins of flax on its arm.

"Here you are," it said, and gave it to her.

"Now, what's my name?" said it.

"Is it Bill?" said she.

"No, it isn't," said it, twirling its tail.

"Is it Ned?" said she.

"No, it isn't," said it, and it twirled its tail.

"Well, is it Mark?" said she.

"No, it isn't," said it, and it twirled its tail harder, and flew away.

When her husband came in, there were the five skeins ready for him. "I see I sha'n't have to kill you to-night, my dear," said he; "you'll have your food and your flax in the morning." And away he went.

Well, every day the flax and the food were brought, and every day the little black impet came morning and evening. And all day the girl sat trying to think of names to say to it, when it came at night.

But she didn't hit on the right one, and towards the end of the month the impet began to look very malicious, and twirled its tail faster and faster each time she gave a guess.

At last came the last day but one. The impet came at night with the five skeins, and said:

"Well, have you guessed my name yet?"

"Is it Nicodemus?" said she.

"No, it isn't," said it.

" Is it Sammie? " said she.

" No, it is n't," said it.

" Well, is it Methuselah? " said she.

" No, it is n't that either! " said it.

Then it looked at her with eyes like coals of fire, and said: " Girl, there 's only to-morrow night, and then you 'll be mine." And away it flew.

She felt very sorrowful, and when the king came in and saw the five skeins, he said:

" Well, my dear, I don't see but what you 'll have your skeins ready to-morrow night, and as I sha'n't have to kill you, I 'll have supper in here to-night." So they brought supper and another stool for him, and the two sat down.

He had eaten but a mouthful when he began to laugh.

" What is it? " said she.

" Why," said he, " I was out hunting to-day, and I got to a place in the wood I had never seen before. I heard a sort of humming in an old chalk-pit, so I got off my horse and went and looked down into it. Well, what should there be but the funniest little black thing you ever saw. It had a little spinning-wheel, and was spinning very fast, and twirling its tail. And as it spun, it sang:

> " ' *Nimmy, nimmy not,*
> *My name 's Tom Tit Tot.*' "

When the girl heard this, she felt as if she could have jumped for joy, but she did n't say a word.

Next day the little black thing looked very full of malice when it came for the flax. And when it brought the five skeins back at night it came right in and sat on the ledge, and grinned from ear to ear, and twirled its tail very fast.

" What 's my name? " it said.

" Is it Solomon? " she said, pretending to be afraid.

"No, it is n't," it said, coming farther into the room.

"Is it Zebedee?" said she again.

"No, it is n't," said the impet, laughing and twirling its tail so fast that you could scarcely see it.

"Don't hurry, girl," it said, "next guess, and you 're mine." And it stretched out its hands at her.

She looked at it and laughed, and pointing her finger at it, said:

> "*Nimmy, nimmy not,*
> *Your name 's* Tom Tit TOT."

When the impet heard her, it shrieked frightfully, and flew away into the dark, and she never saw it again.

THE UNSEEN GIANT

ONCE upon a time there was a giant; no one knew just when he began to live, but he was as old as the earth, that was quite sure.

Nobody had ever seen him or had even known where he lived; he came and went as he pleased, but always invisible. Sometimes he would play all manner of pranks, lift off the roofs of houses and toss them in the air like balls, then he would roll up the big waves ever so high, and many a good ship was buried beneath the angry white foam in the ocean.

Often he would step into the forest and pull up great trees by the roots, flinging them on top of each other, blocking up the roadway with branches and bushes.

Oh, how frightened the people would feel, when he tumbled their houses down about their ears! They had to run for their lives, and even then they feared he would take them on his strong wings high in the air, and dash them on the ground below.

But he was not always cruel, oh, no! Some little children were very sick in the hot city; every one thought they must die. " If there was only a breath of pure air! " cried the mother. Then the big giant felt sorry for the poor, suffering little ones, and swept the cooling mountain breezes along till they flew in the open window and fanned the children while they slept.

There were some tiny seed babies huddled together in a dry milkweed pod. " You'll never grow here," howled the giant, " you must go out in the world if you want to be of any use

438

at all." "But we are so afraid," whispered the timid babies; then the old giant lifted them quite out of their house and carried them to a lovely spot where there was a green moss carpet and a big oak tree, whose leaves had all put on their gay fall dresses. The rain fairies, in their soft, gray cloaks, came down from the skies. "O, the poor, tired seed babies!" they cried, "we 'll put them to sleep"; so they patted them very gently, until they sank into the soft earth bed Mother Nature had prepared for them. Jack Frost tucked them in with a snow-white comfortable, and they slept till spring, then — well, you must ask the oak what became of those babies.

This giant can sing, and you have heard him many a time roaring through the tree tops so loudly that you truly felt afraid.

And then of a winter's night, when you were sitting round the warm fire, listening to the true stories grandma told you of the days when she was young, you have heard him whistle through the keyhole of the front door; no doubt he would have been delighted to walk into the room and stir things up generally, but he was shut out.

"What is this giant's name?" you ask. It is the Wind.

And whence he comes and whither he goes,
Nobody cares and nobody knows,
For never since time began, I ween,
Has this old giant ever been seen.

THE THREE SPINNERS

ONCE upon a time there was a lazy maiden who would not spin, and, let her mother say what she would, she could not make her do it. At last, the mother, in a fit of impatience, gave her a blow which made the girl cry out loudly.

At that very instant, the queen drove by, and hearing the screams, she stopped the carriage, came into the house, and asked the mother why she beat her daughter in such a way that people in passing could hear the cries.

Then the mother felt ashamed that her daughter's laziness should be known, so she said: " Oh, your Majesty, I cannot take her away from her spinning: she spins from morning till night, and I am so poor I cannot afford to buy the flax."

" There is nothing I like better than to hear the sound of spinning," the queen replied; " and nothing pleases me more than the whirl of spinning wheels. Let me take your daughter home with me to the castle; I have flax enough, and she may spin there to her heart's content."

The mother rejoiced greatly in her heart, and the queen took the maiden home with her. When they arrived at the castle, she led her up into three rooms, which were piled from top to bottom with the finest flax.

" Now spin me this flax," said the queen, " and when thou hast spun it all thou shalt have my eldest son for a husband.

Although thou art poor, yet do I not despise thee on that account, for thy untiring industry is dowry enough."

The maiden was filled with inward terror, for she could not have spun the flax had she sat there night and day until she was three hundred years old! When she was left alone, she began to weep and thus she sat for three days without stirring a finger.

On the third day the queen came, and when she saw that nothing was as yet spun, she wondered over it, but the maiden excused herself by saying that she could not begin in consequence of the great sorrow she felt in being separated from her mother.

This satisfied the queen who, on leaving her, said: " Thou must begin work for me to-morrow."

But when the maiden was once more alone, she did not know what to do, or how to help herself, and in her distress she went to the window and looked out.

She saw three women passing by, the first of whom had a great broad foot, the second such a large underlip that it hung down to her chin, and the third an enormous thumb.

They stopped under the window, and looking up asked the maiden what was the matter.

When she had told them of her trouble, they immediately offered her their help, and said:

" Wilt thou invite us to the wedding and not be ashamed of us, but call us thy aunts, and let us sit at thy table? If thou wilt we will spin all the flax in a very short time."

" With all my heart," answered the girl, " only come in and begin at once."

Then she admitted the three strange women, and, making a clear space in the first room, they sat themselves down and began spinning.

One drew the thread and trod the wheel, the other moistened the thread and the third pressed it and beat it on the table, and every time she did so, a pile of thread fell on the ground spun in the finest way.

The maiden concealed the three spinners from the queen, but showed her the heaps of spun yarn whenever she came, and received no end of praise for it.

When the first room was empty, the second was commenced, and when that was finished the third was begun, and very soon cleared.

Then the three spinners took their leave, saying to the maiden:

"Forget not what thou hast promised us; it will make thy fortune."

When the girl showed the queen the empty rooms and the great piles of thread, the wedding was announced. The bridegroom rejoiced that he had won so clever and industrious a wife, and he praised her exceedingly.

"I have three aunts," said the maiden, "and as they have done me many kindnesses I could not forget them in my good fortune; permit me to invite them to our wedding and allow them to sit with me at the table."

So the queen and the bridegroom consented.

When the feast commenced, the three old women entered, clothed in the greatest splendor, and the bride said:

"Welcome, my dear aunts!"

"Alas!" exclaimed the bridegroom, "how is it you have such ugly relations?" and going up to the one with the broad foot, he asked:

"Why have you such a broad foot?"

"From threading, from threading," she answered.

Then he went to the second, and asked:

"Why have you an overhanging lip?"

"From moistening the thread," said she.

And he asked the third:

THE THREE SPINNERS

" Why have you such a big thumb? "

" From pressing the thread," she replied.

Then the prince grew frightened, and said:

" Then shall my lovely bride never more turn a spinning-wheel, as long as she lives! "

Thus was the maiden freed from the hated flax-spinning.

THE WATER-LILY; OR, THE
GOLD-SPINNERS

ONCE upon a time, in a large forest, there lived an old woman and three maidens. They were all three beautiful, but the youngest was the fairest. Their hut was quite hidden by trees, and none saw their beauty but the sun by day, the moon by night, and the eyes of the stars. The old woman kept the girls hard at work, from morning till night, spinning gold flax into yarn, and when one distaff was empty another was given them, so they had no rest. The thread had to be fine and even, and when done was locked up in a secret chamber by the old woman, who twice or thrice every summer went a journey. Before she went she gave out work for each day of her absence, and always returned in the night, so that the girls never saw what she brought back with her, neither would she tell them whence the gold flax came nor what it was to be used for.

Now, when the time came round for the old woman to set out on one of these journeys, she gave each maiden work for six days, with the usual warning: " Children, don't let your eyes wander, and on no account speak to a man, for if you do your thread will lose its brightness and misfortunes of all kinds will follow." They laughed at this oft-repeated caution, saying to each other: " How can our gold thread lose its brightness, and have we any chance of speaking to a man? "

On the third day after the old woman's departure a young prince, hunting in the forest, got separated from his companions and completely lost. Weary of seeking his way he flung himself